Cloaked in Bravery

A Rescue Mission Like No Other

Tony Matthews

First published 2023

Big Sky Publishing Pty Ltd

PO Box 303, Newport, NSW, 2106, Australia.

Phone: 1300 364 611

Email: info@bigskypublishing.com.au

Web: www.bigskypublishing.com.au

Cover design: Big Sky Publishing
Front cover photograph: Selenit, Shutterstock 232487515

Map by Lensie Matthews

Typesetting & indexing: Lensie Matthews

ISBN: 9781923004276

CLOAKED IN BRAVERY

A Rescue Mission Like No Other

TONY MATTHEWS

TABLE OF CONTENTS

Dedication vi
Author's Note vii
Introduction. x
Chapter 1
Early Life and Marriage 1
Chapter 2
The Nine Years War 21
Chapter 3
The War of the Spanish Succession 44
Chapter 4
1706 — Ramillies — Discovery and Discharge. . . . 78
Chapter 5
1707–1708 — The Plundering Continues. . . . 91
Chapter 6
1709 — Malplaquet and the Death of Richard. . . 108
Chapter 7
1710 — *Ne Plus Ultra*. . . . 146
Chapter 8
1711 — The Final Struggle. . . . 155
Chapter 9
1712 — Return Home 163
Postscript 192
Notes & Sources 203
Bibliography 215
Index 217
About the Author 231

Dedication

This book is dedicated with love and admiration to my wife, Lensie

AUTHOR'S NOTE

It is important to note that this book is not a history of the Nine Years War or the War of the Spanish Succession. This author will leave experts on those two conflicts to write their respective histories. The principal focus of this publication is the life and experiences of Mrs Christian Davies, and overall details of the two wars in which she fought are included so that the reader is better able to understand the background to her extraordinary life and adventures. Therefore only those military and battle details that had a direct influence on Christian's career have been included in this publication. I have attempted to present these in a readable form, without, in most instances, going into the depth of detail that would normally be included in a history of a war or of any particular conflict. Having said this, I have included a fair depth of detail concerning a few of the battles in which Christian Davies was involved, including that of Malplaquet as this was the battle in which Christian's husband, Richard Welsh, was killed, and it will be helpful for the reader to be able to understand how that came about as Richard's death was, of course, a pivotal point in Christian's life.

Christian lived in fascinating times and was acquainted with remarkable people including nobility and even royalty. She lived during a period of history when entirely new nations and even empires were being forged on the hard anvil of war, when political plots were almost *de rigueur*, when fanatical religious rancour was rampant (when is it not?) and intrigue, treason and treachery could bring about the fall or elevation of those in high places and alter the map of the world quite dramatically. Yet Christian was a survivor; she was astute enough to recognise danger when she saw it, whether it was physical danger or danger of any other kind. She was courageous, almost to the extent of madness, fearlessly facing cannonballs, volleys of musket-fire or charging cavalry with sabres flying, but she maintained a great love for people, particularly her three husbands, the last of whom she nursed tenderly to her dying day.

People will have different opinions of Christian Davies; some will see her as a strong but perhaps overly-masculine young woman who loved to fight, plunder and even kill — indeed her attitude towards her French adversaries was nothing short of murderous, particularly following the death of her first husband, Richard, at Malplaquet. Others might catch glimpses into her distinctly feminine side to see the soft and caring woman who existed beneath all her bluff and bluster. There is no doubt that Christian was an interesting 'character', full of life and vigour who held more regard for the health, safety and well-being of those she loved than for her own personal safety. She was a woman who believed in justice and fairness and readers will find many examples throughout this book of occasions when Christian took up the cause of those who were unable, for a variety of reasons, to do so themselves. Christian battled successfully with bullies; to right injustices, and had no hesitation in using what today would be termed as 'excessive force' to bring about what she believed was a just and proper result. To Christian, the force required was not excessive, it was simply a way (perhaps then the only way) of ensuring that the vulnerable were protected from the tyrannous.

Other women, of course, have fought in wars. During the Second World War women fought on many fronts, even as highly trained secret agents and resistance fighters. Today the ranks of women fighting on the front lines, particularly in the Middle East, are no longer remarkable but everyday events. However, in the late 17th and early 18th centuries a woman fighting alongside her male colleagues was rare indeed. Christian Davies was a unique woman in every respect; she did not go to war for the sake of making war but to find her missing husband. Her war was one fought for love but she came to love the life and freedoms she found on the battlefields where she was unconstrained and able to do virtually whatever she wanted.

For those who love a story of free spirits, of courage and enterprise then Mrs Christian Davies' story is just such an adventure.

Tony Matthews, 2023.

INTRODUCTION

In 1717, the admissions registrar at the Royal Hospital, Chelsea, took up a quill pen and laboriously wrote in the admissions book for the hospital '... 19 November, 1717. Stair's Dragoons, Catherine Welsh, a fatt [sic] jolly breasted woman', had registered with the hospital and that this woman, who had, '... received several wounds in service in the habitt [sic] of a man,' had been admitted for her valiant behaviour.[1]

This simple entry masked what is certainly one of the most extraordinary stories to come out of the late seventeenth century and early eighteenth century military history of England and Europe, for behind those words is the story of Mrs Christian Davies, mother, wife, foot-soldier and dragoon, who, in two terrible and bloody wars, risked her life and everything that was dear to her in order to find her missing husband.

Christian Davies, 1667-1739, was certainly one of the most remarkable women in British military history. She was born Christian 'Kit' Cavanagh in Dublin, the daughter of a brewer who served in the army of James II after William of Orange had deposed him. Christian was probably in her early twenties when an aunt died, leaving her a tavern in Dublin which she almost immediately took over and managed. Soon afterwards, and contrary to established tradition and social mores, she married one of her servants, a man named Richard Welsh (sometimes referred to as Walsh). However, Welsh was later induced to take a bowl of punch aboard a ship laden with recruits for the armies being formed in the Low Countries for the Nine Years War. He became intoxicated and was carried to Holland where he had little choice but to enlist in what Christian described as Lord Orrery's Regiment of Foot, later the 5th Royals. (Lord Orrery was Charles Boyle — the 4th Earl of Orrery 1674-1731, an author, soldier and statesman).

Determined to find her missing husband, Christian Davies left one child with her mother, and another child — born after her husband's departure — with a nurse. She cut off her hair, dressed herself in her husband's clothing, and finding an ensign 'beating up recruits', she quickly enlisted under the name of Christopher Welsh. After being shipped to Holland she was soon afterwards involved in the Battle of Landen (also given as Lauden) where she was wounded above the ankle and where she, '... heard the cannon play and ... the small shot rattle about ... which put one in a sort of panic.' The wound she received laid Christian up for two months but during subsequent fighting she was taken prisoner. Later, however, she was exchanged — a quite usual military procedure during this period — and sent back to the Allied lines. Soon afterwards a young girl fell in love with Christian, believing her to be a man, and Christian, in an endeavour to protect the girl's honour, was forced to fight a duel with a dragoon, inflicting such a severe wound that it was initially thought the man would die. Christian was imprisoned over this event for a short period. After being discharged from her regiment she engaged in a regiment of dragoons, which later became the famous Royal Scots Greys, being present at the 1695 Siege of Namur.

After the Peace of Ryswick, and not having found any trace of her husband, Christian returned to Ireland — unknown and unrecognised — so much had she changed during the years she had spent under arms. Christian visited her children but being too poor to pay for their expenses she decided not to reveal herself to them.

When the War of the Spanish Succession broke out in 1701 Christian again enlisted in a final effort to find her missing husband. She rejoined her old regiment and over the following years saw a great deal of action. During the second bloody attack at Schellenberg (July 1704) she received a musket ball in her hip that was never extracted. After a period of convalescence she fought in the Battle of Blenheim (August 1704), and was later ordered to guard a batch of prisoners. At this time she accidentally came upon her husband whom she had not seen for many years. However, by this time, Richard, who believed that he would never again be allowed to return to England, had found another woman, a Dutch lady to whom he had promised marriage. Christian forgave Richard and asked him not to reveal her identity; to say that she was his brother so that they could remain together.

All through the campaigns fought by the armies under the command of the English captain-general, John Churchill, the Duke of Marlborough, Christian Davies continued to hide her true identity so that she could remain with her husband. At Ramillies, in May 1706, she went through the thickest of the battle unharmed but after the fight had ended a shell fell from a church steeple and exploded. A piece of shrapnel struck Christian in the back of her head, fracturing her skull. She was trepanned and suffered terribly for ten weeks. However, during the course of her operation her true gender was discovered and she was forced to admit to her remarkable subterfuge. The news spread quickly and Christian became something of a celebrity and war hero. Her commanding officer, Brigadier Preston, presented her with a silk dress; her husband was brought to her and she was released from military service with a substantial bonus. The chaplain of the regiment insisted that there should be a new wedding to which all the officers were invited.

However, Richard Welsh, it seems, was still involved with the Dutch woman. Sometime later, at Ghent, finding her husband in a public house with this woman, Christian was so enraged that she cut off the woman's nose with a knife. For this attack Christian was sentenced to a period on the 'stool' — a particularly hideous device.

At the December 1708 Siege of Ghent (which had fallen to the French the previous July) Christian once again followed her husband during the thickest of the battles, as she did for many years afterwards. Sadly, Richard was killed during the ferocious Battle of Malplaquet. When Christian heard the news she went in search of Richard's body amid the bloodied debris of the battle. She found a robber stripping Richard's corpse and Christian fought him off. She then dug a grave and buried her husband's remains. According to eyewitness reports, she would have thrown herself into the grave had she not been prevented from doing so. Christian's grief was so great that she tore flesh from her arms with her teeth.

Christian was twice more married — once to another soldier who was also killed. After returning to England, Queen Anne presented Christian with £50 and a pension of a shilling per day for life. However, Lord Treasurer Oxford (Robert Harley) in a characteristically miserly mood, soon afterwards succeeded in reducing the pension to just fivepence per day.

In June 1722 Christian marched, '... with streaming eyes and a heavy heart' at the funeral of John Churchill, the Duke of Marlborough. Her third husband was later taken ill and although by this time Christian herself was an old woman, she nursed him until she caught a cold which turned into fever. She died on 7 July, 1739. Christian Davies was reportedly buried in the grounds of Chelsea Hospital, a detachment of soldiers firing a volley over her grave, although other reports claim that she was interred at St. Margaret's Church, Westminster. There are no records extant to demonstrate which of these is correct.

The information for this book comes from two principal sources. Some years prior to her death Christian Davies either wrote or dictated an account of her experiences during the European campaigns. For approximately 200 years it was believed that this account was written by Daniel Defoe but more recently has been attributed to Christian herself, and, indeed, the text was written as an autobiography in the first person. Additionally, Defoe had died about nine years before this first edition was published and in the days prior to any kind of copyright law it was not all that unusual for booksellers and publishers to use the name of a well known author in order to sell more copies of their publications, particularly when that author was deceased and could therefore not protest the misuse of his or her name. Four editions of this first book appeared between 1740 and 1743 so evidently it did sell well. The possibility that the book was written by Defoe has also been discounted by J. R. Moore in his checklist of the writings of Daniel Defoe (2nd edition, 1971). Christian's book was reprinted by Peter Davies of London in 1928.

The original edition: *The Life and Adventures of Mrs Christian Davies Commonly Called Mother Ross*, London, R. Montagu, (printer) 1740, was presumably embellished either by Christian Davies herself or by the bookseller who printed the edition. It was published the year after Christian's death. Because of this it is difficult to estimate with any precision how much of the story is factual and how much is fanciful, and a certain degree of licence must be allowed for dialogues Mrs Davies herself attributes as truthful, but which were written many years after the events and possibly not by Mrs Davies at all.

The second principal source also suffers from these problems. *The British Heroine, or An Abridgement of the Life and Adventures of Mrs Christian Davies, Commonly Called Mother Ross*, was reputedly written by an army surgeon, Dr J. Wilson, who is also reported to have served in the European campaigns at the same time as Mrs Davies. His account of the events was published in London by T. Cooper in 1742, although much of the information contained in this now obscure publication seems to have been extracted, sometimes almost verbatim, from Mrs Davies' own memoirs, published two years previously. This version is so close to the original publication that it is almost certainly the same book but published as a biography rather than an autobiography.

It is necessary therefore, when reading this biography, to take into account the fact that Christian Davies, while being an extraordinary woman, was not reticent in speaking or writing of her adventures in a somewhat over-enthusiastic manner. She was proud of her accomplishments and more especially proud of her courage, strength and prodigious stamina which allowed her to live her life as the equal of any man during a time when strength and aggression were the fundamental cornerstones of self preservation.

Appear weak when you are strong,
and strong when you are weak.

Sun Tzu,
The Art of War.

CHAPTER 1

Early Life and Marriage

If we can believe the reports published since 1739 concerning the life of Mrs Christian Davies then it is certain that this woman was one of the most remarkable in the history of the British military. Yet the question remains, can these reports be relied upon for absolute accuracy? During the course of her life, and for a number of years after her death, there were various publications concerning the life and exploits of Christian Davies, some of them major works. However, the information for these publications seems to have come principally from Christian herself and as time often distorts the facts such reminiscences must be treated with caution. Since those first publications very little has been written about Christian Davies' experiences, apart from a few articles in now obscure newspapers and the occasional synopses in more contemporary books. Yet despite this lack of accredited information, it certainly seems clear that Christian's experiences during the wars of King William and Queen Anne were remarkable, even for those difficult times. As Dr J. Wilson — who apparently had fought in the same campaigns — reportedly wrote in 1742:

> The most lively descriptions our novels and romances give us of great and virtuous ladies are but a faint resemblance of this extraordinary woman, who was in reality all that fancy and fiction have attributed to others. ... She was a brave soldier, a tender mother, an affectionate wife, a true lover of her country and a pattern of patience under a continuous series of misfortunes. In short, she was an honour to the fair sex.[1]

Wilson's 'biography' has been criticised by later historians who claimed that many of the stories attributed to Christian Davies were often embellished by Christian herself. This may be the case but in the book attributed to him Dr Wilson stated:

> Though many passages in the following history may appear very extraordinary and even incredible to those who were never acquainted with Mrs Davies and her manner of life, yet I must beg leave to assure my readers that I have had so strict a regard to truth and impartiality through the whole piece that nothing is inserted but what I either knew myself to be fact or had from authorities which I thought unquestionable, and in order to make the history yet more complete, and to remove any objection that might be made to the truth of it, I have carefully compared it with an account that was taken from her own mouth at several times while she was at Chelsea, then corrected by some memoirs she left behind her and published soon after her death. But I think no gentleman can question the authority of this history who has had the least acquaintance with the officers of the army under whom she served, or been conversant with. The newspapers of that time ... abound with the surprising exploits of our undaunted heroine. ... The greatest objection that I have heard brought against her living so long in the army undiscovered is the difficulty of performing a certain natural office which soldiers are obliged to do, not only standing but frequently in public and even at the head of a regiment. However, Mrs Davies easily accomplished this by means of a silver tube painted over and fastened about her with leather straps. This urinary instrument our heroine sold in Flanders for seven pistols after she had thrown off the habit of the male sex and resumed that of her own, but she greatly repented having parted with this uncommon

> implement when she came to England where, by the prodigious concourse that came daily to see her, she found that a good livelihood might have been procured by showing it as a curiosity.[2]

Christian (also known as Catherine) Davies was born in Dublin in 1667. Her father was a brewer — evidently a successful one — for Christian later stated that he had employed at least twenty people.[3] Christian's mother, who had reportedly received a sound education from her father, Bryan Bembrick, in the bishopric of Durham, ran a small farm which was owned by the family. Christian wrote in her autobiography:

> My father was remarkable for industry and vigilance in his affairs which employed his whole time in town, he never saw my mother but on Sundays, except [when] some extraordinary business required his visiting the farm.[4]

Young Christian was reputed to have been something of a tomboy, despite the relatively good education afforded her. She learned to read and write — talents rarely seen among the Irish working class of the 17/18th centuries, but she disliked academic pursuits, preferring instead to be at the farm assisting her mother. Dr J. Wilson, reputedly Christian's first biographer, later recorded:

> ... she was never better pleased than when following the plough or using the rake, flail or suchlike instruments which she could manage with near as much strength and skill as her mother's menservants.[5]

Christian described herself as having, '... patience indeed to learn to read and become a good needle-woman, but I had too much mercury in me to like a sedentary life.'[6]

By the time she was eighteen years of age Christian was largely ungovernable. She rode a horse like a man, usually with no saddle or bridle; she was wild, tempestuous, unruly and a source of constant concern to her parents.

She later wrote:

> I used to get astride upon the horses and ride them bare-backed about the fields, leaping hedges and ditches, by which I once got a terrible fall and spoiled a grey mare given to my brother by our grandfather. My father never knew how this mischief happened, which brought me under the contribution [debt] to a cowherd who saw me tumble the mare into a dry ditch, and whose secrecy I was obliged to purchase by giving him, for a considerable time, a cup of ale every night.[7]

Christian herself later told of an incident when she and a number of other young women, the youngest being seventeen years of age, were rolling happily down a small hummock — with little care for the undergarments they were displaying — when an unnamed nobleman (the Earl of C–d, as Christian wrote) passed by in his coach. Seeing this feminine display the earl stopped the coach to watch. The girls, however, quickly stopped playing and the earl called them to him. He promised each of them a crown if they would continue with their display. The girls acceded to the man's request — a crown (five shillings) during the 1680s was a large sum when the average working wage was only a few pounds per year.[8]

However, political events forming in England and on the Continent were soon to change Christian's idyllic life forever.

King James II's allegiance to the Protestant Church had long been suspect and because of this there were always going to be major problems within his dominions — particularly in predominantly Protestant Ireland. James took Eucharist in the Roman Catholic Church in 1668 or 1669 but his conversion to Catholicism was kept secret for some time and he continued to attend Anglican services until 1676.[9]

James's first wife, Anne Hyde, (whom he married prior to his ascendancy to the throne), the daughter of Charles II's chief minister, Edward Hyde, also converted to the Catholic Church prior to her death in March 1671. (Their daughter, Mary, would become Queen Mary II and rule in conjunction with her husband William III).

In 1673 the English Parliament passed the Test Act which required all civil and military officials to disavow the doctrine of transubstantiation (the Roman Catholic doctrine of the conversion in the Eucharist of the whole substance of the bread into the body and the wine into the blood of Christ, only the appearance of the bread and wine remaining) and to denounce a number of other customs of the Roman Catholic Church as being both superstitious and idolatrous. They were also required to receive the Eucharist under the auspices of the Church of England. Charles II's brother, James, however, who had not then ascended to the throne, refused to do so. He relinquished his post as the Lord High Admiral and his conversion to Catholicism became public knowledge.[10]

James's second marriage that same year (20 September, 1673) was to the staunchly Roman Catholic Mary of Modena, an Italian princess, fifteen years of age. The wedding, a Catholic ceremony, was by proxy. Mary arrived in England on 21 November and an Anglican marriage ceremony was held but this did little more than recognise the Catholic ceremony. Mary was distrusted by many of the English who regarded her as being an agent of the Pope. When a defrocked Anglican clergyman named Titus Oates began to spread rumours of a Papist plot to murder King Charles II and to put James on the throne, a wave of anti-Catholic hysteria swept the country and some members of parliament even suggested that the crown should go to Charles's illegitimate son, James Scott, the 1st Duke of Monmouth.[11]

At James's accession to the throne on 6 February, 1685, following the death of King Charles II, there was widespread discontent. Interestingly, Charles had converted to Catholicism on his deathbed and having no legitimate sons his brother, James, succeeded him.

The English Army was then increased by some 20,000 men; Catholic officers were appointed and an ecclesiastical commission was established with sweeping powers to suppress all anti-Romanist preaching. One after another Anglican officials were dismissed from their positions.

James faced armed rebellion on two fronts: one led by James Scott, the Duke of Monmouth and the other by Archibald Campbell, the 9th Earl of Argyll. Campbell's insurrection from Scotland was easily defeated but Monmouth's small peasant army in the south was a little more difficult to deal with. Monmouth had declared himself king at Lyme Regis on 11 June, 1685. He attempted to raise recruits to his cause but only managed to form a small army. However, James's army (with a great deal of help from John Churchill, later Duke of Marlborough) finally defeated Monmouth at the Battle of Sedgemoor. Monmouth was captured and executed at the Tower of London and the king's judges, principal among them being the now infamous Judge Jeffreys, condemned many of the rebels to transportation or indentured servitude in the West Indies. The trials of these men came to be known as the Bloody Assizes and about 250 rebels were executed.[12]

These rebellions forced James to increase his standing army even further and command of some regiments were given to Catholics without the necessity for their commanders to take an oath under the Test Act. James allowed Roman Catholics to occupy many of the highest offices in the country and he even received at court the papal nuncio, Ferdinand d'Adda, who was the first papal representative at court since the reign of Queen Mary I.[13]

When Mary of Modena bore James his first surviving son, (James Francis Edward Stuart) on 10 June, 1688, and it became clear that James's successor would also be a Catholic, a group of leading English statesmen sent a letter to William of Orange, the son of Mary (princess royal), eldest daughter of Charles I (executed by Oliver Cromwell in 1649) inviting him to bring an army to England to take the throne from James. (James's earlier son, Charles, also born to Mary of Modena had died of smallpox when little more than a month old [December 1677]). One of these petitioners was John Churchill, the future 1st Duke of Marlborough, who, deserting James II, had promised William that if he invaded England he and the troops under him would serve William's cause.

When William, Prince of Orange, invaded England, landing at Torbay on 5 November, 1688, and advanced rapidly on London, King James II's staunchly Catholic and autocratic reign quickly came to an end. James fled, throwing the Great Seal of the Realm into the Thames River. However, he was caught in Kent and placed under guard. The deposed king was subsequently allowed to escape to St. Germain, (because William did not want him to become a Catholic martyr). James would later (March 1689) land in Ireland with French troops where the Irish Parliament still recognised him as the true monarch. There James worked on building a significant army which would ultimately face William's troops at the historic Battle of the Boyne.

Meanwhile the newly crowned King William III and his wife, Queen Mary II, (James II's daughter) saw the passing of the Bill of Rights which, *inter alia*, declared that henceforth no Catholic would be permitted to ascend the throne. The Bill also prevented any English monarch from marrying a Catholic.[14]

At this time Christian Davies' father, like thousands of other Catholic Irish, was strongly incensed by the loss of their Catholic monarch. He sold much of his possessions, his crops of corn and other items of his trade to a neighbouring farmer named Ascham, and with the money raised and using much of his financial reserves, he raised a troop of horse and under his command the men set off to join James's army.

The transaction between Christian's father and Mr Ascham had been made without the knowledge of Christian's mother and this lack of communication — or trust — soon afterwards led to a bloody feud between Christian's mother and her neighbour. Christian wrote:

> After my father was gone to the army my mother sent reapers into the field to cut the corn, these met with others sent by the then proprietor upon the same errand. Words immediately arose and they very soon came to blows, making use of their sickles, a desperate weapon. The noise reached my mother's ears, who, not without some difficulty, and having regaled them in her house with a good breakfast and strong liquors, they were at length appeased and dismissed.[15]

The horse which Christian's father rode was reputed to have been something of a rogue and no other man was willing to mount him. However, Christian seemed able to manage the animal; she fed and saddled him regularly, and to the amazement of onlookers would often mount him and, '... draw and snap the pistols, to the terror and amazement of her friends.'[16] Christian was proud of her capabilities with horses and especially proud of her achievements with her father's horse. She later stated:

> I had so often fed him with bread and oats that he would stand for me to take him up when at grass, though he would have given twenty men work enough to catch him. When I once had hold of him I would put on his bridle and lead him into a ditch and bestride him bare-backed. I have often mounted him when saddled and took great pleasure to draw and snap the pistols and have not seldom made my friends apprehend for my life. I mention this not

> as worth notice, but only to show my inclinations while a girl were always masculine.[17]

Christian seems to have been fascinated with military matters; even as a teenager she recalled being intrigued and animated when she had heard martial music during the proclamation of King James II in 1685. She subsequently wrote of this event:

> I was employed to stack wheat and was on the top of one [haystack] near fifty-four foot high when I perceived in the road near our farm the judges and other magistrates in their robes, preceded by kettledrums, trumpets and heralds in their rich coats coming up the hill in order to proclaim King James. Animated by the martial music and desirous to have a nearer view of this glorious sight which, with the glare of the gold and silver coats, the heralds, trumpets and kettledrums wore, had, in a manner, dazzled my sight. I leaped down, ran to, and cleared with a leap a five-barred gate which was between me and the road they passed, calling to my mother to come and see the show, as I imagined every man there at least a prince. My mother, [who was a Protestant — author's note] hearing the procession was to proclaim [the Catholic supporter] King James, went back and wept bitterly for some time, but would never tell me the reason for her tears.[18]

An early indication of the young woman's courage came shortly after her father had left to fight for King James's cause. The precise date seems uncertain but Christian later recorded the event of her mother worshiping at the Protestant church in Leslip when Papists sealed up the church-door with butchers' blocks and other large pieces of timber, evidently with the intention of murdering the Protestants inside. Christian's own account of the event recorded:

> My mother was then in the church; I was home, but, hearing the noise and fearing my mother might receive

> some hurt I snatched up a spit and thus armed sallied forth to force my way and come to her assistance, but being resisted by the sergeant, I thrust my spit through the calf of his leg, removed the things which blocked the door, and called to my mother, bidding her come, for the dinner was ready.[19]

During this conflict the minister, a Reverend Malary, the clerk and several other people were wounded and Christian was arrested for assaulting the sergeant. However, during Christian's defence the magistrate trying her case (who must have been a Catholic) was advised of her father's endeavours in the army of James II, and the young girl was freed.[20]

Meanwhile, on 14 June, 1690, King William III arrived at Garrickfergus in Ulster from where he marched south to take Dublin and crush James II. James decided to meet William at the River Boyne, about thirty miles from Dublin. William and his well-trained, well-armed, regular troops, some 36,000 strong, arrived on the banks of the Boyne on 30 June, the day before the battle. While surveying the fords over the river William himself was wounded in the shoulder by artillery shrapnel.

James's Jacobite forces numbered approximately 23,500 men and the battle took place close to the town of Drogheda on the east coast of Ireland. It commenced on 1 July, 1690.

The ebb and flow of the battle seemed for a while to be gaining ground on neither side and the natural river barrier created major tactical problems for both sides. However, James's forces were eventually defeated. They retired in good order across the River Nanny at Duleek, fighting a successful rearguard action which prevented William's men from trapping them there. About 2,000 men were killed during this battle, three-quarters of whom were Jacobites. Following the battle the Jacobite army abandoned Dublin which William occupied two days later.

Meanwhile James had fled, initially to Dublin and then to Duncannon before returning to exile in France. He crossed the English Channel in a vessel especially prepared in case of defeat and arrived safely at Saint-Germain-en-Laye in France. However, infamy was to follow him there. Because he had so quickly abandoned his Irish supporters James went on to become known in Ireland as *Séamus an Chaca* (which translates variously as either 'James the Shit' or 'James the beshitten' but the general meaning is fairly obvious).[21]

Following the defeat of James's forces at the Battle of the Boyne, Christian's father, along with an associate, a handsome lieutenant in the French Army, returned to Dublin where, fearing reprisals against them by troops searching for survivors of James's army, they went into hiding. However, about 3 a.m. the following morning the two soldiers were alarmed by the noise of several friends who had also fled from William's forces. Thinking that these were troopers searching for them, they made a hasty exit from the house.

A dialogue has been recorded of the conversation that was allegedly held between Christian's father and mother at this time, and while this dialogue has been attributed to Christian's memory of the events, there is no proof that this is the case and in fact the conversation may well have been the product of her publisher's imagination. Even so, it is worth recording. Christian was alleged to have written:

> While they were saddling, my father took a short but sorrowful leave of his wife and children, whom, with tears in his eyes, he blessed and recommended to the Divine protection; then turning to my mother, 'My dear,' said he, 'do not be dejected, comfort yourself that whatever misfortunes befall us we suffer in a just cause, and for having done what is the duty of every loyal subject; at least my conscience tells me that I have acted as I ought and as I was

> bound to do by my oath of allegiance from which I know no power on earth that can absolve me. The Lord giveth and the Lord taketh away, blessed be the name of the Lord. His wants are inscrutable and I humbly submit to his decrees which are all founded in wisdom. As for you, keep at home your children and be their support, for you being a Protestant need apprehend no danger from the enemy. May they hereafter repay your maternal care and tenderness by a filial duty, and prove your comfort, but never torment yourself with uneasy thoughts for your unfortunate husband. Think of me no more.'
>
> 'God forbid,' said she, and bursting into a flood of tears. My father, who could not bear to see her weep, as he loved her with a sincere tenderness, ran out of the room and he and the officer, mounting their horses, fled with precipitation.[22]

Christian added that her mother could not sleep for the remainder of the night and roamed the house alone. The children however, '... did not take their father's departure so much to heart, and lay in till daybreak.'[23]

Approximately twelve months later came news that James II's supporters in Ireland, the Jacobites, had been defeated at the Battle of Aughrim where General Godert de Ginkell, the Williamite's Dutch commander, had obtained a victory over Marquis de St. Ruth (General Charles Chalmont).

Following the defeat of James at the Battle of the Boyne, his Jacobite supporters had retreated behind the River Shannon which acted as a massive moat around the province of Connacht. The Jacobites had strongholds in Sligo, Athlone and Limerick which guarded the routes into Connacht. From there the Jacobites hoped for military assistance from France's Louis XIV — a strong supporter of James's cause and his protector in France.

The Jacobite line of defence had, however, been penetrated by General Ginkell's forces when they crossed the Shannon at Athlone, capturing the town after a particularly bloody siege. The commander of the Jacobite forces, General St. Ruth, had not moved his troops quickly enough to prevent the fall of Athlone. Ginkell then marched through Ballinasloe towards Limerick and Galway until he found his route blocked by St. Ruth's army at Aughrim. The date was now 12 July, 1691, and among St. Ruth's army was Christian Davies' father. The Jacobite army was principally composed of Irish Catholics, while the Williamites were made up of English, Scottish, Dutch and French Huguenots with some Ulster Protestants. Each army was approximately 20,000 in number.

The Jacobites were entrenched in a fairly strong position along the crest of a ridge known as Kilcommadan Hill which was lined with stone walls, hedgerows and earthworks thrown up by the defenders. On the left was a large bog through which there was only one causeway. This was overlooked by Aughrim village and the ruins of an ancient castle. The other flank was open ground where St. Ruth placed his best troops.

General Ginkell opened the battle by attempting to assault the open flank with infantry and cavalry. However, in the face of determined Jacobite resistance this attack soon slowed and stopped. The fighting had been so fierce that the grass was reported to have been slippery with blood and the site later became known as 'Bloody Hollow'. A frontal assault was then attempted against the centre of the Jacobite defences on Kilcommadan Hill. This too failed. Three separate attacks were driven off with heavy losses and the Williamites were chased into the bog where many more were killed or drowned.

Ginkell was now left with only one remaining option: to attack along the causeway through the bog on the Jacobite left. With such a narrow line to defend, St. Ruth should have been able to hold the position easily. However, his men were running short of ammunition. The problem was compounded when it was discovered that some of the British manufactured musket-balls would not fit into the muzzles of the French-supplied muskets. The struggle continued for some time and at one period St. Ruth was heard shouting '... they are running, we will chase them back to the gates of Dublin.' Yet as he attempted to rally his cavalry he was decapitated by a cannonball. The Jacobite positions then quickly collapsed and their troops, including Christian's father, completely demoralised by the sudden death of their commander, fled the field, many retreating to defend Limerick. It was estimated that some 7,000 men died during this battle, and one witness, a man named George Storey, who observed the scene from a distance, said that the hill looked like it was covered by a flock of sheep.[24]

After the Battle of Aughrim the English forces laid siege to Limerick (for the second time, the first being 1690) where many of the survivors of the Battle of Aughrim had fled.

General Ginkell's troops surrounded the city and bombarded it, opening a breach in the walls. The Williamites then attacked the earthworks which had been thrown up surrounding the walls, sending the Jacobite defenders fleeing towards Limerick. However, the French defenders of the main gate refused to open it to their allies and about 800 Irish Jacobites were slaughtered or drowned in the River Shannon. A treaty (known as the Treaty of Limerick) was soon signed which promised to respect the civilian population of Limerick and to tolerate the Catholic religion in Ireland. There was also an agreement which protected Catholic-owned land against confiscation and guaranteed safe passage to France of the remainder of the Jacobite army. Ten thousand Jacobite soldiers and about 4,000 women and children subsequently left Ireland in what became known as the Flight of the Wild Geese. However, the terms of the Treaty of Limerick were later rejected in the Protestant dominated Irish Parliament.[25]

It was during this siege that the handsome French officer who had accompanied and later fled with Christian's father following the Battle of the Boyne, was also killed. When the body of the officer was stripped it was discovered that she was a woman. This strange event may well have been a factor in Christian's later actions.[26]

Christian's mother, meanwhile, had not been idle; realising that William's forces could never be defeated by James's disorganised, ill-informed and poorly trained troops, she had managed to obtain a pardon for her husband so that he could return to his old profession unmolested by the new authority.

During the Battle of Aughrim, Christian's father had been badly wounded, however, he was recovering, and intended returning to Dublin when one of his servants, a Papist named Kelly, stole one of his horses and deserted to General Ginkell's army. This event was reputed to have so affected Christian's father that his health rapidly deteriorated; he caught a fever and soon afterwards died. Upon his death and despite the pardon, all his assets were seized.[27]

How this event affected Christian and her mother is not clear, although almost certainly it reduced them financially, and as their late husband and father had led such an active part in the army of King James, they almost certainly went in fear of further retribution, especially so after the decisive battle at Aughrim when William's army had taken over almost total control of Ireland.

By now, however, Christian had blossomed into a reputedly attractive young woman, hot-headed, certainly, strangely independent, strong-willed and also physically strong, attributes she would badly need in later life. Yet Christian had no shortage of suitors. One of these was a second cousin on her mother's side of the family, a man named Thomas Howel, (later Reverend Howel [also reported as Howell]) who was a student and Fellow of Dublin College. Howel courted Christian for approximately two years. He offered her marriage — an offer she refused because in light of her late father's financial losses she could not bring a dowry to the marriage and feared that she would force Howel to live in poverty for the remainder of his life. Howel ignored Christian's quite reasonable protestations and continued an ardent courtship. Christian was equally determined and continued to refuse. She later wrote:

> When we eagerly wish a thing, we seldom examine thoroughly the consequences which may attend the possession of what we desire, and if we cannot help seeing the evils ... we easily satisfy ourselves with arguments which flatter our inclinations, however weak. This was his case, for when I laid before him the certain poverty which would attend his marrying a woman without a fortune, he removed the objection, at least as to his own part, with the airy prospect of preferments in the church, and in the interim with what money he could get by a school, sufficient, as he flattered himself, to maintain me like a lady. ...When I represented to him the deplorable condition of a clergyman's widow, with, possibly, a number of children, he answered that economy should ward against that evil. I, who looked upon all this as a castle in the air, would not consent to what he wished and ... very seriously begged of him to give over his pursuits, but to no purpose. He continued his visits and solicitations which were more frequent, longer and more urgent than usual.[28]

One day, while making the beds in her mother's house, Christian was surprised by Howel who raped her, or, as Dr J. Wilson recorded in 1742: '... deprived her of that which is justly esteemed the pride and glory of virgins and ought to be preserved with as much caution and concern as life itself.'[29]

Christian's own account of the event was not glossed over and in her memoirs she claimed that prior to the attack she had enjoyed the amorous attentions of Howel and that she had caught '... the contagious desire.' It was only when Howel had thrown her upon the bed that things had begun to get out of hand and, as Christian wrote, '... he added force to vows of eternal constancy and marriage and with little resistance on my side, throwing me upon the bed deprived me of that inestimable jewel which a maiden ought to preserve preferable to life.'[30]

Christian was, quite naturally, devastated by the attack. She lost her gaiety, became despondent, morose, irritable and sad. She tore at her hair and claimed that she was not far from madness.

Her mother remonstrated with her but Christian would not tell her of the event, saying only that she needed a change of air. Her mother agreed and the young woman was sent to an aunt who kept a public house in Dublin.

Coming from her mother's farm in the country, Dublin must have been quite a shock to a young girl. At that time it was a dirty city, overcrowded and pestilent, with people jammed into old tenement buildings for which the landlords charged exorbitant rents. The city had a far larger percentage of single-room tenements than any other city in Ireland and tens of thousands of people were living in dwellings which were quite unfit for human habitation. Conditions such as these did not change for many decades.

Whether or not Christian's move to the city was a sound one is difficult to say. The aunt's public house was near Dublin College and Christian was often brought into contact with her former attacker who was studying there, although she avoided him as much as possible. Finally, however, in the new surroundings and with different work to complete, Christian recovered from her deep depression. For the following four years she lived and worked with her aunt. When the ageing woman died, she left the public house and all its furnishings to Christian.

Christian later stated:

> I now received the reward of my prudent behaviour. I lived in ease and plenty. My business was considerable,

> I got money apace and was esteemed by all my neighbours and acquaintances. Never woman was in a happier situation for I was at the height of my ambition and had not a wish to make. In a word I was thoroughly content and had reason so to be, till love, too often the bane of our sex, love who has not seldom ruined noble families, nay, destroyed cities and lain kingdoms waste, envious of the calm I enjoyed, came to imbitter [sic] my peace, disturb the tranquillity of my life and make me know, by experience, the short duration of all sublunary satisfaction.[31]

It was during her time at the public house that Christian met Richard Welsh, a servant of her aunt and now Christian's employee. Christian was attracted to Richard and the attraction was evidently mutual. However, Richard was somewhat shy and refrained from making any advances towards his employer. Christian therefore made it known to a mutual friend that she found Richard attractive and that any advances he made would not be rejected outright. Heartened by this news Richard was excited but still dubious. If he made such an advance and was rejected it could have meant losing his job. He was assured by the mutual friend that this would not be the case and soon afterwards he cautiously made his feelings known to Christian who was secretly delighted. Yet she would not allow herself to be carried off so easily. She coldly instructed Richard to carry on with his work, but the thaw had started. Undaunted, Richard continued with his objectives and slowly Christian admitted that she had feelings for him. She described him as being, '... a well made person with a handsome, manly face, and with a generous open temper, sober, vigilant and active in business, very regular in life and modest in his behaviour.'[32]

Christian was now torn between a growing attachment for Richard and the knowledge that, should she marry him, her life would irrevocable change — possibly for the worse. She later stated:

> ... he was, or appeared to me, a man whom any woman might love without having her good sense called to question. My pride at first made me endeavour to stifle this growing passion, and I tried to conquer it by reason. I thought it would be a [poor] reflection upon me to marry my servant and I was sensible that it might be to the disadvantage of my fortune ... but love and reason seldom agree and when once that despotic tyrant gets possession of the heart he will also rule the head ... the sight of Richard Welsh overturned the strongest resolutions that I could make, his name was music to my ears, if I did not see him no other object could please my eyes, and I knew no other happiness but in possession of Richard Welsh. Though my pride and reason were thoroughly vanquished, yet my modesty held out, for I thought it indecent and a reflection on my sex to make the first overture. This caused me many a restless night.[33]

By the end of the week Richard had asked for Christian's hand in marriage and his proposal was accepted, although according to Christian's own account of the proposal the ground over which Richard was treading was filled with seeming dangers. She claimed that when he first broached the subject of his love for her she had made it difficult for him and put on, '... an air of severity which, however, he might plainly see was counterfeit.'[34] She castigated him, stating that the cause of his passion was simply idleness and ordered him back to work. Richard, however, persisted, claiming that he loved her deeply and that he would do anything to win her love. Finally she relented and said that she would consider talking with him on a man-to-woman basis that evening after the inn had closed. Christian claimed that Richard had seized her in his arms and, '... almost stifled me with kisses. I never before was so well pleased though I pretended to be terribly angry and threatened if he was ever rude again I would make him repent it.'[35]

That evening Richard went to Christian's bedroom, telling her maid that there were accounts to be settled. The marriage proposal itself was a strange one, Richard claiming that by marrying her he would not be jeopardising her relative wealth. He said that he would not become an overbearing landlord nor would he want any part of her money. Christian wrote of the event:

> He then threw himself on his knees and grasping mine in a sort of ecstasy he continued: 'I love you for yourself, not for your money, of which I will never pretend to be other than a steward would you consent to make me the happiest man alive.' I bid him to get up and, as it was late, to leave me to go to bed and I would consider on what he had said.[36]

Despite Christian's outward rejection the outcome was obvious — possibly even to Richard himself.

According to Dr J. Wilson:

> Richard proved a careful, tender and obliging [husband] ... and, as he promised, left his wife as much mistress of her effects as she was when single, thus they lived a happy pair for four years in which time she had two fine boys and was big of a third child when the fickle goddess, to show herself ever variable, reversed their blissful state with a fate not more grievous and insupportable than it was surprisingly odd and casual.[37]

CHAPTER 2

The Nine Years War

When William III (with Mary II) had ascended to the throne of England in 1689, one of his first major military decisions (apart from defeating James in Ireland) was to send a large English force to aid the Dutch Army which was then fighting its old adversary, the French. Louis XIV, the king of France, was continuing to dispute Dutch territory, as he had since the English and the French, as allies, had made a sudden and quite unprovoked attack on the Dutch in the spring of 1672. William had later managed to break the alliance, leaving France to fight alone for Dutch territory, thus the taking of the English throne and the sending of English soldiers against the French was a masterstroke of military irony.

The War of the Grand Alliance, or the War of the League of Augsburg, later known as the Nine Years War, (1688-1697), was one of the bloodiest and most costly wars in England's history. It was fought for a variety of reasons over much of western Europe. Historians today are divided over Louis XIV's precise reasoning and foreign policies, but it is widely believed that the French king wished to secure his borders against future invasion through Germany and the Spanish Netherlands, and also to create a stronger and economically more powerful France.

Recruitment for the Nine Years War was by a variety of methods, principally conscription; one-in-seven English adult males served during the campaigns. The strain of paying for the vast field army reduced England to a financial crisis and France too was almost bankrupt because of its shattered economy.

As these events unfolded, Christian's life was indeed about to change and would never be the same again. At this time she obtained her beer supplies from a man named Forrest, an alderman living in St. James Street, Dublin. The account for the supply was paid monthly. The precise date of the following event is uncertain, but it appears that payment of the account was Richard's responsibility and during one of his visits to St. James Street with a payment of approximately £50, he met an old friend and soon afterwards went mysteriously missing.

When Richard did not return to the tavern that evening, Christian was, quite naturally, worried for his safety. She sent people to search for the missing man but with no success; all she could discover with certainty was that Richard had visited the house of Mr Forrest in the company of another man and Christian concluded that this other person had killed Richard, either for the money or for reasons unknown. During the following days Christian's anxiety increased and there was still no news. She was reported finally to have become so distressed that she could no longer attend to the business of the tavern, and she left its management in the hands of a friend.

As the months passed Christian's belief that her husband had been murdered deepened even further. Twelve months after his disappearance she purchased suits of mourning clothes for herself and her children, and once again took over the management of the tavern.

Soon afterwards, however, Christian received a letter written by Richard:

> Dear Christian,
>
> This is the twelfth letter I have sent you without receiving any answer ... which would both surprise and very much grieve me did I not flatter myself that your silence precedes from the miscarriage of my letters. It is from this opinion that I repeat my account of my sudden and unpremeditated departure and the reason for my having

enlisted for a soldier. It was my misfortune when I went out to pay the alderman the £50, to meet Ensign C...m, who, having formerly been my school-fellow, would accompany me to the alderman's house, from whence we went, at his request and took a hearty bottle at the tavern where he paid the reckoning. Having got a little too much wine in my head I was easily persuaded to go on board the vessel that carried recruits and take a bowl of punch, which I did in the captain's cabbin [sic], where, being pretty much intoxicated, I was not sensible of what was doing upon deck. In the interim the wind sprang up fair, the captain set sail with what recruits were on board, and we had so quick a passage that we reached Helvoetsluys [today Hellevoetsluis in the Netherlands — author's note] before I had recovered from the effects of the liquor. It is impossible for me to paint the disorder I was in, finding myself thus divided from my dear wife and children, landed on a strange shore without money or friends to support me. I raved, tore my hair and cursed my drunken folly which had brought upon me this terrible misfortune, which I thought to remedy by getting [a] ship to carry me back. But there was none to be found. The Ensign, who possibly did not intend me this injury, did all he could to comfort me and advised me to make a virtue of necessity and take on in some regiment. My being destitute and unknown compelled me to follow his advice, though with the greatest reluctance and I now am, though much against my inclination, a private centinel [sic] in Lord O..y [Lord Orrery — author's note] Regiment of Foot, where I fear I must pass the remainder of a wretched life under the deepest affliction for my being deprived of the comfort I enjoyed while blessed with you and my dear babies ... Your unfortunate but ever-loving husband, Richard Welsh.[1]

Christian was reputed to have screamed and then fainted when she read this letter. Neighbours who heard her rushed to her aid and brought her around, after which she began crying and would say nothing to her friends but, 'Oh my dear Richard, must I never see thee more?'[2]

Christian fainted again several times and was finally taken to bed. Richard's letter dropped from her hands and her friends quickly read its contents. They tried to comfort her but she was inconsolable. That night she could not sleep and by the following morning she had made her decision: she would disguise herself as a man by dressing in one of her husband's suits of clothes and sail to Flanders where Lord Orrery's (Charles Boyle, the 4th Earl of Orrery) regiment was then billeted.

Preparations for Christian's journey were comprehensive. She left her eldest son with her mother, her second son having died some time previously. The infant child was placed in the care of a nurse. Christian's household goods were left with some friends who had extra room in their house and who promised to look after them until Christian returned.

Christian then turned her attention to her own appearance. She cut her hair short, dressed herself in her husband's clothes, donned a hat and wig and purchased a silver-hilted sword which she belted to her waist. She covered her breasts, which, as she later wrote, '... were not large enough to betray my sex,' with a thickly quilted waistcoat. It was against the law to export more than £5 out of Ireland so Christian sewed fifty guineas into the waistband of her breeches.[3] She then went in search of the recruiting posts. The press later reported, '... and finding Ensign Lawrance beating up recruits at the Golden Last (tavern), she enlisted under the name of Christopher Welsh.'[4]

Christian subsequently wrote:

> I went to the sign of the Golden Last where Ensign Herbert Lawrance, who was beating up for recruits, kept his

> rendezvous. He was in the house at the time I got there and I offered him my service to go against the French, being desirous to show my zeal for his majesty King William and my country. The hopes of soon meeting with my husband added a sprightliness to my looks which made the officer say I was a clever brisk young fellow, and having recommended my zeal he gave me a guinea enlisting money and a crown to drink the King's health.[5]

Christian was drafted to Captain Tichbourn's company of foot in a regiment commanded by the Marquis de Pisare. After a brief stay in Dublin she and her fellow recruits were shipped to Holland where they landed with their company at Williamstadt, marching to Gorcum, (Gorinchem) where the regimental colours and horses were given to them.

The following day they began their march to Geertruidenberg (in English 'Saint Gertrude's Mountain. Today the city is in the province of North Brabant in the south of the Netherlands), and finally the long march to Landen in Belgium where the recruits were incorporated into their respective regiments in the Grand Alliance Army (referred to as the Allies within this text) which was then shortly expected to go into action, as Christian, perhaps somewhat nervously, explained, '... the enemy being very near within cannon shot.'[6]

This was a fairly typical recruiting operation of the day; young men (and in this instance a young woman), taken from the streets of London, Dublin, Manchester or from any city or hamlet throughout Britain or Ireland, and shipped almost immediately to the scene of the fighting with little or no training. Training was cursory and usually received on the field. These were the years of blunt, unsophisticated warfare. Musketeers were drilled prior to the battles they fought and stood seven or ten to a row, allowing each row ample time to load their slow, clumsy and inaccurate weapons. The days were yet to come when the

British Army had trained its recruits in the art of fast weapons loading, with more sophisticated muskets, firing in rows of just three or four. Likewise, the foot-soldiers were given a pike, sometimes a sword, and relied on their sheer numbers, physical strength and a large amount of luck to win the day. Sword-fighting was rarely the clever, sophisticated and dashing art portrayed today in countless films. Men armed with swords were almost always quite untrained in their use and the weapons were generally used simply as long, slashing butcher's knifes; one would simply hack away at an opponent while the opponent hacked away at you. It was just a matter of who could survive the worst of the injuries which would, as a matter of course, be inflicted once close-quarters battle had commenced. Pikes were even worse; heavy brutal weapons that could inflict mortal wounds from a relatively safe distance.

The wars in the Low Countries at this time were cumbersome, slow moving affairs — wars of troop movements and siege — tens of thousands of men marching from point A to point B on one day to counter the movements of the enemy, and marching back the following day to counter any countermove by opposing forces. It was a season-by-season campaign when commanders in the field were more concerned about siege methods and supplies than fighting battles on the open field. Supplies were almost always a major problem for the troops who often relied on scavenging and looting in order to fill their bellies. Into this confusing, demoralising mass of brutality, bloodshed and seething humanity, Christian Davies marched beside her fellow soldiers.

The Battle of Landen took place on 29 July, 1693, and the belligerents were the forces of King William III and Louis XIV. This was to be Christian's baptism of fire. The French were led by François Henri de Montmorency-Bouteville, duc de Pincy, known generally as the duc de Luxembourg (Duke of Luxembourg). Luxembourg was a more than capable military commander and a force to be reckoned with. He had been born in Paris on 8 January, 1628, the son of the Comte de Montmorency-Bouteville who, sadly, had been executed six months before the birth of the child for taking part in a duel with the Marquis de Beuvron. Luxembourg's military career commenced during the War of Devolution (1667-1668) when he served as a lieutenant-general. He later fought against the Dutch and gained a high reputation. In 1673 he made one of the most successful and famous retreats in history by withdrawing from Utrecht to Maastricht with only 20,000 men in the face of 70,000 enemy troops. This successful retreat, saving many lives, placed Luxembourg in the foremost ranks of French generals. In 1675 he was made a marshal of France and the following year placed at the head of the army of the Rhine. In 1677 he stormed Valenciennes and in 1678 defeated the Prince of Orange at St. Denis.

However there was a dark side to his otherwise distinguished career. Luxembourg had been incarcerated for a while in the notorious Bastille in Paris over what had been known as *L'affaire des Poisons* (the 'affair of poisons'), the most dramatic murder scandal to take place during the reign of King Louis XIV which involved a number of aristocrats and even reached into the inner circle of the royal court. The case involved elements of deliberate poisoning and even witchcraft.

L'affaire des Poisons began when Marie-Madeleine-Marguerite d'Aubray, the Marquise de Brinvilliers, conspired with her lover, Captain Godin de Sainte-Croix, to poison Marie's father, Antonine Dreux d'Aubray and two of Marie's brothers in order to inherit their estates. There were also rumours that Marie had previously used poisons to murder poor people during her visits to hospitals. Faced with these charges, Marie fled but was subsequently arrested in Liége. Forced to confess under torture, Marie was sentenced to death after undergoing what was known as the 'water cure'. On 17 July, 1675, Marie was made to drink sixteen pints of water; she was then beheaded and her remains burned at the stake. Her lover had evaded much the same fate by conveniently dying of natural causes in 1672.

However, this was only the beginning. The trial of Marie was an international sensation and drew attention to a number of other mysterious deaths. Even King Louis, fearing that he might be the subject of a poison attack, forced several of his servants to become food- and drink-tasters. Authorities arrested numbers of fortune-tellers and alchemists who were suspected of selling 'potions' to suspected killers; these potions were euphemistically named 'inheritance powders'. Under torture some of these alchemists provided the names of their clients who had purchased poison powders. The most famous of these alchemists was a 'witch and midwife', Catherine Deshayes Monvoisin, who named a number of extremely important people, including François Henri de Montmorency-Bouteville, the duc de Luxembourg and even the king's mistress, the Marquise de Montespan. Catherine Monvoisin admitted that she and the king's mistress had performed black masses and used aphrodisiacs in order to gain and keep the king's favour.

To try the many cases involved in *L'affaire des Poisons* a special court, the *Chambre Ardente* (the burning court) was set up. Catherine Monvoisin was sentenced to death for witchcraft and on 22 February, 1680, she was burned at the stake. Some thirty-four people were subsequently sentenced to death for poisoning or witchcraft while two more died under torture. The Duke of Luxembourg, however, managed to evade this kind of terrible justice.[7]

Luxembourg was subsequently released from the Bastille, no doubt enormously relieved to escape the fury of Louis' harsh laws, and a flood of military victories followed including the triumph he was now to find at Landen.[8]

Here the French fielded an army of some 80,000 men while the English and Dutch Armies totalled about 50,000. From the 18th to the 28th of July Luxembourg had drawn together his superior forces to face the Allied lines which lay in a semicircle from Elissen, on the right, to Neerlanden, along the Landen Brook. King William had no intention of retiring over the Gete River and dug in along a strong line running from Laar through Neerwinden to Neerlanden. It is not intended to go into details of the battle within this brief discourse (Christian provides some details below) but following furious fighting including three separate attacks by the French on the Allied lines and a final successful cavalry charge, William III was forced to retreat over the Gete River, hundreds dying as they attempted to cross. The bulk of the Allied army was only saved because of William's stubborn rearguard action. Casualties included 9,000 French and 19,000 British and Dutch.[9]

Like the other recruits, Christian's field training was cursory, but according to her own account she excelled in it. Shortly after her arrival at her regiment she was posted as a night guard at the bedchamber door of the Elector of Hanover. While on guard the French went into action close by against the Allied forces and the cannon-fire and rattle of musket-shot were tremendous. This was Christian's first experience of warfare and she later admitted that it frightened her. 'I heard the cannon play and the small shot rattle about me which at first threw me into a sort of panic, not having been used to such rough music, however, I recovered from my fear,' she later wrote.[10]

After being relieved Christian was ordered by Lord Cholmondeley (pronounced Chumly) to return to her regiment, however, as she was walking back to the troop-lines she was wounded by a musket ball in one of her legs. Cholmondeley saw the incident and ordered her to be carried from the field.

Fortunately the musket ball missed the bone of Christian's leg and the wound was not severe. Had the bone been hit it would almost certainly have meant the amputation of her leg, and possibly death, as field surgery at that time was notoriously ineffective and carried an extremely high mortality rate.

Christian herself wrote a captivating account of the Battle of Landen, describing the masses of dead:

> The Duke of Luxemburg [sic] having invested [laid siege to] Huy, the 18th of July, 1693, King William, to make a diversion, detached the prince of Wirtemberg with twenty battalions and forty squadrons, which forced the French lines in Flanders, and put the country under contribution. This detachment and another the king had sent off to cover Liége, greatly weakened our army. Luxemburg, who had just carried Huy, laid hold on so favourable an opportunity, and drawing together all his forces, as if he had a design upon Liége, on the 28th, about four in the afternoon presented himself before the allies, who being sensible that they were much the weaker, had posted themselves between the Geete [Gete] and the brook of Landen. The fatigue of a long march, and the day being so far spent, made him defer the battle to the next day; but this delay gave King William an opportunity to have secured his troops, by retiring in the night to Zoutleeuw, but by his majesty rather choosing to wait the enemy, fortified the front of his camp, guarded all the passes, placed his cannon to the greatest advantage, and in a word, took all possible precaution to give the French general a warm reception.
>
> At four the next morning the French advanced in good order, within cannon-shot of our intrenchments [sic], that they might have time to raise their batteries, after which, the battle began at the village of Laar, with the left wing of our army, where a terrible slaughter was made. The foot, [soldiers] which were posted behind the intrenchments, suffered the enemy to advance very near to our cannon, and then firing upon them, covered the field with dead bodies, and swept down whole battalions which lay dead in the same ranks and order as

they advanced. The French, notwithstanding, made two vigorous attacks, but did not get an inch of ground from us, and their obstinacy only augmenting their loss, they gave over on that side about eleven o'clock, but it was to begin again with equal violence with our right wing, which was posted at the village of Neerlanden. The enemy here met with the same reception, and being repulsed, they made so considerable a movement backwards, that we thought them quite dispirited, and sick of the undertaking; but they, leaving some troops to keep the main body and our left in play, marched with the major part of their forces, and their cannon to the village of Laar, to make one more attack upon our left wing, which was both more vigorous and bloody than the two preceding. The allies defended themselves with equal bravery, til borne down by numbers, they were forced to abandon the village of Laar, and the ground between the intrenchment and the brook. The French horse, having by this advantage an opportunity to extend themselves, trod under foot all that opposed their passage, and fell upon the rear of the infantry which defended the trenches. As it was now impossible to drive them out of the post they had won, King William, seeing all efforts in vain, ordered the retreat to be sounded. Some few corps retreated in good order, and without confusion, which were mostly Dutch, but the rest took to flight in such disorder and precipitation, that the bridge broke down, and the enemy made bloody havoc of us; whole regiments threw themselves into the Geete, [Gete River] to gain the opposite side, and such numbers were drowned, that their bodies made a bridge for their flying companions, and saved them from the fury of the conquerors. The king, indeed, lost the battle with about sixteen thousand men, the French, say twenty thousand ... the king [William III] not only performed the part of a general, but even of a subaltern officer,

> for he alighted no less than four times to lead on foot to the attack; and was at the head of the squadron, commanded by Lord Galway, in the hottest part of the battle; he had two horses killed by [near] him and a musket-ball went through his sash.[11]

Christian later wrote that because of her wound she had been unable personally to witness the details of the battle she describes, but added that she was on the spot at the time and obtained all the information firsthand from her fellow soldiers who had actually taken part in the events.

The Duke of Luxembourg, who had engineered the successful Battle of Landen, was not to live long after the event. He accomplished little the following year (1694) with the exception of a successful march from Vignamont to Tournai in the face of a heavy enemy presence. He then returned to Versailles for the winter, became ill and soon died (4 January, 1695). In his last moments he was attended by the well known French Jesuit priest, Louis Bourdaloue, (1632 to 1704) who, following Luxembourg's death, is reported to have stated, 'I have not lived his life, but I would wish to die his death.'[12]

Two months after her wounding at Landen (around the end of September or in October 1693) Christian was again fit for active service. However, by now the summer campaigns were drawing to a close and Christian's regiment was ordered into winter quarters at Geertruidenberg.[13]

The campaigns in Europe during the wars were principally fought during the summer months. Winter turned the countryside into a semi-frozen quagmire where thousands of soldiers became bogged down; it was almost impossible to move the regiments from one position to another and the problems of supply were considerably heightened.

During this, her first winter quartering at Geertruidenberg, Christian and many of her fellow soldiers were ordered to assist the Dutch in repairing the dykes which had been ruined by marine worms. Christian and an ensign named Gardener were almost drowned when the tide unexpectedly flowed over where they were working.[14]

During the next season's campaigns (1694) when the Allied forces were involved in complicated marches and counter-marches. Christian Davies and sixty other English and Dutch soldiers were captured by the French and taken to Saint-Germain-en-Laye, where they were imprisoned for a short period.

There is something of a mystery over this event as Christian herself later admitted that the captured soldiers were 'stripped'. How Christian managed to conceal the secret of her gender is not known, although perhaps they were only partially disrobed or simply stripped of their weapons. She herself later wrote of the event:

> During this peaceful campaign, as we were foraging, the French came unexpectedly upon and took three score of us prisoners, stripped us and by very tiresome marches conducted us to St. Germains en Lay [sic]. The first night the Dutch and English were promiscuously imprisoned but the next day King James's queen caused the English to be separated, to have clean straw every night, while the Dutch had none.[15]

For the English at least, conditions were certainly not as poor as many prisoners would have expected. They were set to work but given a farthing a day to pay for tobacco. They were also issued with a pound of bread and a pint of wine each day. The Dutch prisoners, on the other hand, were given just half a pound of bread a day, drank water rather than wine and, according to Christian, '... lay almost naked in filthy dark prisons without other support.'[16]

The handsome and courageous Duke of Berwick, James FitzJames, the illegitimate son of James II and his mistress

Arabella Churchill [sister to the Duke of Marlborough], who was then serving in the French Army and who would be decapitated by a cannon ball during the Siege of Philippsburg in June 1734, paid frequent visits to the prison to ensure that conditions were passable, if not comfortable. Some of the prisoners were offered lucrative allowances to join the French forces and seven of them signed under Louis XIV. Berwick himself was by now a highly valued commander in the French Army but he would later (1695) be attainted for treason and lose all his titles. However, Christian declined the offer to join with the French, stating that she had already taken an oath to King William and her honour would not allow her to break that oath.[17]

Christian was kept prisoner for only nine days when she and the remaining men were exchanged for a like number of French prisoners. The English went soon afterwards to the palace where James II and his second wife, Mary of Modena, were then resident under the protection of Louis XIV. They thanked Mary for obtaining better conditions for them and Mary spoke directly to Christian who later wrote: 'She told me I was a pretty young fellow and it grieved her much that I had not my liberty sooner.'[18]

Soon afterwards the summer campaigns of 1694 ended and the regiment was once again ordered into winter quarters.[19]

That year (1694) King William's wife, Queen Mary II, had died of smallpox leaving William as sole monarch. Theirs had been a sad marriage. They had wed as part of Charles II's foreign policy and Mary had at first loathed her husband, thinking him quite repulsive. William was twelve years her senior and maintained an ongoing relationship with his mistress, Elizabeth Villiers, who was a lady-in-waiting to Mary. However, Mary had later come to love her husband, despite his unfaithfulness.[20]

Christian recalled that when news of the queen's death arrived, the regiment's drums and colours were put into mourning.[21]

During the winter quartering of 1694/95 Christian became involved with a burgher's daughter. The young girl was attracted to Christian's fine good looks and slim figure. Christian admitted that she was well versed in the arts of wooing a woman as she had been courted many times herself. Her exact words were, 'As I had formerly had a great many fine things said to myself, I was at no loss in the amorous dialect.'[22]

According to Dr J. Wilson's account:

> Mrs Davies, whose grief for her husband was drowned in the hopes of finding him, began to indulge her natural gaiety of temper and lived very merrily. In her frolics she made her addresses to a burgher's daughter who was young and pretty, ran over all the tender nonsense employed on such occasions, squeezed her hand, sighed often when in her company, looked foolishly and practised upon her all the ridiculous airs which she had often laughed at when they were used as snares against herself. But these arts had an effect which Mrs Davies did not wish for. The poor girl grew really fond of her and was uneasy whenever she was absent.[23]

Having become involved in such an affair, largely, it seems, for her own amusement, Christian now found difficulty in extricating herself without bitterly disappointing the young woman. Dr J. Wilson, records that at this time a sergeant of the same regiment also became attracted to the burgher's daughter. However, the girl was not interested; she refused to accept any attention from the sergeant who soon afterwards attempted to rape her, tearing the clothes from her back. The girl was saved by the intervention of several neighbours. As soon as she had recovered, the girl went to Christian and demanded that she revenge the attack. Christian was incensed and readily agreed that something would have to be done. She was relieved from duty and went in search of the sergeant whom she found soon afterwards.

Christian recalled that she was:

> ... so irritated at this account that I could hardly contain myself. I was seized with a tremor all over my body, often changed colour and, had I not been prevented by my duty, I should that instant have sought and killed him.[24]

Once she had found the girl's attacker, Christian verbally assaulted him and challenged him to a duel. Dr J. Wilson recorded Christian's alleged words:

> How durst you sir attempt the honour of a woman who was, for ought you know, my wife. The action is base in itself and ought to be the quarrel of every man in the regiment, as it casts a reflection on the whole corps. But I am principally concerned in this insult, for I am sufficient to chastise your impudence and require immediate satisfaction for the affront.[25]

The sergeant called her a 'proud, prodigal coxcomb' to which Christian angrily retorted, 'I leave Billingsgate language (foul language as used in the working class suburb of Billingsgate, London) to women and cowards. I am not come to a tongue battle, Mr Serjeant [sic] but to exact a reparation of honour.'[26]

The two withdrew to a place where they could fight, and, surrounded by onlookers, they drew their swords and began the duel. Christian drew blood with her first thrust and the sergeant retaliated by wounding Christian on her right arm. But before the sergeant could recover from the thrust and cover his guard Christian plunged her blade underneath his and wounded him in the thigh. The sergeant parried, thrust towards her breast and hit her again in the right arm, but the wound was slight as the sergeant was now losing blood rapidly and had become considerably weakened. Christian later recorded that had the fight continued she would almost certainly have killed the man. However, at that moment a line of musketeers arrived and arrested both the duellists. Christian was placed in a prison-cell and the sergeant was sent to a hospital where it was generally thought he would soon die of his wounds.

Sitting in her cell, Christian had time to reflect on her actions. She sent a note to the burgher's daughter telling her of the events. The girl went to her father who soon made a representation to King William and secured a pardon for Christian. The pardon stipulated that she was to be paid her arrears, her sword was to be returned to her but she was to be discharged from the regiment.[27]

After her release Christian went to thank the young girl for taking her problem to her father. Wilson later recorded what were purported to be the young girl's words. 'Had I been so prudent you would not have ventured your life and I should not have given the world any ground to censure my conduct, for how may people interpret your being warm in my cause? This consideration makes me throw off the restraint of my sex and propose to you the screening my honour by our marriage.'

Christian was reported to have replied: 'My dear, you offer me the greatest happiness, will you give me leave to ask you of your father?'

The girl reportedly answered: 'You cannot imagine a rich burgher will give his daughter to a foot-soldier, for though I think you merit everything, yet my father will not view you with my eyes.'[28]

Christian had been expecting such an answer and had known beforehand that she would be refused by the burgher. It was her way out of an embarrassing and rather awkward situation. She told the girl that she could not see her doomed to the life of a soldier's wife, following the regiment for years in dirty and dangerous encampments, and she promised to try to obtain a commission which the girl's father might view in a better light. What became of the relationship is not known, but it seems that it largely ended at this point.

Christian later admitted, 'Thus I got off from this amour without loss of credit.'[29]

Christian's discharge from the regiment was made so that the wounded sergeant could not take any revenge upon her. Not wanting to break into her stock of guineas, Christian now entered into service with the Royal Regiment of Scots Dragoons (later [1707] renamed the Royal North British Dragoons (also known as the Royal Regiment of North British Dragoons) which would subsequently become a part of the famous and historic Royal Scots Greys).

Interestingly, when first formed, the dragoons had spent their early years in suppressing prohibited Presbyterian assemblies in Scotland. The history of the Royal Regiment of Scots Dragoons had commenced in May 1678 when three independent troops of Scots Dragoons had been raised in order to quell the 'Coventanters', a militant body of Scots who were strongly opposed to the enforcement of the episcopacy. Dragoons were not, technically, cavalry, but mounted infantry armed with both a sword and short musket called a 'dragon' from which the derivative 'dragoon' was later formed.

In 1681 under the orders of King Charles II these had been regimented into the Royal Regiment of Scots Dragoons. They were numbered as the 4th Dragoons in 1694. They later went through several name changes but were finally recognised as the Royal Scots Greys (from the colour of their horses). The regiment would have a rich history, fighting not only in the War of the Spanish Succession but also at the Battle of Waterloo in 1815 when Sergeant Charles Ewart, after a ferocious fight, managed to capture the French Imperial Eagle standard of the 45th French Regiment. The eagle insignia now forms part of the regimental cap-badge. The regiment also saw action during the Crimean War, the Boer War, the Great War and were part of the Eighth Army during the Second World War until finally being amalgamated into the 3rd Carabiniers (the Prince of Wales

Dragoon Guards) in July 1971 to form the Royal Scots Dragoon Guards (Carabiniers and Greys) and equipped with Challenger tanks. Their regimental base is Edinburgh Castle.[30]

Christian remained in quarters until the following season when her new regiment was ordered to provide support work for the historic and particularly bloody Siege of Namur in July/August/September 1695.

In order to understand the complexities of this siege we need to travel back slightly in time. During the winter of 1691/92, the French had created a 'grand plan' for the destruction of their enemies including a design to invade England in an effort to support James II's attempts to regain his throne, and also for a simultaneous attack on Namur in the Spanish Netherlands. The French hoped that the attack on Namur would either force the Dutch to make peace or, alternatively, its capture would be an important pawn in future negotiations.

The French had captured Namur in 1692 when the Duke of Luxembourg had lain siege to the city. King Louis himself had been present during that military operation. Following the French occupation the city's defensive works had been considerably improved principally because the citadel had now become the most strategically important fortress in the Spanish Netherlands.

Yet the attempted invasion of England had been a complete failure due principally to the supremacy of the British Royal Navy. The engagement had been fought off the tip of the Cherbourg peninsula and ran for six days. The French fleet of forty-four rated vessels under the command of Admiral Tourville had been able to put up a strong resistance against the eighty-two British ships commanded by Admirals Rooke and Russell. However, the French were forced to disengage the attack. Some ships escaped but fifteen of them had sought the safety of Cherbourg and La Hogue. These were subsequently destroyed by British seamen and fireships. With the British now completely in control of the English Channel, the invasion of England was abandoned.[31]

However, the date was now 1695 and with France on the defensive at Namur, King William III and Maximilian II Emanuel of Bavaria began their siege of the city on 2 July that year. Approximately 80,000 Allied troops formed the besieging force. By the following day the city had been completely invested. Interestingly, the man who had designed the original defensive positions of the city, Baron Menno van Coehoorn, was now in charge of directing the siege-works against Namur. Baron Coehoorn was a Dutch soldier and military engineer of Swedish extraction and was responsible for a number of innovative siege warfare techniques including the design of a small mortar called the 'Coehorn' (sic), which he invented and used so effectively against French fortifications. His expertise would be used in the later Sieges of Bonn and Huy and he would die of apoplexy in 1704 while en route to consult with Marlborough.[32]

The outer fortifications of Namur were overcome by 18 July and five battalions of a combined English/Dutch force launched a concerted attack against the Brussels Gate of Namur. The general assault commenced on 3 August and the French commander, Louis François, the duc de Boufflers, offered to surrender the city under truce while the dead and wounded were collected and the French retired to the citadel of the fortress. This offer was accepted and the truce held for six days. Officers from both sides were exchanged as hostages while the truce was in effect.

Upon re-commencement of hostilities the French made an attempt to draw the Allied armies away from Namur by the bombardment of Brussels, the capital of the Spanish Netherlands. However, this tactic was unsuccessful. The bombardment lasted from 13 to 15 August and failed to draw any troops away from the Namur siege.

Another month of bitter fighting passed before Boufflers finally offered to surrender the citadel. The date was now 1 September, 1695, Boufflers had lost 8,000 of his 13,000 men. The Allies had lost 12,000. Fourteen regiments from England,

Scotland, Ireland and Wales had taken part in this historic battle.[33]

What active part Christian Davies and the Royal Scots took during this famous battle is not certain, although it seems their role was one more of support rather than direct action. The dragoons had been deployed to the Netherlands in 1694 and served in the traditional role of reconnaissance and security duties. Apart from skirmishes they were reported not to have taken part in any major battles during their time in the Netherlands. However, in their support role Christian would probably have witnessed many of the events at Namur. She later recalled one particular assault on the city:

> Never was a more terrible fire seen, for no less than sixty large battering pieces and as many mortars played incessantly on the outworks which rose one above another in form of an amphitheatre. ... Notwithstanding we lost a thousand men in this assault and had as many wounded.[34]

The fall of this vitally important strategic centre had pinned down William's army through an entire summer campaign but its capture, along with the earlier capture of Huy, had restored the Allied position on the Meuse. It had also secured communications between the Allied armies in the Spanish Netherlands and those on the Moselle and Rhine.[35]

Following the fall of Namur, and with winter approaching, the Allied soldiers were ordered into winter quarters for 1695/96 at a town which Christian named as Boss but may have been Bost near Tienen (Tirlemont).[36]

While in quarters Christian became involved with another woman who, having been rejected by Christian, accused Christian of being the father to her child. Christian was angered but could do little if she wished to continue her masquerade. She took possession of the child and cared for it, but infant mortality was extremely high during this period, especially in the disorganised and unhygienic conditions of large military camps. Despite giving it all care possible, the child died just a month after being placed in Christian's charge.[37]

King William returned to Holland on 17 May, 1696, with the intention of reopening the campaigns in the Low Countries. Half the Dutch Army was drawn up near Tienen (Tirlemont), under the command of Prince Nassau-Sarbruck, Veldt-marshal of the States, who, with the Elector of Bavaria, was to observe the French forces then in camp at Fleuris. The second part of the Dutch Army, commanded by Prince Vaudemont was stationed near Ghent with the intention of opposing Marshal Villeroy (also known as Villeroi) and his French forces. King Louis XIV had already been suing for peace; a tentative truce was called and after a series of conferences the formal peace was signed at Ryswick in October that year. King William reviewed his army and disbanded a large number of troops, one of whom was Christian Davies.[38] The Scots Greys were returned to garrison duties in Scotland where they would remain from 1697 to 1702.[39]

During all these campaigns Christian had discovered no clues to her husband's whereabouts, and after the bloody years of fighting it now seemed quite reasonable to suppose that he had been killed.

Christian took passage aboard ship for Dublin where she found her mother and children. However, dressed as a man, hardened by military life, neither her mother nor her children recognised her. Although it was an emotionally difficult decision, Christian had little money; she knew that she would one day again go away to seek Richard, and so decided to remain incognito. Christian later recorded:

> I found means to converse with them, [her mother and children] but I was so much altered by my dress and the fatigues I had undergone that not one of them knew me,

> which I was not sorry for. The demand the nurse had upon me on account of my youngest child, being greater than suited with my circumstances to discharge, I resolved to remain incog.[40]

What exactly became of Christian during the following five years is not known. It is only known that she found ways of making a living without breaking into her capital while awaiting another opportunity to re-enlist in the military in search of her husband. It seems likely that during this hiatus she again returned to running some kind of tavern, as she did in later life, and probably also worked as a cook, making pies and other small, easily prepared meals so popular in the days when few houses had cooking facilities and many people relied for their meals on the plethora of pie-carts and meat-roasting establishments found on the streets of the city.[41]

CHAPTER 3

The War of the Spanish Succession

Christian's opportunity to search again for Richard came in 1701 with the outbreak of the War of the Spanish Succession when England and its allies declared war against France. It was to be a war of attrition controlled by four military geniuses: Marlborough, as commander-in-chief of the united armies; his ally Prince Eugene of Savoy, reputed to have been one of the most successful military commanders in European history, pitched initially against two brilliant French commanders: Marshals Claude Louis Hector de Villars and Louis François, duc de Boufflers.

The War of the Spanish Succession broke out in 1701 and ended with the treaties of Utrecht and Rastatt in 1713-1714. It was fought principally by several European nations. These included the Spanish loyal to Archduke Charles; the Holy Roman Empire, Great Britain, the Dutch Republic, Portugal and the Duchy of Savoy, against the Spanish loyal to Philip V of France and the Electorate of Bavaria. The reason for the war was the possible unification of Spain and France under one Bourbon monarch — a unification that would have altered dramatically the balance of power in Europe. The war would result in the recognition of Philip as King of Spain. However, he would be forced to renounce his claim to the French throne and also to cede many of Spain's possessions to England and its allies, partitioning the Spanish Empire in Europe.

Many allies of England entered the war not only because they feared for their own possessions but also to acquire new possessions in the form of territories and forts or castles. This outlook led to a serious conflict of needs — leaders torn between offensive activity and defensive passivity.

Louis XIV was supported by Spain. Spain's King Charles II had conceded that Louis's grandson, Philip, the Duke of Anjou, (who became Philip V of Spain) was to be the successor to the Spanish throne. France's other allies included Bavaria and Cologne. With Louis on the throne of France and Philip now on the Spanish throne, there grew such a powerful alliance and military might that it seemed little could be done to prevent the two powers from ruling supreme in Europe. Added to this was the vexing problem of trade in South America and the West Indies. These lucrative trading centres were also to be affected by the combination of military powers. This was especially so when the Spaniards offered a French company the exclusive rights to import Negro slaves into the South Americas — a contractual agreement that greatly affected English ship-owners. Militarily, the situation in Europe looked grim. When Philip V of Spain was acclaimed in Madrid, the French immediately moved large forces to Belgium and many Dutch garrisons were interned without a shot being fired. Despite the fact that preparations for war were immediately made in England, facing such overpowering might of the combined French and Spanish forces, the Dutch were largely unable to defend themselves. The English peacetime forces were not strong enough to lend any real aid, and alone, the Dutch were virtually helpless. Mons, Namur, Léau, Venlo and many other smaller positions along the Dutch defensive barrier were all taken by Louis. All the hard-won victories of the Grand Alliance taken during the Nine Years War were easily and quickly retaken by the French.

Spain had changed sides and was now an enemy of the English. The Dutch barrier had fallen into French hands, Louis occupied Cologne and Treves and all the Channel ports. He also controlled the Meuse and Lower Rhine and his forces extended from Namur through Antwerp to the sea. It was now clearly evident that it was Louis's intention to invade Holland. With this sobering reality before them, the English were faced with the prospect of more than ten years of bitter struggle, but it was a struggle from which not just an England, but a British Empire would finally emerge.

Soon after the outbreak of war Christian Davies took ship to Holland, having had her, '... martial inclinations awakened,' where she again enlisted in the Scots Greys, the regiment being recalled from garrison duty in Scotland in 1702.[1]

Christian was present at the Battle of Nijmegen and at the Siege of Kaiserswerth on the banks of the Rhine, which was besieged on 16 April, 1702, principally because the fortress at Kaiserswerth was a bridgehead where the French could easily cross the Rhine to support potential allies.[2]

For political reasons France and the United Provinces restrained themselves from declaring war until 15 May, about a month after the Siege of Kaiserswerth had commenced, but if not a war in name then it was certainly a war in action.[3]

Sometime between six and seven o'clock on the morning of 15 June, 1702, a month after the official declaration of war and after two months of fierce fighting which included a French diversion at Nijmegen, the governor of Kaiserswerth capitulated. The capitulation was signed shortly before midnight that day. This opened the way to Son and Neuss which also later fell into Alliance hands, freeing the way to Bonn which, as we shall see, would come under siege in May the following year (1703).[4]

The capture of Kaiserswerth, although often attributed to the Duke of Marlborough, was largely effected by Dutch troops. Marlborough was not actually appointed (defacto) commander-in-chief of the Grand Alliance armies until 30 June — two weeks after the surrender of Kaiserswerth.[5]

It is not known where Christian was actually based during the Siege of Kaiserswerth; in her reminiscences she fails to mention her actual movements during the time of the siege. However, it was during this time that a party of dragoons — which included Christian Davies — under the command of

Major-General Dompre, was detached from the English Army and sent forward. They came into contact with a 'superior number' of French cavalry and a fierce battle followed during which the French were put to flight with heavy losses. Christian fought during the thickest of the fighting, although she was unharmed, and was later commended for her bravery by her officers.[6]

Christian later recalled:

> About the middle of the siege a party of horse and dragoons were detached from the army under the command of Major General Dompre, I was in the detachment. We fell in with a superior number of French cavalry and put them to the run, with a considerable loss on theirs, and little loss on our side. I had here the good fortune, though in the thickest of the engagement, to escape without hurt, and to be taken notice of by the officers.[7]

In order to understand the military events and chain of command which existed during this period it is necessary to step back a little in time. King William III and John Churchill, the later Duke of Marlborough, had never liked each other but despite their differences the king had decided that Marlborough would be the best choice as the leader of the English Army.

However, Churchill's fortunes were about to take on an even more dramatic turn for the better. On 20 February, 1702, King William III fell from his horse and was mortally injured. He would die on 19 March. William and Mary had no children and therefore Anne, the daughter of James II and James's first wife, Anne Hyde, was the heir apparent to the throne. She was crowned Queen Anne of Great Britain on 8 March that year. Anne had been born at St. James's Palace, London, on 6 February, 1665, and at the time of her ascendancy to the throne was married to the Protestant Prince George of Denmark, the couple having wed on 28 July, 1683.[8]

While King William's attitude towards Churchill had been cool, to say the least, the new queen was quite different. Sarah Churchill, John Churchill's wife, was Anne's 'Lady of the Bedchamber' and one of the queen's most intimate friends. Churchill had supported Anne during her difficult relationship with William and Mary, and Anne was now about to reciprocate. Anne made Churchill the master-general of ordnance, a post he had long desired, appointed him a knight of the garter and promoted him to the post of captain-general of her armies at home and abroad. Sarah was made 'Groom of the Stole, Mistress of the Robes and Keeper of the Privy Purse.' Combined, John and Sarah Churchill were earning in excess of £60,000 per annum and enjoyed an unrivalled influence at the royal court.[9]

With the death of William III there were many questions regarding the effectiveness of the Grand Alliance between England and the United Provinces, and John Churchill was sent to the states general at the Hague to act as Queen Anne's plenipotentiary. He was received on 31 March, 1702. Churchill made an important speech to the states general promising Anne's support for the coming war and in May 1702 the Alliance, as we have seen, declared war. John Churchill returned to England.

However, there were now concerns over who would become the supreme commander of the Alliance forces. William had named Johan Willem Friso as his successor while the King of Prussia and also Prince George of Denmark, Anne's husband, were more than a little interested in succeeding William as 'stadholder'. William's death had also brought a vacancy to the post of captain-general of the Dutch Army and the appointment of a supreme commander was an immediate concern to the Dutch. Friso was considered as being too junior to fill the post and several senior generals were not considered to be suitable material for such an elevated position. Queen Anne wanted her husband, Prince George of Denmark, to be appointed supreme commander but it was not a popular choice as the prince lacked the experience to command such a vast army in the field. The Dutch also did not wish to have a royal person at the head of the Alliance. Finally, on 30 June, 1702, the states general provisionally appointed John Churchill as supreme commander of the Anglo-Dutch forces.[10]

The decision was problematic; John Churchill did not have much experience in commanding a large army in the field but he was now being placed at the head of the English, Dutch and hired German forces. There were at least a dozen Dutch and German generals who had considerable battle experience and these men were now required to take orders from their far less experienced senior. However, as we shall see, John Churchill was to prove himself a more than able commander.[11]

On 26 July, 1702, 50,000 Anglo-Dutch troops under Marlborough's command marched south, forcing the French commander, Boufflers, also to march south, retreating to Brabant. This manoeuvre provided the Allies with additional territories and allowed Marlborough to lay siege to the Meuse fortresses north of Maastricht including Venlo, Stevensweert and Roermond.[12]

On 29 August, 1702, the town and inner citadel of Venlo were surrounded; they were taken six days later. Christian Davies' company of horse was not involved directly in the attack on Venlo and was instead sent to forage for food in the surrounding countryside. Christian recalled, '... The poor peasants fled before us, leaving their implements of husbandry in the field.' Christian's horse trod on a scythe during this foraging campaign and, '... was cut in so dangerous manner that I despaired for its recovery, though he at last was again fit for service.'[13]

The capture of Venlo on 22 September, 1702, was followed by other successful campaigns against the towns of Stevensweert and Roermond which were both besieged and taken — Stevensweert in two days and Roermond in three.

By October that year the Allied armies had cleared the Meuse of all French garrisons as far as Maastricht and appeared at Liége where they made preparations to attack the two heavily defended forts. For three days the citadel was bombarded with cannon-fire until a massive breach in the defence-works was made. When the breach was considered large enough the Allies assaulted it on the afternoon of 23 October, carrying the half-moon defence and mounting the breach with swords in hand. Dr J. Wilson stated that the Allies, '... made a cruel slaughter', during which the English troops particularly distinguished themselves.[14]

Christian added:

> The English in particular distinguished themselves in this assault, for they mounted at a place called the ... six hundred steps, for so many there are, and steeper than any pair of stairs I ever saw in my life.[15]

The reward for this attack was huge. The Allies captured thirty pieces of cannon, 20,000 florins and a great many other items of value. Wilson continued:

> Mrs Davies got but little of the plunder, except a large silver chalice and some other pieces of plate which she afterwards sold to a Dutch Jew for a third part of their value.[16]

Christian, ever eager for her share of the plunder, later claimed, '... as the citadel was taken by assault, few of the garrison escaped with life, and not one of those who did, carried off with them rags enough for a cut finger.'[17]

The next objective was, as Christian described, 'the fort of the Curthusians' on the far side of the Meuse. The French garrison there knew they had no chance against the combined might of the Allied armies and within a few hours they capitulated.

The French marched out of the fort the following day leaving vast quantities of bread and wine, much to the delight of the Allied troops in general and Christian in particular.[18]

This ended the first campaign in Flanders for 1702. Christian Davies and her regiment were ordered into winter quarters at Venlo, and several days later the regiment was detailed as one of the guards to accompany John Churchill along the banks of the Meuse. The group became lost in the darkness and waded into a pigsty where Christian stole one of the piglets — a common enough occurrence during these campaigns when military supplies were of poor quality and often non-existent. However, a regimental corporal attempted to steal the animal from Christian and a violent argument followed. The corporal drew his sword and slashed at Christian's head. She fended the stroke with her arm, the blade slicing the sinew of one of her fingers. Christian pulled a pistol from her belt, reversed it and struck out one of the corporal's eyes.[19]

Christian seemed unaffected over the encounter, later recording that she returned to her quarters and simply had her wound sewn up.[20]

It was during this episode that the Allied commander, John Churchill, was also almost captured by the French. Christian later recalled:

> In the interim our general was taken prisoner by a party of thirty-five soldiers; but got off by means of a sham pass. The next day we heard of this incident, but not of his having escaped. The garrison, as the earl was entirely beloved by all the forces, was greatly alarmed, and the governor of Venlo, placing himself at our head, marched straight to Guelders, to which place he imagined the earl had been conducted, threatening to come to the utmost of extremities if he was not delivered up. In the mean while, he received certain advice of our general being in safety; on which we marched back to our quarters,

> without attempting any action, and soon after had the joyful news of the queen having rewarded his [John Churchill's] virtues with the titles of Marquis of Blandford and Duke of Marlborough [see details below] on which the rejoicings customary were made, and we were regaled at our bonfires with good liquor.[21]

Christian had never given up hope of finding her husband alive although by now it seemed there was little chance of success; more than a decade had passed since she had last seen Richard and during that time English troops had fought in almost all of the major battles in Europe. The death toll had been extraordinarily high and it seemed unlikely that Richard could have survived those vicious campaigns. Despite her misgivings, during the quiet of winter Christian had time to make enquiries about her husband but with no success. She later wrote that she was distracted by her inactivity and thoughts of her lost husband made her pensive and sad. To combat these feelings of despondency she finally took recourse to, 'wine and company which had the desired effect ... and I spent the season pretty cheerfully.'[22]

Following the highly successful campaigns of 1702 Queen Anne publicly proclaimed John Churchill as the 1st Duke of Marlborough. It was to be one of his greatest achievements but a success that would be tinged with tragedy and sorrow. On 20 February, 1703, Sarah and John Churchill's son and heir, also named John Churchill, while studying at Cambridge University, died of smallpox, plunging the newly created duke and his wife, Lady Sarah into the depths of sorrow.[23]

The following month, March 1703, still grieving, the Duke of Marlborough left London to place himself in command of his armies in Europe and to begin the summer campaigns against the French and her allies. Marlborough went firstly to the Hague to plan the forthcoming season's strategies with his allies, and later invested the town of Bonn. Christian wrote of this event:

> We opened the trenches before Bonn and the fort on the other side of the Rhine on 3rd of May in the night. Our fire was so brisk and we pushed on our attack with so much fury that the garrison of the fort set fire to their barracks, blew up their magazines and got into the town sheltered by the smoke. On the 12th the breach was large enough for a regiment to mount at a time, we carried the covered way, made a lodgement on the palisades, and everything was ready for a general assault when Monsieur d'Alegre [the commandant at Bonn — author's note] hung out a white ensign. The capitulation was signed that night.[24]

The Scots Greys were employed at this time in their traditional roles of reconnaissance and screening for the main army. One of the regiment's most notable actions for early in 1703 was the capture of a major French convoy which included a large shipment of gold bullion. However, sadly, Christian makes no mention of this event in her memoirs.[25]

It is not clear what part Christian Davies took in the campaigns of the 1703 season but she wrote of the various campaigns including the sieges of Huy and Limbourg. Christian later stated:

> When our army drew near to Huy, the garrison withdrew into the castle, and we took possession of the town. Before I proceed, I must take notice of one action, which had liked to have slipped my memory. Monsieur de Villeroy, [also shown as Villeroi] some time before we opened the trenches before the town, spread it abroad that he would give us battle; upon which our army drew up, but he not liking our countenances, altered his mind ... and retired into his lines. Our lieutenant, with thirty of our dragoons, fell in with a party of forty horse of the enemy, but they took to flight at the first fire, and we pursued them to the barriers of their intrenchments [sic]; and being there ordered to stand our ground, we maintained it, in the

> midst of many smart fires, till we had taken a view of the enemy's situation, which was the errand of our regiment and some others sent upon.
>
> The Baron de Trogné opened the trenches before Fort St. Joseph on the 17th of August ... and the next day, ground was broke before Fort Picard. They surrendered on the 27th, and Count Sinzendorff taking possession of the place for the emperor, we prepared for another siege. Monsieur de Bulau, lieutenant-general of the Hanoverian troops, was, on the 8th of September, detached with twenty-four squadrons to invest Limbourg, and the rest of the troops designed for this siege having joined him, they immediately carried part of the suburbs, and on the 21st took the lower town. As the garrison was pretty much straitened in what was still in their possession, five battalions were left to blockade and starve them to a surrender, but tired with this tedious method, on the 26th the besiegers began to batter the place with forty-two pieces of cannon from four batteries and with twenty mortars. The fire continued very vigorous till about the next day at noon, [27 September, 1703 — author's note] when the governor seeing great part of the rampart demolished, beat the chamade, and surrendered prisoners-of-war. However, all the officers were handsomely treated, and nothing taken from them, or even their soldiers, arms excepted.
>
> The grand army did nothing more this campaign, than observe the enemy.[26]

It is not intended to go into the complexities of political and military machinations during the end of 1703 and beginning of 1704; however, following the resignation of Marshal Villars and further French successes in south Germany, a new army under Camille de Tallard, was assigned the task of taking Vienna in 1704, thus knocking Emperor Leopold out of the war and virtually collapsing the Grand Alliance.

That year Marlborough, ignoring the demands of the Dutch, marched his English and Dutch forces southwards to Germany with the intention of preventing the Franco-Bavarian army from advancing on Vienna. Prince Eugene simultaneously marched his Austrian Army northwards from Italy with the same intention. Marlborough and Eugene would later face Tallard's French forces at the historic Battle of Blenheim (also known in some countries as the Second Battle of Höchstädt).[27]

However, before Blenheim could take place Marlborough would face further obstacles including the bloody Battle of Schellenberg which was fought in July 1704, the battle being named after the village situated on high ground behind the city of Donauwörth (Christian Davies referred to it as Donawert). Here the Scots Greys would participate in the assault not as mounted dragoons but as dismounted infantry, later chasing the French on horseback.[28]

Marlborough commenced his 400 kilometre march from Bedburg, close to Cologne, on 19 May, 1704, and within five weeks had linked his forces with those of the Margrave of Baden. It was the task of the Allies to induce the Elector of Bavaria, Maximilian II Emanuel, to abandon his allegiance to King Louis XIV and once again to rejoin the Grand Alliance. However, to force this issue the Allied armies needed to secure a fortified bridgehead on the Danube through which supplies could pass into the elector's heartland. In order to achieve this, Marlborough selected Donauwörth as the crossing point.

Once it had been realised that Donauwörth was Marlborough's objective, the elector and his co-commander, Marshal Fredinand de Marsin, sent the Count d' Arco with some 12,000 men from their main camp at Dillingen as an initial force to hold the heights at Schellenberg. It was planned that this initial force would quickly be reinforced by the main army.

Marlborough decided against laying siege to the enemy's forces, time being essential to his plans, so he planned to attack before the enemy could make the position impregnable. He had received word that Prince Eugene's adjutant general, Marshal Tallard, was marching through the Black Forest with some 35,000 troops to reinforce the Franco-Bavarians at Schellenberg.

Marlborough's men were camped at Armerdingen and Count d' Arco had received intelligence as to their positions and believed that he had at least a full day and night to prepare his defences at Schellenberg.

Christian Davies would be heavily involved in this battle, just one of about 22,000 Allied troops who would throw themselves against the enemy fortifications in three separate and very bloody attacks.

At three o'clock on 2 July, 1704, the Allied armies began to break camp for their march to the killing grounds. Marlborough was personally in charge of the initial assault force of some 5,850 crack troops who had been drawn up in groups of 130 soldiers from each of the battalions under his command. Behind these 'storm-troopers' came approximately 12,000 Allied infantry — British, Dutch, Hanoverian and Hessian troops.

Marlborough fully realised that a frontal assault would be costly in lives but he was very keenly aware that if the position could not be captured by nightfall then the main Franco-Bavarian Army would arrive to defend the position and it would become almost impossible to take without a lengthy siege.

Marlborough's artillery commander, a man with the rather apt name of Colonel Holcroft Blood, opened a devastating fire on the enemy from a position near Berg, the cannon-fire being reciprocated by Count d' Arco's similar response from Gustavus's Fort, a position near Boschberg Wood.

(Colonel Blood was an interesting man and his father, the infamous 'bravo and desperado', Colonel Thomas Blood had, in 1671, attempted to steal the Crown Jewels from the Tower of London.[29] Colonel Holcroft Blood would also play an active role in the Battle of Blenheim (see below) and die at Brussels on 30 August, 1707, leaving just forty shillings to his wife, Elizabeth Blood, and almost all the remainder of his estate to his son (also named Holcroft Blood) and his mistress, Dorothy Cook).[30]

At 6.00 p.m. that evening (2 July, 1704) a force of just eighty grenadiers from the 1st English Foot Guards was sent forward with the unenviable task of drawing the enemy fire, thus enabling the Allied commanders to gain a better understanding of the defenders' strong-points. The main Allied force was following closely behind. However, as the Allied lines drew closer the men became very easy targets for the French and Bavarian musketry. Showers of deadly hand-grenades were also rolled down the slopes towards the attacking troops and savage hand-to-hand fighting subsequently took place. However, the Allies failed to penetrate the Franco-Bavarian defences and were forced to withdraw. General Johan Wijnand van Goor, who had led the attack, was killed during this dramatic first assault.

The second assault on the Bavarian defences was also completely unsuccessful. The English Redcoats, including Christian and her Scots Greys, and the Dutch soldiers in their smart blue uniforms advanced towards the Bavarian lines in long rows, led by their courageous commander Count von Styrum. Once again the colourfully clothed Allies made perfect targets for the Bavarian musket-balls and fuse-spluttering hand-grenades. The Allied attack faltered and died and in complete confusion the English and Dutch fell back. The Bavarians, intoxicated with their twin successes, fixed bayonets and surged over their barricades to pursue the retreating Allied troops. It was only the timely intervention of English Guardsmen, assisted by dismounted cavalry, which prevented a total rout and forced the Bavarians to return to their defensive positions.

By now, however, Marlborough had received intelligence that the defences which linked the town walls with the hill breastworks were being only sparsely manned. These defences were quickly attacked and easily breached, defeating the two battalions of infantry and some cavalry which had held the positions. Marlborough then launched his third and final attack along a much broader front. This forced the defenders to spread their fire which reduced its effectiveness. A simultaneous flanking movement surprised the Bavarians and they were finally forced to fall back in confusion. Complete panic spread throughout the Franco-Bavarian troops and as they fell back Marlborough unleashed thirty-five squadrons of murderous cavalry and dragoons (including the now remounted Scots Greys) to chase the defeated foe. Shouting: 'Kill, kill, destroy,' the mounted Allied troops raced into the ranks of the fleeing French and Bavarians, cutting them down with swords and lances. The pontoon bridge over the Danube collapsed with the weight of the fleeing troops and about 5,000 were drowned in the quickly moving river. Others attempted to flee and hide among the marshes and reeds but were hunted down and slaughtered like sheep.

The Elector of Bavaria arrived just too late to reinforce the garrison at Schellenberg. As he came upon the abandoned town he was in time only to see the flight of its terrified defenders and the subsequent massacre of the fleeing troops. He then drew out his garrisons from Neuburg and Ratisbon and fell back across the River Lech, near Augsburg.

The defeat of the Franco-Bavarian troops at Schellenberg had a severely detrimental impact of the ability of the Franco-Bavarian forces to face the Allies during the remainder of the campaign. Of the 22,000 Allied troops who had been involved in the battle some 5,000 had become casualties and the hospitals set up by Marlborough at Nordlingen were completely swamped with wounded. The battle also highlighted the dangers faced by senior officers who frequently led such attacks. During the battle the Allies lost no fewer than six lieutenant-generals and twenty-eight brigadiers, colonels and lieutenant-colonels.[31]

Christian Davies had been one of the casualties. During the second unsuccessful attack she had been shot in the hip with a musket-ball; the ball lodged between two bones and could never be extracted. The wound was not severe, although for a while it seemed that Christian would be a cripple for the remainder of her life. After she had been hit she had refused to be carried off the field, but propped herself against a tree and cried out words of encouragement to her fellow Redcoats as they continued to hurl themselves against the seemingly impregnable Bavarian defences.[32]

After the third attack and subsequent surrender, Christian allowed herself to be carried to a field-hospital near Schellenberg where she was examined by three surgeons, all of whom failed to discover her true gender. One of these surgeons was Dr J. Wilson who reportedly later wrote Christian's 1742 biography.

The plunder taken during this battle was also great; Marlborough's men captured sixteen pieces of cannon, thirteen standards and colours, all the tents and baggage and the plate of the Count d' Arco. At the city of Donauwörth itself, the plunder was even greater: three pieces of cannon, twelve pontoons of copper, twenty thousandweight (20,000 lbs) of powder, three thousand sacks of flour and huge quantities of oats and other provisions. While she was in hospital Christian received her fair portion of this loot which she almost certainly sold to the many Jewish merchants who habitually followed the campaigns in order to buy such items. The action had cost more than 3,000 Allied dead or wounded including General Johan Wijnand van Goor who had been struck in an eye with a musket ball and killed. The Duke of Luneburg had been badly wounded and died before the fight had been won.[33]

Having garrisoned Donauwörth the Allies quickly took the smaller towns of Rain and Aicha, taking Aicha at the point of their swords. At Aicha about 500 of its defenders were put to death and the remainder taken prisoner, although Christian did not take part in this massacre as she was lying in hospital at the time.[34]

The way was now open to the centre of Bavaria. Dr J. Wilson, stated:

> ... so that the inhabitants were greatly alarmed and many of them quitted their houses. Even the Electress did not think herself safe in Munich, though she had eight thousand regular troops about her, but desired shelter of the Archbishop of Salzburg. In short, the Allies ravaged the country, pillaged about fifty villages and forced the miserable inhabitants to seek refuge in the woods.[35]

Christian recalled that the Allies did not discriminate; they burned the houses of both the peasants and the gentry.[36]

After such a successful Allied campaign, the Elector of Bavaria, expecting to have his country laid waste, held a council of war in an open field and it was decided to abandon his camp at Lauingen (Lawingen) and to reinforce the Bavarian Army. Several garrisons were drawn out of quarters and set in defence of Augsburg where a large percentage of the elector's financial reserves were stored. The elector set the burghers to work in fortifying the position, digging trenches and other defensive barriers including a massive ditch fifty feet wide and proportionally deep. Here the elector sat and waited for some relief in the form of the French Army, a relief which finally arrived under the command of Marshals Villeroy and Tallard at the beginning of August that year (1704).[37] However, nothing could save the Electrate; various towns fell, either through force or treaty, the electress and her children were captured, the elector stripped of office and his subjects disarmed. Dr J. Wilson stated:

> In a word Bavaria was treated as a conquered country and Count Lewenstein-Worthem was made governor of it. This Electorate was miserably plundered, the Allies sparing nothing, but killing, burning, or otherwise destroying whatever they could not carry off. The bells of the church were broken to pieces and Mrs Davies, having left the hospital, time enough to have a share in the plunder, filled two bed-ticks with bell-metal, men's and women's clothes, some velvets and about a hundred Dutch caps, all of which she sold for four pistols to a Jew who followed the army to purchase the pillage. She likewise got several pieces of plate, etc., which the same ... merchant had at his own price.[38]

In Christian's own words, she stated that she left the hospital, '... in time enough to contribute to their misery and to have a share in the plunder'.[39]

Christian was fit enough to take part in the Battle of Blenheim, one of the major battles of the War of the Spanish Succession, and although she was reputed to have been in the thickest part of the fighting she came through unharmed.

Here the Scots Greys fought as part of Ross's Brigade and served as dismounted cavalry in the actual attack.[40]

The decisive Battle of Blenheim, which brought about the complete defeat of Bavaria, was fought on the banks of the Danube around the small village of Blenheim and has gone down in history as one of the turning points in the war. The complete victory of the Grand Alliance under the Duke of Marlborough would save Vienna from the Franco-Bavarian forces and thus prevent the collapse of the Grand Alliance. Blenheim would see Bavaria knocked out of the war; King Louis XIV's hopes for a rapid victory would be shattered and France would lose some 30,000 casualties including its commander, Marshal Tallard who would be captured and taken as a prisoner-of-war to England.

When the two huge armies came to face each other in August 1704, there was some disparity in their strengths, particularly their artillery. The Grand Alliance with the Duke of Marlborough and Prince Eugene of Savoy could muster approximately 52,000 men (including at least one woman), and sixty-six cannon. The French and Bavarians under the duc de Tallard and Ferdinand de Marsin mustered 56,000 men and ninety guns. Some of the Grand Alliance senior officers attempted to remonstrate with Marlborough, pointing out the considerable superiority of firepower. However, Marlborough was adamant that the battle should take place. He stated that he realised the dangers but it was absolutely necessary in order to save Vienna that the Franco-Bavarian forces should be defeated and that he relied on the bravery and discipline of his troops, though outnumbered, principally in artillery, to carry the day.[41]

The battlefield at Blenheim stretched along a front of approximately 6.4 kilometres. The Danube effectively covered the right flank of the Franco-Bavarian Army and the left flank contained the hills of Swabian Jura. A small stream, the Nebel, lay at the front of the French line. The village of Blenheim lay on the French right, close to the point where the Nebel flowed into the Danube. The village was surrounded by hedges, gardens, meadows and fences.

Marshal Tallard believed that the Franco-Bavarian positions were so strong that Marlborough would not risk attacking them but would wait for the French to move forward. However, at 2.00 a.m. on the morning of 13 August, forty Allied squadrons were sent towards the Franco-Bavarian lines. An hour later the main Allied force began to follow in eight separate columns. They reached Schwenningen by 6 00 a.m. and were then just three kilometres from Blenheim. It was planned that Marlborough, commanding 36,000 troops, would attack Tallard's force of 33,000 on the left and capture the village of Blenheim. Meanwhile Prince Eugene commanding 16,000 men would attack the 23,000 troops on the right wing. With the French flanks under pressure, Marlborough would then cross the Nebel and attack the French centre, delivering a crushing blow.

The battle continued for most of the day and resulted by 4.00 p.m. in many of the Franco-Bavarian troops being virtually besieged in the village of Blenheim.

The raging battle now paused; Marlborough wanted to attack upon the entire front but Prince Eugene, after hours of desperate fighting, needed time to reorganise. An hour later, at 5.00 p.m. fourteen hours after the Allied troops had first moved forward, all was in readiness along the entire Allied front. Two lines of cavalry were moved to the front of Marlborough's battle-line behind which came two lines of infantry. French cavalry attempted to break the attack but the Franco-Bavarian troops were tired and ragged and the cavalry was put to flight. The exposed infantry on the plain now tried one last desperate measure and attempted to form a square. However, Colonel Blood's highly accurate and close-range artillery fire decimated them. The troops, without any kind of support or cover, died almost to a man.[42]

Those who managed to escape the Allied onslaught on the plain ran for their lives plunging in desperation into the Danube where approximately 3,000 were drowned. Others were cut down by Marlborough's highly efficient and very murderous cavalry.

All that remained were now those troops still besieged in Blenheim. Bitter hand-to-hand fighting took place in the village and houses were burning fiercely. The defenders were resolute; they had seen what had happened to their fellow soldiers who had been defeated on the plain, the thousands drowned in the river, the hacking down of fleeing and defeated troops, and were desperate to prevent the same happening to them. The French were initially able to repulse every attack and the slaughter among the Allied troops was immense. However, defeat was inevitable and by 9.00 p.m., after eighteen hours of marching and fighting, the French infantry finally and fearfully laid down their arms. The Battle of Blenheim was over and Marlborough was the most famous soldier of his age. Even the Tories in London, Marlborough's most savage opponents, who had warned that if Marlborough should fail they would, '... break him up like hounds on a hare,' could not restrain their admiration for the duke.[43]

The Scots Greys fared well during this action. Although they had been sent to fight as infantry at the village itself, they were attacked by a savage charge of French regiments but with the assistance of Hanoverian troops were able to beat back the charge. Despite being deeply involved in hand-to-hand fighting, the Scots Greys did not experience a single fatality during this action, although many were seriously wounded.[44]

After the Battle of Blenheim, Christian Davies was detailed to act as one of the guards for the prisoners-of-war, most of whom were in poor condition, many of them naked. The prisoners were taken north-west towards the garrison of Breda. It must have been a lengthy march of several weeks. At the Plain of Breda, near the end of the march, while the prisoners were resting for a meal, an event occurred that was again to change Christian's life. Each prisoner was allowed a pint of beer and a pennyworth of bread and cheese and both the guards and their charges were pleased that their long march would soon be coming to an end.[45]

While the large group was resting, Christian noticed that there were many women — camp followers — who were crying for those who had died during the battles of Schellenberg and Blenheim, while others were congratulating the men who had fought and survived. Here, however, Christian saw a woman who was clearly overjoyed at the survival of one man whom Christian thought she recognised. On closer examination she suddenly realised that the man was none other than her long-lost husband, Richard.

Christian recalled:

> I was so divided between rage and love, resentment and compassion, that the agitation of my mind had such a visible effect on my body and was so plainly discernible in my countenance that my comrade asked me what it was that troubled me, that I changed colour and trembled as I did all over me. I had a pot of beer in my hand and had not the power to utter more than: 'Take the beer, I can hold it no longer.'[46]

Dr J. Wilson later wrote:

> Seeing him caressed [by] this Dutch woman, for so she was, raised in her [Christian] so great an indignation that she was resolved to banish every tender thought that might plead in his favour, and wipe the idea of him out of her memory. She was so divided between rage and love, resentment and compassion, and the agitation of her mind had such a visible effect on her countenance that her comrade asked her what was the occasion that her colour changed, and she trembled in such a manner. After some little time, having recovered her spirits, she answered that the sudden and unexpected sight of a brother whom she had not seen for twelve years before occasioned the disorder he observed. She then begged her comrade to ... ask him if his name was not Richard Welsh, and when he had [last] heard from his wife and children. He did so and brought her word that as he was the first man upon command she might speak with him at the main guard. Hardly had he delivered these few words when the drums and trumpets sounded a march. Upon their arrival at Breda, after the prisoners were secured and Mrs Davies had performed her duty, she went to the main guard in search of her husband.[47]

Christian could not find her husband at the guardhouse but was told that Richard was in a public house behind the guard-block. She walked to the tavern and pushed her way through the bar-room to the kitchen where she found Richard drinking with the Dutch woman. Christian ignored the couple and asked the landlady to provide a private room and a pint of hougarde — a white beer. Here Christian reflected on what she would do. She drank some of the beer and washed her eyes and face with the remainder to hide the fact that she had been crying. After calling the landlady to bring another pot of beer she asked her to tell Richard that she would like to speak with him in private. The landlady delivered the message and soon afterwards Richard came to the room. Christian sat with her back to the window so that her face was in shadow. She greeted him by name and asked when he had last heard from his wife and children. Richard reportedly answered: 'Sir, I have heard no news of them these twelve years though I have written no less than a dozen letters which I am apt to believe have miscarried.'

Christian replied: 'I believe sir, you do not lay that to heart, since a number of pretty girls here can easily compensate the absence of a wife. You doubtless find it so.'

Richard replied: 'Sir, you take me for a villain and you lie, I do not find it so.'[48]

It is difficult to know if there is any basis of truth in this alleged record of the conversation between Christian and Richard. It matches well with that record allegedly given by Christian in her own autobiographical writings, but it may well have been only the result of her publisher's imagination.

However, after this alleged conversation Christian started trembling with emotion at Richard's words and as he moved closer he saw that the stranger was indeed his wife. He ran to her, placed his arms around her and kissed her, weeping for joy. She disengaged herself and stood looking at him. The narrative reportedly continued:

> Yes Richard, 'tis I who have been so long in search of an ungrateful ... husband; what a ... reward have I met with for abandoning peace and plenty ... for leaving my poor babes, my aged mother, my friends, my relations and my country, to expose myself to the hardships, fatigues and dangers of a soldier's life in search of a husband whom I have at last length found in the arms of another woman. What fault of mine, if not over fondness, could make you cruelly desert me and your children?[49]

Richard was said to have replied:

> My dear Christian, do not imbitter [sic] the joy I feel in thus meeting with you, by such cruel and undeserved reproaches. Had you received any of my letters you must have learnt that my misfortune, not my fault, was the cause of our unhappy separation.[50]

Christian replied:

> I wish I had not received that which you said was your twelfth [letter]; for my tenderness would not let me believe you capable of a falsity, as I now am convinced you are; it was the fatal receipt of that letter which ruined my peace by going in search of it. Yes, that letter made me resolve to undergo all dangers, rather than not find you out; had it not come to hand I might have been still undeceived in the belief of your death; time would have mitigated my grief, and forgetting you, as I am a witness you did me, I might have continued at this time in easy and happy circumstances, have enjoyed the comfort of my friends and relations, and have done my duty to my children in taking care of their education and settlement, instead of being harassed with fatigues of war, and my poor infants exposed to the hazard of being brought up as vagabonds. I have at length found you, but so altered

> from the just and endearing husband you once were, that I had rather have had the assurance of your death, than see you thus survive your affections which I was once fool enough to believe nothing could take from me.[51]

Richard reportedly answered: 'Believe me they are still as warm towards you as ever; pardon my faults, which I acknowledge.'[52]

At this point the Dutch woman suddenly appeared at the door of the room and demanded to know why Richard had left her alone, referring to Richard as, 'My dear'.[53] Richard allegedly flew into a rage, shouting at her that she should not refer to him in such a manner and that if she again interrupted him or followed him he would kill her.

Christian now turned angrily on him stating: 'It is not manly to use a woman ill, especially if you have seduced her, as I doubt you have with a promise of marriage. In such case I shall hold her innocent.'[54]

Christian then turned to the woman and asked if Richard was her husband. The woman confirmed that Richard was husband in everything but the ceremony, as they had lived together as man and wife for several months. Christian then told her that Richard had been married to her for more than twelve years and that he had children by the marriage, adding that the Dutch woman should have nothing more to do with him. Christian ended: '... if you value your own reputation or safety, or have any regard for him, avoid him for the future.'[55]

The Dutch woman reportedly burst into tears and a bitter scene followed during which she vilified Richard for promising marriage when he could not legally carry out that promise. Christian finally calmed them both and the Dutch woman went away — still in tears — vowing never to see Richard again.

By now Christian was in no mood for romance. She roundly denounced Richard for his philandering and told him that despite the hardships she had endured in search of him she had become used to the army's way of life and intended to continue in military service as a man, and that she would pose as his brother.

Richard remonstrated with her, telling her that she had endured years of hardship already and that to have her by his side and not to be able to be her husband would be an inhumane torment, ending, '... do you call this love, would you banish me from your bed?'[56]

But Christian's resolution was firm, and she told him that he had forfeited the right to her bed by taking another woman to his. She added that she would continue as a man until either killed, wounded or discovered. Finally Richard relented and they sat together for a long time reminiscing of the days when they had lived together in Ireland as man and wife. Finally Christian gave Richard a piece of gold, telling him that she would look after him as much as possible but that he should consider her only as a brother until her gender was discovered or until the end of the war. In the privacy of their room they embraced passionately and left soon afterwards, returning to their respective posts. They saw each other every day in camp but Richard kept his promise and treated her only as a brother. When the French prisoners had been fully secured in the camp Christian and Richard returned to their respective regiments. By now the summer campaigns were ending and after the Siege of Landau, Christian's regiment was ordered into winter quarters in Holland, leaving the foot-soldiers — Richard among them — in Bavaria.[57]

During the winter break Christian took leave and visited the Hague and from there travelled to Rotterdam and Amsterdam. While at the Hague Christian experienced a brief relationship with another female, one of several such relationships. It was, apparently, an innocent encounter but as has been seen earlier in this publication Christian was not adverse to 'courting' a person of her own gender, even if it was only for fun.

Travelling to the town of Delft on what she called a 'shcoot', but which was probably a barge or 'schute', Christian later wrote:

> I obtained leave to visit the Hague, certainly the most beautiful village in the whole world: from thence I made a tour to Rotterdam, and ... happening to sit by a pretty Dutch girl, I told her she was very handsome. She returned, that I was very complaisant, but she did not know any one to whom she would more willingly appear agreeable; for I was a pretty young fellow. 'I find', said I, 'your banter will soon silence me; I said that you were handsome, because you are really so, and you are turning me into ridicule for speaking my sentiments; indeed, what I said was needless, because you cannot but be conscious of your own perfections; but out of the fullness of the heart the mouth speaks.'
>
> 'The very reason', replied she, 'that, before I was aware, I spoke my thoughts, which are altogether as sincere as your compliment.'
>
> 'Were they so, I should be the happiest man in the whole army of the allies.'
>
> 'And, could I make you that happy man, it would, perhaps, make me the most miserable woman.'
>
> 'Then you are of opinions that a soldier cannot make a good husband.'
>
> 'That is not my reason; it is, I should be in continual apprehension for your life, and never know a minute's peace in your absence.'
>
> 'Such a confession might make any man vain, though from a person of much less merit; but I have too great an opinion of your good sense to flatter myself that your heart corresponds with your tongue: no, you thought my declaration impertinent, and you have a mind to revenge

yourself, by first raising my vanity, and then laughing at my credulity.'

The schoot was, by this time, arrived at Delft; we all went across that town, which is the worst paved in Holland, to take another schoot at Amsterdam. I gallanted my pretty frow [Frau] through the street, said all the fine things to her I could think of, and was so importunate to know her place of abode, and to have leave to wait on her, that she let me, at length, know it was without [outside] the gate, near the Scotch dike; and added, that if I was sincere, and my intentions honourable, she would give me leave to see her home, when we should come to Rotterdam, and should not be displeased with my future visits. In a word, at our arrival, she gave me her hand to help her out of the schoot, and conducted me to her lodgings, where she called for a bottle of wine to refresh me. I drank a glass or two before any but a servant appeared; but, not long after, a sister came in, who embraced her, and asked who I was. She told her that I was a gentleman belonging to the English forces [for I had told her, in our passage; she could not otherwise have known, as I was dressed genteelly in a plain suit], and that she was indebted to me for many civilities. The sister made me a compliment, and said her mother would thank me, were she not indisposed. On this, my fair one begged me to excuse her waiting on her mother, and with a surprise, said, 'The maid told me she was well.' I told her I would take a more convenient time to pay her my respects; and withdrawing, went into the town and got a lodging on the Scotch dike, [dyke] in a house where a Scotch serjeant [sic], of my acquaintance, going to Scotland to recruit, then lodged. His name was John Beggs. ... We were glad to see each other, supped together, and, over a bottle, I told honest John what a fortunate adventure I had met with in my passage. 'I assure you', said, he, 'you have reason to call it fortunate, for they are mighty virtuous young ladies: there are three sisters and the mother, who live together, and are noted for their extensive charity. I have the honour to be well with, and visit the family: if you consent to it, we will wait on them tomorrow.' I was glad to hear this character of the family, as I thought I might pass the few days I intended to stay at Rotterdam, in an agreeable, amusing way.

The next morning honest John showed me the town; we saw the town-house and anatomy chamber, the shambles, and the statue of Erasmus, with the house where that great man was born, and then, being tired of rambling, went to our quarters to dinner; after which, we set out to visit my new female acquaintance. We were carried into the same parlour I had been in the evening before. John bid the maid bring a bottle of wine, and tell the lady of the house he was there. I reprimanded him for his freedom, and told him I thought he took as much liberty as if he was in a public house. 'Oh', said he, 'they allow me to take what liberty I please: they are the best-natured family in Holland.' At that instant my fellow-traveller came in, whom my friend John taking hold of, pulled upon his knee, and she suffered him to take such liberties as convinced me that there was not a family of more extensive charity; for they made no distinctions of rank, nation, or religion. She asked John if I was his acquaintance. He told her I was: 'Then', said she, 'as the gentleman made me a great many fine speeches in the schoot, and I really like him, do you take my sister, and oblige your friend and me, by my convincing him that I thought him a pretty fellow, as well as said so.'[58]

Christian was evidently incensed by either the young woman's words or her actions in sitting on John Beggs' lap and '... taking such liberties'. She later wrote:

> I was greatly shocked at my disappointment, and had much ado to prevent my treating her in a very rough manner, when she threw her arms round my neck and would have kissed me. I pushed her rudely off, saying, I had mistaken a fiend for an angel. I would have gone directly out of the house, but she clapped herself before the door, and told me, I must first pay the bottle of wine I had the evening before. Upon being told it was a guder. I threw down the money, and flew out of the house in a rage; my friend paid the other bottle, and followed me, laughing as if he would never have given over. When he could get the better of his fit, he asked me if I did not think myself fortunate in so virtuous an acquaintance.[59]

Christian subsequently returned to her quarters ready for the 1705 summer offensives against the French-held cities of Huy, Maastricht, Liége, and other smaller centres and strongholds such as Tienen (Tirlemont).

Following the Battle of Blenheim, the Duke of Marlborough and Prince Eugene once again separated, Eugene took his army to Italy while Marlborough remained in the Low Countries. The year 1705 brought little success to either side. Marlborough attempted to invade France down the Moselle but this proved unsuccessful and resulted in a stalemate which would not be broken until 1706.

Christian Davies later recalled some of the 1705 campaigning in the following manner:

> We marched out of our winter-quarters, and encamped between Maestricht [sic] and Liége. The Duke of Marlborough arrived at the Hague on the 14th of April, where he stayed but a few days before he set out to place

himself at the head of the army. The foregoing campaign it was agreed to provide good magazines in Germany, which his grace relying upon, took the better part of the army, after he had reviewed us, and directed his march towards the Moselle, to join the Germans betimes, not at all doubting but the French would draw off from the Low Countries a considerable number of their forces, and send them the same way to oppose the allies: but they were too well informed of the neglect of what had been agreed upon; were satisfied the duke would lose a great deal of time in waiting for the Germans, and were therefore determined to take advantage of their delay, and undertake some important expedition of the Maes. The Dutch army, not being strong enough to keep the field, was intrenched [sic] under the cannon of Maestricht. The French, quitting their lines on the 27th of May, encamped at Vegnacourt, and at Val-Nôtre-Dame, and having sent a detachment over the Maes, they, the next day, invested Huy. The town, which was defenceless, immediately surrendered, upon condition that the burghers should keep their privileges, that the garrison should have liberty to retire into the castle, and that the French should not fire from the town on the castle, nor the others from the castle upon the town. On the 30th, at night, the trenches were opened before Fort Picard, which was carried on the third assault, with all its outworks. They, immediately after the reduction of this fort, with all possible expedition, raised new batteries against the others, and made such a terrible fire with thirty pieces of cannon and twenty mortars, that Cronstrom, who was governor, was obliged to surrender prisoner-of-war on the 10th of June.

The French taking Huy, and laying siege to the citadel of Liége, together with the want of magazines on the Moselle [by which neglect the duke's army began to suffer], and the distance the Germans were off rendering it impossible to join him time enough to undertake anything considerable on that side, obliged the duke to quit the Moselle. His grace was no sooner arrived in the neighbourhood of Maestricht, but the French abandoned the city of Liége, raised the siege of the citadel, and withdrew, as usual, into their lines. The army being now united, took the field, and, in few days, retook Huy; and by the advice of his grace the Duke of Marlborough, resolved to attack the enemy's lines, by the shelter of which they had avoided a battle. To this end we decamped on the 17th of July, and marched straight to their lines, to attack them at one and the same time at Heilisheim, near the village and castle of Wang, and at the villages of Nederhespen and Oostmalen. The vanguard, being, at break of day, arrived at the place of rendezvous, Count Noyelles immediately assaulted the castle of Wang, which, after a small defence, he carried, and entering the lines with the runaways, seized on the barriers, and drew up in order of battle.

Three battalions, with the like rapidity, possessed themselves of the village and bridge of Heilisheim, within a quarter of a league of Wang, and took post within the lines. Lieutenant-General Schultz, with as great facility, made himself master of the villages of Overhespen and Nederhespen; by which, our horse and dragoons having openings to enter the lines, his grace led us on, and formed us to make head against the enemy; their corps nearest to the places of attack were in motion at the first alarm, and about fifty squadrons and twenty battalions advanced to dispute the hollow way. Our horse, sustained by some of the foot, made our way; and the duke, at our head, charged the French horse so briskly, that he broke, entirely routed them, and made himself master of eight pieces of cannon. The rest of the French, who were advancing to support the foremost corps, seeing their horse take to flight, thought it no shame to follow their example. The glorious success of this attack of the French lines, the honour of which, as it was just, every one attributed to the Duke of Marlborough's advice, conduct, and intrepidity, was followed by the taking of Tirlemont, where a French battalion was made prisoners. The French army, which was obliged to retreat, some towards Namur, and others towards Louvain, found means to unite, and intrench [sic] themselves behind the Dyle. The duke would have attacked them here, but being opposed by the Dutch, we had a three days' march for nothing, which the duke resented so much, that the States, to give his grace satisfaction, removed General Schlangenburg, who made the opposition. After we had continued some time in view of the enemy, near the abbeys of Ulierbeek and Park, on the 29th of August the duke marched to Leuwe, which was invested the same day by fifteen battalions, and the same number of squadrons, notwithstanding its situation is in the middle of a morass. Lieutenant-General Dedem, who commanded this body of troops, having, on the 2nd of September, possessed himself of an advanced redoubt, which was raised on the avenue to the town, between nine and ten that night opened the trenches on the side of the gate of St. Tron, pushed on his works within two hundred yards of the covered way, and the batteries being soon ready to play, the Baron du Mont, who commanded in the place, offered to march out, [surrender] if all military honours were allowed him. This being rejected, he and his garrison were compelled to yield themselves prisoners-of-war on the 5th of the same month.

Our army having levelled the French lines, broken the sluices, and demolished the outworks of Tirlemont, to prevent the enemy from keeping garrison in it in

> the winter, we marched to Herenthals, and his grace made a tour to the Hague. On his return to the army, we besieged Sanduliet. The trenches were opened on the 26th of October, and the garrison, in three days, forced to surrender prisoners-of-war. The taking of this town putting an end to the operations of this campaign, his grace the Duke of Marlborough went to Vienna, and was received with the highest marks of distinction. The emperor confirmed him prince of the empire, erected the district of Mildelheim into a principality for him, and gave advice of it to the diet of Ratisbon, enjoining them to receive a deputy of this principality, and to give him place in their sessions. The news of this being brought us, before we left Tirlemont, we were regaled with liquor, and made great rejoicing.[60]

The services of Christian Davies during the 1705 period have not been recorded, only that she and her regiment were again sent into winter quarters in Holland at the end of the year and while in quarters they received replacement recruits to fill the ranks of the men who had been killed during the previous summer; they also received fresh horses.[61]

CHAPTER 4

1706 — Ramillies
Discovery and Discharge

In London the political situation at the beginning of 1706 was one which still strongly supported the war and it was Marlborough's plan to march overland to Italy. The United Provinces accepted this plan but on the proviso that he took no Dutch troops with him. However, events forced Marlborough to reconsider and the Dutch government instructed its deputies to capture and control as many towns and fortresses in Flanders as possible. Marlborough was extremely pessimistic about achieving any positive results in Flanders during 1706. He believed that the French would remain largely on the defensive during the campaign, possibly losing a few fortresses or towns, but that would not win the war for the Allies. However, Louis XIV was of a different opinion. He believed that an active and aggressive year of fighting could achieve significant results for the French.[1]

During the winter break of 1705/06 the French had strongly fortified their positions. At Leuven, the capital of the province of Flemish Brabant, (Leuven is the Dutch spelling; in French it is known as Louvain), some twenty-six kilometres east of Brussels, they had stockpiled masses of hay, oats and other supplies, including a large quantity of ammunition. The period of rest had strengthened French resources considerably and also their willingness to fight. Rather than wait to be attacked as they had in the past, they would now sally out to challenge Marlborough's forces, meeting them at Ramillies, north of the city of Namur where battle would quickly commence. The two opposing forces opened hostilities at about two o'clock on the afternoon of 23 May, 1706. Ramillies was a fairly evenly opposed battle. The Duke of Marlborough with the Dutch commander Count Overkirk facing Marshal Villeroy and Maximilian II Emanuel. The Allied forces numbered some 62,000 men, ninety guns and twenty mortars compared to the forces of France, Bavaria and Spain with 60,000 men and sixty-two guns.[2]

The year had commenced aggressively and successfully for the French, having gained some early successes in Italy and Alsace, and King Louis XIV now pressed Marshal Villeroy to bring Marlborough to battle in the Spanish Netherlands. In accordance with these demands, Villeroy set off at the head of his army, leaving Leuven (Louvain) and marching towards Zoutleeuw (Léau). Marlborough was also ready to do battle and assembling his forces at Tongeren, near Maastricht, he advanced towards the Mehaigne River and the Plain of Ramillies where the French were forming their battle-lines.

Here the Scots Greys, serving in Lord John Hay's Brigade of Dragoons, would take an active part in the action. They would force their way into the village of Autre Eglise, pushing back the French who had held the position. After passing through the village they would encounter the impressive *Regiment de Roi* (King's Regiment). These the Greys would defeat, capturing their colours. It was also to be the battle during which Christian Davies would be revealed as a woman.[3]

The actual battle itself was a complex affair but after four hours of fierce fighting Villeroy's army was completely defeated, Marlborough having caught his enemy in a tactical vice. The French were driven back, with Christian Davies, as usual, in the thick of the fighting. The remnants of the French Army scattered in all directions and thousands of men were captured along with a great quantity of ammunition, artillery, wagons and baggage. The rout of Ramillies was described as being the most shameful and disastrous of French defeats. Casualty figures vary but according to John Millner's memoirs, *Compendious Journal* (1733), 12,087 soldiers in Villeroy's army were killed or wounded with a further 9,729 captured. Another estimate gives the casualty figure as high as 30,000 with losses by desertion actually doubling that number.[4]

The Allied success at Ramillies opened the way, with the whole of the summer campaigns ahead of him, for Marlborough to capture a range of major cities and fortresses. The French commander, Marshal Villeroy, would be unable to stem the relentless march of Allied victories for that year.[5]

The Duke of Marlborough subsequently wrote to Lord Treasurer Oxford (Robert Harley), (who would later be responsible for reducing Christian's pension from one shilling to fivepence per day and also be one of those infamously responsible for Marlborough's impeachment) stating that with the whole of the summer campaign still ahead of him, with the grace of God he (Marlborough) should make best use of the time and cut a swath into as many French-held positions as possible.[6]

However, after the Battle of Ramillies a stray shot from a mortar battery situated in a steeple exploded near Christian and a piece of shrapnel struck her on the back of her head. She was taken on a stretcher to a small village named Meldert near Leuven (Louvain) and trepanned by an army surgeon. For a while it seemed that Christian — like many other trepanned patients — would die, but she lingered, hovering between life and death for ten weeks before finally recovering. Yet Christian's long-maintained subterfuge was now over. During the operation the surgeons quickly realised that she was a female and informed the commanding officer, Brigadier Preston, that a woman was serving in the ranks.[7]

Christian later recalled:

> I suffered great torture from this wound, yet the discovery it caused of my sex, in the fixing of my dressing, by which the surgeons saw my breasts, and by the largeness of my

> nipples, concluded I had given suck, was a greater grief to me. No sooner had they made this discovery but they acquainted Brigadier Preston that his pretty dragoon [so I was always called] was, in fact, a woman.[8]

Dr J. Wilson later wrote:

> He, [Preston] was very loth to believe it and did her the honour to say he had always looked upon her as the prettiest fellow and the best man he had. His incredulity made him send for her supposed brother who, finding the secret discovered, acknowledged that she was his wife and that he had had three children by her. The news of this discovery spread far and near, and brought Mrs Davies an abundance of visitors.[9]

The regimental commander, Lord John Hay, was advised of the situation and conducted his own investigation, questioning Christian's friends and tent-mates, all of whom protested that they had had no idea that Christian was a woman. Richard was again sent for and he recounted to Lord Hay what he knew of Christian's adventures as a man during the main campaigns in which she had served. He told Hay why Christian had become a soldier, details of his own enforced recruitment, and how they had finally found each other. Hay was suitably impressed. He ordered that Christian should want for nothing and that her pay as a soldier should continue in full while she was recovering from her head-wound. He also sent her some shirts and sheets. The regimental commander gave her a silk gown and all the officers donated something in which she could dress. However, much to her chagrin, Christian was dismissed from the service and soon after her recovery she visited Lord Hay who remonstrated with her over denying Richard her bed. Christian was alleged to have replied: 'My Lord the discovery of my sex has now removed the cause and I have no objection to living with my husband, as 'tis the duty of an honest wife.'

Hay was said to have replied: 'Well, I am satisfied we will have a new wedding.'[10]

Lord John Hay had been born circa 1668. He was the son of John Hay, the 2nd Marquess of Tweeddale. Hay was commander of the Royal Scots Greys from 1704 until his death on 25 August, 1706.[11]

A new wedding between Christian and Richard was indeed arranged and all the regimental officers were invited; the officers kissed the bride and Christian received many bridal gifts. However, although Christian was devoted to Richard, the role of a wife was a prosaic one compared to the excitement and dangers she was used to experiencing as a dragoon on active service.

Christian was now in the rather uncertain position of not receiving any pay so she began work as an army cook, preparing meals for the troops and returning to Richard's quarters each evening. However, this too did not suit Christian's adventurous spirit and her increasing need for adventure and war-plunder. She resigned as a cook and became a sutler — a camp-follower — providing provisions for the men. She placed herself close to the forward lines of Richard's regiment prior to its going into action — a position guaranteed to be rewarded in the best loot during and after the fighting.

Christian later wrote of those days when she was first discovered:

> I conceived [a child] the first night, having never known [a] man except my husband, but at the time I was surprised. ... An idle life was what I could never [get] away with, beside I was under a necessity, having now no pay, to do something for a support, wherefore I undertook to cook for our regiment, returning to my husband's quarters every night. I did not long carry on this business as the close attendance it required prevented my marauding which was vastly more

> beneficial. After I had given over my cooking I turned sutler and, by the indulgence of the officers, was permitted to pitch my tent in the front while others were driven to the rear of the army.[12]

It should, perhaps, be emphasised that looting at this time was a natural part of any warfare. Troops, often poorly paid and hungry, considered that the acquisition of loot was a part of the pay and reward for their dangerous service, although technically it was a crime punishable by death. A comparable example may be made of the privateer ships then sailing the English Channel and Atlantic — small, heavily armed vessels, thick with sails and crewed by men who joined the ships for no other reason than the prize money involved in capturing French vessels and sailing them to English ports where the cargoes and the ships themselves would be sold and the profits divided up on a specified percentage basis to the officers and men. The armies of the Duke of Marlborough operated in a similar fashion, although there were no organised percentages, every man looted as much as possible, generally selling the looted items to Jewish camp-followers.

The capture of Ramillies was a significant turning point in the war; with the French forces disorganised and demoralised, the way lay open for penetrating deeply into the French lines, and French fortresses in their dozen were attacked and fell in rapid succession.[13]

One of Marlborough's principal problems was that of a supply route to the sea. The French-held port of Ostend was conceived as the perfect harbour to bring in such supplies but first it would have to be captured. Marlborough went to the Hague to consult with the states general and immediately after his return he invested Ostend by land while Admiral Fairborne blockaded the port by sea. The town could not be totally cut off without first capturing Fort de Plasendaal on the canal of

Brugge (Bruges). Ostend was renowned as a difficult objective well used to fortification and siege, yet a concerted attack on the fortifications saw it capitulate on 4 July, 1706, after just three days.

Menen (in French Menin) was next placed under siege with 200 pieces of cannon brought from Maastricht and Holland. It held out for eighteen days before its surrender. The army remained at Menen to repair the destroyed defences and to fill the breaches. The capture of Menen was followed by successful attacks on Dendermonde, '... which made a more obstinate resistance than expected,' as Christian Davies later wrote, but capitulated in early September, 1706. The Siege of Aeth, (Ath) with forty battalions was next undertaken.[14]

During this prolonged Allied push, Christian Davies was well enough to take up her position in the front of the lines working now as a sutler and hoping for rich pickings as the French forces fell before the might of the Grand Alliance commands.

Richard Welsh was involved in the fighting for Aeth and when a general movement was ordered to one side, Richard left Christian cooking food in a large pot as he moved forward. Christian continued cooking as the battle raged, and when the meat was cooked she covered the pot with cloths so that the steam and heat could not escape. She then crept through an enemy-occupied village, a distance of some five miles, with her pot of food on her head, in an effort to find her husband's position.

A later report stated:

> Having found her husband, she set the broth and meat before him, she invited her colonel and other officers who were not a little surprised at the risk his wife had run, and that she could bring it hot such a length of way. Lord Auverquerque, [the troops' commanding officer — author's note], who was come to thank the officers and soldiers for their diligence, stood talking to some of the

> former, when Mrs Davies, looking through the sandbags, saw a [French] soldier who came out of the town to gather turnips. She took a piece [musket] out of one of the soldier's hands and called to an officer to see her shoot him. 'Tis possible they were just then perceived for the instant she killed the man, a musket shot from the town came through the sandbags, split her under-lip, beat one of her teeth into her mouth and knocked her down ... Her husband ran to take her up imagining she was shot through the head, but she convinced him to the contrary by spitting the ball and tooth into her hand.[15]

Christian's recollection of the event included: 'Both [the enemy's] shot and mine, with which I killed the soldier, were so exactly at a time that none could distinguish whether I fell by the recoiling of the piece or the enemy's ball.'[16]

Following this incident a surgeon sewed up Christian's lip and Lord Auverquerque, who had witnessed the event, gave her a present of five pistols.[17] The wound seemed not to have overly concerned Christian, although she was certainly fortunate to have survived. The musket shot which struck her must have travelled a considerable distance and therefore its force would have been largely spent before it struck her in the mouth. Quite unmoved by her narrow escape, Christian remained that night with her husband in the trenches until his regiment was relieved the following morning.[18]

A few days later the French at Aeth beat the chamade to indicate that they were ready to surrender as prisoners-of-war. Soon afterwards Marlborough's armies marched into winter quarters at Ghent.[19]

The year 1706 had been a decisive one for the Allies: King Louis XIV had been severely humbled and was now secretly negotiating for peace. Marlborough had kept his promise to Robert Harley to make good use of the summer months and town after town had fallen under Allied control.[20]

Richard Welsh's regiment was now quartered in Ghent and it was here that Christian gave birth to her child. However, in the harsh conditions of that bitter winter, with food in short supply, the infant lived for only about six months.[21]

Christian Davies was, however, a tough and resilient woman. She recovered quickly from the death of her child and soon afterwards took a position as an assistant cook. During this period she was involved in another event which displayed both her quick anger and her physical strength. A later report claimed:

> While she was in this service the cook had one day orders to dress something for Mr Stone, the surgeon, which was ready for the table when Lieutenant St. Leger came into the kitchen and would have it for himself. The cook would not yield to it and the lieutenant knocked him down. Mrs Davies, irritated at the injustice of the action, ran to the lieutenant, collared him, threw up his heels, and in the fall he broke his leg. Mr Damper, Mr Stone, and several others ran in, and everyone allowed her to have been in the right. Mr Stone [the surgeon] refused to set his leg, which was done by a French surgeon, but after such a bungling manner that it was no small mortification to him who was a tall, strong, well made, black man and had no small opinion of himself.[22]

It was as well that Christian had not been serving in the army as a regular dragoon at that time; had she still been in the army she could well have faced a firing squad, or the noose, for attacking an officer. However, as a civilian woman no military charges could be brought against her. Christian later recalled that the man in question had been, '... very much the bully'. She added, '... His misfortune became a standing jest, for whenever he was quarrelsome in company, he was menaced with me.'[23]

Some years later Christian again met with this man in a coffee-house and a companion asked the man if he knew Christian. He replied that he knew her face but could not put a name to her. Christian told him her name and asked if he had forgotten who had broken his leg. The man, according to Christian's own account, stated, 'Damn her, she is strangely altered, she is grown fat.' To which Christian allegedly replied: ''Tis true in my person I am altered, but not in my temper; for should I see you knock down, as you did, a man of much inferior strength as was our cook, I might perhaps give you another broken leg.'[24]

The man abused her, '... which he could do as well as any officer in the army,' and then left the coffee-house.[25]

Soon after the event in the cookhouse Richard's former mistress took a lodging in Ghent close to the barracks where Richard and Christian were living, and one lunchtime she invited Richard to dine with her at a tavern. Christian soon began to look for him and was informed that he had been seen at the tavern with the Dutch woman. Christian's well known quick temper soon flared and she ran to the tavern where she found Richard and the woman sitting together in a small cubicle. Without thinking, Christian grasped a carving knife and struck at the woman, cutting off her nose which was left hanging to her face with only a shred of skin. Richard leapt over the table and ran to the main guardroom for a doctor who soon afterwards sewed the woman's nose back onto her face, although she was terribly disfigured by the scars.

Richard was taken before his colonel who severely reprimanded him and confined him to barracks. Christian was also punished. She was placed onto a turning stool and whirled around until she was violently sick. A later report stated:

> This stool is like a round cage, big enough to hold one person fixed upon a spindle in which the criminal is exposed to the ridicule of all the bystanders. After she

> had undergone this punishment she was conducted out of the gates of the town with great ceremony. Mrs Davies afterwards acknowledged that the violence of her temper, which was a very jealous one, carried her too far on this occasion, for in the place where she found them they could not have wronged her, nor had she any reason to think her husband had been guilty of any criminal familiarity with the woman. ... The woman who raised this jealousy, [later] married at Groeningen, where Mrs Davies often afterwards met her ... as she was mortified at the figure she made by the amputation of her nose and its being stitched on again.[26]

Shortly after this event a man and woman were executed for committing a murder. The man had been married to a woman at Oudenaarde. The couple had had three children and the wife was pregnant with her fourth child. However the husband had been having an affair with a young servant girl for some considerable period and the two plotted to kill the man's wife so that they could be together permanently. The husband purchased some poison and gave it to the girl so that she could place it in the wife's gruel. The husband then travelled to Ghent so that he could not be accused of the crime. The servant girl placed the poison into the food, and, as was later reported:

> The poor woman swelled amazingly and was in the utmost torture. Her little boy, about nine years' old, hearing his mother cry out in her agonies, ran and brought her relations, but nothing could relieve her, and it being evident that she was poisoned, the maid was secured, who, imprisoned, confessed that she had put something into her mistress's water-gruel by her master's order.[27]

After receiving this confession, four men were appointed to watch for the husband's return to the town. When he appeared at around sunset that day he was arrested, charged with the murder, and almost certainly tortured to obtain a full confession which came just a few days later. The trial was a foregone conclusion; both the man and his mistress were sentenced to death and executed the following day, the woman being beheaded and the man broken on the wheel.[28] This man's punishment was a particularly brutal form of execution, the victim being strapped to a large wheel and an executioner armed with a heavy metal cudgel performing the task of despatching him. He broke first one leg, then an arm, another leg, a second arm, right and left cheekbones, right and left ribcages, the sternum, the nose, shoulders and, if the victim were still alive at this time, delivered the *coup de grace* by crushing his skull.

The report continued:

> After the execution was over they were hung in chains, the woman by the heels and the man by the neck. Mrs Davies and others marching that way sometime after this execution, [by which time the corpses had become desiccated and brittle] one of the company [who] observed a bird go in and out of a certain part of the woman's body that may be easily guessed at, cried out, '... there's a bird's nest,' and named the place which modesty forbids us to repeat. However, Mrs Davies went to search and pulled out five young birds just fledged to the amazement of all that beheld them. ...
>
> Sometime later, [after Christian had returned to England] near Holloway, as she was walking one summer's evening, she observed a multitude of people taking notice of a bird flying in and out through the sockets of a man's eye, hung in chains. When Mrs Davies told the mob she was assured a bird had built her nest there, in general they hooted her with scorn, but offering to lay a wager of a crown to prove her assertion, she was soon taken up and, procuring a

> ladder from a neighbouring house, she clapped it against the gibbet, mounted it and drew out a wren's nest with five eggs. The man who had laid the wager with her wanted to be off and thought, because she was a woman, to laugh her out of it. But she, not being used to such trifling, declared if he would not give her the crown she would have it out of his bones.
>
> 'Well,' replied the fellow, 'you shall have it if you can get it.'
>
> 'Shall I,' said she, 'I'll try that.' Upon which she flew at him giving and receiving several smart blows until at last she seized him by the collar, tripped up his heels, laid him across her knees, pulled down his breeches and gave him three or four slaps on his bare bum, among several hundred spectators who applauded her revenge with loud huzza's. That done she seized him by the legs and shook his money out of his pocket upon the ground. She took up her crown, telling him she should take but her own and he might go to the devil with the rest. He took the remainder, put up his breeches and sneaked off with a following mob at his tail. This recounter proved very lucky to Mrs Davies, for the engagement stopped several gentlemen to see the event of it, and among them a collection was made of eight pounds fourteen shillings which she carried home in triumph.[29]

Following the success at Ramillies, Marlborough was acclaimed by the English Parliament and his titles and estates were made perpetual for his heirs in order that Marlborough's deeds would never be forgotten.[30]

CHAPTER 5

1707 – 1708
The Plundering Continues

What became of Christian during the campaigns of 1707 following the mandatory winter hibernation at Ghent is not clear. Marlborough's manoeuvres were limited during 1707, the main weight of the war against the French being pressed in the south by Prince Eugene's forces which were amassed against Toulon.

By that year the Allied armies in Flanders totalled about 90,000 men comprised of ninety-seven battalions and 164 squadrons. The French were considerably superior with Marshal Vendôme (Louis Joseph de Bourbon, Duke of Vendôme) having about 110,000 men under his command.

It was expected that 1707 would be a year of bitter fighting. The resounding victory at Ramillies in May 1706 and the subsequent capture of Ostend, Dendermonde and Aeth only added to the Allied victories on the wider fronts. In Italy, Prince Eugene of Savoy had defeated the French Army under Marshal Fredinand de Marsin and the duc de Orléans which had caused them to abandon the Siege of Turin. Meanwhile on the upper Rhine, Marshal Villars had been forced onto the defensive as much of his army had been withdrawn to bolster the French troops facing Marlborough in Flanders.[1]

Marlborough arrived for the summer fighting in May that year (1707) when his armies were concentrated near Brussels. He marched his forces in the direction of Soignies while Marshal Vendôme counter-moved by marching the French Army to Gosselies. Marlborough immediately retreated to Brussels as the

Dutch field-deputies had been issued with instructions that their forces were to avoid battle at any cost.

However, on 10/11 August, 1707, the Allied army left Meldert, near Brussels, and marched to Genappe in an attempt to turn the French flank. The French forces, believing that they might be cut off, retreated to Seneffe, the Allied troops, floundering in the mud and torrential rain, following in their wake. It was a cat-and-mouse game of military chess which resulted in little if any gains on either side although apparently Marlborough captured about 4,000 French stragglers.[2]

The 1707 campaigns petered out with both sides roughly occupying the same ground they had at the beginning of the season in May that year.[3]

While the campaigns of 1707 were relatively simple and fruitless, those of the following year would be far more exhausting and bloody.

In 1707 the Act of Union had been proclaimed which brought together Scotland and England, creating the United Kingdom — a move which was not well accepted by many of the Scots and it was believed in France that a rising in Scotland could be provoked which would bring about the destruction of Queen Anne's reign.

Therefore, by 1708 the French were preparing to attack the British by landing forces at Scotland led by the son of the late James II, James Francis Edward Stuart, thus enabling the 'Old Pretender', as he became known, to lay claim to the English throne. James II had died of a brain haemorrhage at Saint-Germain-en-Laye on 16 September, 1701, and his son, James Francis Edward Stuart, had been recognised by his cousin, King Louis XIV, as the rightful English king. The Old Pretender's Jacobite supporters proclaimed him James III. James declared himself as being king and was recognised as such not only by France but also, unsurprisingly, by Spain and the Papal States. In England James was attainted for treason on 2 March, 1702, and all his titles, including that of Prince of Wales, were forfeited.

When the plans for the Scottish invasion became known to the Allies, the heads of the United Provinces pledged their full support for Queen Anne. Marlborough arrived at the Hague to discuss plans and strategies and it was decided that in Flanders the Allied forces should attempt a repeat of their successes at Blenheim. The French had decided to open their summer offensives with a landing in Scotland led by the Old Pretender and a concerted effort to retake their lost possessions in Flanders. To do this they had amassed some 110,000 men, compared to about 90,000 men in the Allied commands.

Dunkirk was the departing point for the French fleet on their mission to land James Francis Edward Stuart in Scotland. At the French port they had assembled six major ships-of-the-line and a number of frigates. The forces consisted of about twelve battalions and a large cache of weapons with which to arm insurrectionist Scots. Most of these ships were driven back by the British fleet under Admiral George Byng, 1st Viscount Torrington, but several ships managed to get through to Scotland including the vessel carrying James, the Old Pretender, which arrived safely at the Firth of Forth. Yet it was to be a futile gesture.[4]

Christian Davies later wrote:

> On the 5th of March, 1708, the king [Louis XIV] went to St. Germains [Saint Germain-en-Laye] to take his leave of the Pretender*, and, in wishing him a happy issue, made him a present of a sword set with diamonds, worth fifty thousand livres, desiring him to remember that it was a French sword. Having made a suitable comment to the king, the Pretender took his leave of the dauphin and other princes of the blood, and that very day set out for

Dunkirk from whence he set sail the 17th, at night, with a number of volunteers, big with the hopes of being joined by such malcontents in Scotland, where he designed to land, as were adverse to the Union, [between England and Scotland] and with the troops which followed, and the assistance of such Scots, to submit [conquer] the whole of Great Britain.

The designs of France being timely discovered, the English and States-general soon got ready a fleet of forty men-of-war under the command of the late Lord Torrington, [George Byng 1668-1733] who, with all the sail they could crowd, [onto the masts] followed the French, having advice of their departure and course.

In the mean while some English troops drawn out of Flanders, were sent to England by the way of Ostend. The Pretender came to anchor near Edinburgh; fired the number of cannon agreed upon with his partisans; and hoped the signal would raise some thousands of malcontents, who would take arms to support his pretensions. On the certain assurances made him of an insurrection, preparations were making [being made] to disembark his troops, but the English, by a great deal an over-match for the French, appearing in sight, suspended the landing. A council was held, in which it was resolved to send three ships to the town to land their troops in case they perceived any commotion in their favour; but these having the mortification to find none ... they were obliged to drop the enterprise, and make the best of their way to the coast of France. ... Thus the Pretender returned to Dunkirk the beginning of April, and all his hopes were dissipated in smoke; the unsuccessful project only served to irritate the allies against France, and brought them to a resolution of acting with more vigour than they had done yet.[5]

* The Pretender would lead another rising in 1715, shortly after the accession of George I, landing at Peterhead and advancing with a small force as far south as Scone where he intended holding a coronation. However, upon learning of the approach of a strong force under the command of the Duke of Argyll, James retreated to Montrose, the Highlanders dispersed into the mountains and James embarked from Montrose for France, his efforts completely defeated. He subsequently married Maria 'Mary' Clementina Sobieski, the granddaughter of the 'warrior king' of Poland, John Sobieski, and accepted an offer from the Pope to live in Rome. He died there on 1 January, 1766, and was interred in the crypt of St. Peter's Basilica at the Vatican. His first son was Charles Edward Stuart, also a 'Pretender' famous as Bonnie Prince Charlie; a second son, Henry Benedict Stuart, became a Roman Catholic cardinal.[6]

Meanwhile, unlike 1707, the 1708 campaigns in Flanders were to be particularly aggressive. The French Army was commanded by Marshal Vendôme but nominally also by King Louis XIV's eldest grandson, the Duke of Burgundy. However, Burgundy appeared unwilling to take orders from Vendôme and began overruling Vendôme in important military matters without the backing of the king. Thus the French Army found itself with a kind of dual command structure which necessitated referring vital matters to King Louis at Versailles.

On 26 May, 1708, the summer hostilities commenced with the French marching to Soignies. Marlborough was now behind the Dijle where he was waiting for Prince Eugene of Savoy and his forces.

It was the French intention to reverse many of its defeats of the previous years. Rapid French deployment delivered Brugge to them on 5 July and Ghent fell on 8 July. With these two important centres in their hands, the French commenced a siege on Oudenaarde, (also known as Oudenarde or Oudenard) a siege that was soon lifted because of subsequent Allied manoeuvres which would lead to the historic Battle of Oudenaarde.[7]

When Marlborough's forces crossed the Scheldt River (Dutch: Schelde River, French: Escaunt River) below Oudenaarde, the battle commenced on 11 July, 1708.[8]

Marlborough's attacking forces of some 8,000 men marched fifty miles in just sixty-five hours before they reached the bridges of the Scheldt. Marshal Vendôme could not believe that the Allied forces were already upon him and he rode out to assess the situation himself. Marlborough commanded the left and central lines, giving command of the right wing to the brilliant Austrian general, Prince Eugene of Savoy. The French fought tenaciously but without any specific order-of-battle or battle-plan, and the fighting was extremely confused throughout the entire day, a large portion of the French forces not even being brought into action. For those who *were* brought into action the particularly bloody fighting was at close-quarters among the villages, woods and streams, and did not cease until after darkness had fallen. By that time the French forces were demoralised, confused, and divided into two segments; some 40,000 of them were surrounded by the Allies, a further 40,000 stood helplessly on a ridge above the battle area. Marlborough, realising that little more could be achieved in the darkness, ordered his men to cease firing and to lay upon their arms. During the night most of the surrounded French troops escaped through the Allied lines and Marshal Vendôme hastily took the remnants of his force and retreated towards his newly captured Ghent. A quarter of his army had been either destroyed or dispersed, and the Allies had captured some 7,000 prisoners.[9]

This victory altered the course of the war. Marlborough wanted to march on into France, but Prince Eugene disagreed, insisting that the massive French fort at Lille should first be captured as it would have been militarily dangerous to leave such a powerful French fortification and large numbers of French troops in the rear of the Grand Alliance armies. Marlborough demurred to the younger man and so the Siege of Lille was commenced. It was to be the largest and most complicated siege in the annals of eighteenth century warfare.

Lille was one of France's five major cities at that time and its fortress was the strongest in the region, possibly the strongest in all France, having been designed by Sébastien Le Prestre de Vauban (later the Marquis de Vauban). Its massive walls protected a garrison of approximately 15,000 troops under the command of Marshal Louis François, the duc de Boufflers.

The siege itself was under the control of Prince Eugene of Savoy, while Marlborough remained in a fluid position to ward off the superior French forces.

Although, as we have seen, Christian did little during the 1707 campaigns she was evidently still in Europe that year and ready to take part in the bloody Siege of Lille. Christian only wrote in her memoirs that between the French capture of Ghent (July 1708) and the Allied attack on Lille (August 1708) she took part in a horse-race with an officer near the town of Courtray. Christian wrote that she was going to the town to purchase provisions when she met Colonel Cholmondeley on horseback. She added:

> ... The colonel, who was of a gay, lively temper, and pretty much of what we call the wag, seeing me go into the town, waited for my coming out, that he might divert himself by teasing me, which he did not a little delight in. I carried my provisions on a mare; the colonel had a small black stonehorse, which, when he saw me returning, he turned loose, and the horse, like a brute as he was, began to be very rude with my poor beast, and in his rough courtship broke my four bottles of wine. I was so irritated at this that having driven away his unmannerly tit, I pursued the colonel with stones, but he eluded my anger by his flight, and told the officers, that his stonehorse had an amour with Kit Welsh. [Christian Davies] Some time after this, as I was upon my mare, in a dress convenient for my vocation, Mr Montgomery,

> captain of the grenadiers in Lord Orkney's regiment,* began to ridicule my habit, and make a jest of my poor beast. I offered to run her against his horse for a pistole, [sic] and we would both ride. Brigadier Godfrey, who was [close] by, laid another pistole on my side. We both went to the place chosen to run upon, and starting at the beat of drum, placed to give the signal, he suffered me to keep pace with him some time, but finding he was going to leave me, I made a furious push at him, flung man and horse into a ditch, and thus won the race. The brigadier laughed heartily at my stratagem, the captain was half angry, but I got a couple of pistoles [for the brigadier gave me that he had won], and did not much concern myself, nor should I have given myself any trouble had he been irritated, for I may safely say, I had a little fear about me as any man in the army.[10]
>
> *(Lord Orkney's Regiment of Foot, the Royal Scots, was the oldest regiment in the British armed forces. Lord Orkney was George Hamilton, the fifth son of the Duke of Hamilton. George Hamilton had served as a company officer in the regiment when his uncle, the Earl of Dumbarton was its colonel. Lord Orkney had taken command of the regiment in 1692 and was to remain at the head of the regiment through many of its most active years.)[11]

The Siege of Lille, which commenced on 12 August, 1708, was certainly the most difficult and complicated piece of military action of that year. Defended, as we have seen, by Marshal Boufflers with a garrison of some 15,000 men, it was a massive undertaking. 16,000 horses were employed in dragging Marlborough's siege-trains from Brussels, a line of communication which had to be protected by a large percentage of the duke's armies. For week after week Marlborough bombarded the city with his heavy batteries and launched a series of very bloody assaults against the French trenches. Marshal Vendôme and his army marched to the south of Lille and attacked Marlborough's forces, and at the same time Boufflers launched an attack against the weakened Allied positions surrounding the city. In addition to this the French launched a dangerous thrust with some 20,000 men to cut off Marlborough's lines of communications with Ostend, and Major-General Webb with Brigadier Count Nassau-Woudenburg, with an inferior force, were dispatched by Marlborough to meet this new threat. Christian's husband was a part of this force and, naturally, Christian followed the troops.

Christian later wrote:

> ... the Duke of Marlborough advanced beyond Menin [Menen] almost as far as Marquette, to be at hand to sustain us. We were joined by a second detachment of twelve battalions and twenty-eight squadrons, and met the [British] convoy at Hoogleden [probably Hooglede — author's note] where we had advice that Monsieur la Motte was marching with a body of twenty-three thousand men and better, to attack it [the convoy] near Wenendal and our generals posted, on each side, a regiment in the coppice, with orders to lie snug, and not to fire until they were sure of taking the enemy in the flank. Hardly was this disposition made before the enemy appeared in sight. They formed the infantry into four lines, and the horse in as many, and entered the defile to attack the escort; but they were no sooner within our ambush but they were saluted with a general discharge on either hand, which put their right and left into a thorough disorder; they, however, formed again very soon, and even made two battalions give way a little, but Albemarl's* regiment coming up to oppose their passage directly in their front, kept them in play, and gave time to make some fresh troops advance. Seeing themselves attacked in front, and open on the flanks to an incessant fire, the two wings were forced in disorder up their centre, and all of them returning the way they had come, hastened out of the defile, where they left

> four thousand of their dead, and some pieces of cannon. The French general not being able to lead on his third attack, was obliged to retreat and suffer the convoy to pass. We had not above six or seven thousand men, so that they were above three to one. The conduct of General Webb greatly contributed to this victory, however he paid dearly for by the wounds he received.[12]...
>
> *This was almost certainly Arnold Joost van Keppel, the 1st Earl of Albemarle [note difference in spelling].[13]

Christian also profited from the engagement and later boasted of her plunder, adding:

> I got a fine bay horse with silver-capped pistols and lace housings and pistol bags. I sold my horse to Colonel Hamilton for nine pistoles, my pistols to Captain Brown for five crowns and the lace of my furniture, excepting what I reserved to lace the knees of my husband's breeches, [I sold] to a Jew at five livres an ounce. [14]

During the Siege of Lille one incident of significant historical note concerned the actions of the Chevalier de Luxembourg (not to be confused with the Duke of Luxembourg who had died thirteen years earlier in 1695 q.v.) and became known as, *l'affaire de Poudres* (the gunpowder incident). The chevalier, with about 2,000 horsemen, managed to pass through the Allied lines and succeeded in delivering 40,000 lbs of badly needed gunpowder to the French defenders. [15]

While the town was under siege, Christian one day was foraging for food and plunder when she entered an abandoned chateau where she found a basket of eggs and some cocks and hens which, in the language of the camp she described as, 'corporals and their wives'. The following day she returned to the chateau to explore it more thoroughly and was unexpectedly captured by a group of French soldiers. They took her food, mare and forage and were arguing over who should have her clothes when an officer appeared. Christian, who was again dressed in men's clothing, told the officer that she was the son of a well known regimental commander and strangely, the officer released her. Christian hurried back towards her own lines, noticing as she did so that the French were bringing up a large number of cannon. She later wrote:

> I made the best of my way to the Duke of Argyll's quarters, where I found his grace and the Lord Mark Kerr at chess. I asked them with some warmth, in a language which only became a soldier, and a freedom allowed my sex, what they meant by having no better intelligence, and idling their time at chess while the French were on the point of cannonading us. I had, in returning from my chateau, observed all the hedges lined and the cannon ready to play upon us. The Lord Mark Kerr, surprised to see his grace pay any regard to what I had said, told him, I was a foolish drunken woman, and not worth notice: to which the duke replied, he would as soon take my advice as that of any brigadier in the army. He then asked me my reasons: I told him, and had hardly done it, when he found my intelligence true, and that we had scarce time to get into the lines for safety. Sir Richard Temple's and How's regiments were ordered to clear the hedges, and the duke would have gone with them, and probably never returned, had I not prevented him by keeping back his horse; for both these regiments were cut to pieces before our horse and train of artillery came up, which soon drove them to the main body of their army. The enemy cannonaded the Duke of Argyll's quarters so soon, that there was no making a bed for him there; and he was obliged to take up with one of straw of my making, and Colonel Campbell for a chum. They had no candles, but

> I had two of wax taken out of a priest's house, and hung up one over their heads in a paper lantern. Here they slept very comfortably, and I took the opportunity to steal the duke's wine for the poor fellows upon the guard, who I thought wanted it to comfort them: I had left but two bottles, which occasioned the duke's butler making a great uproar. In the morning his grace gave me a pistole for my early intelligence.[16]

Soon afterwards, on 22 October, 1708, severely weakened by the savage fighting, the city of Lille finally fell. It had cost the Allies some 12,000 casualties. The success was primarily due to the safe arrival of the reinforcements and stores from Ostend. The city's citadel, however, under the determined resilience of Marshal Boufflers, held on for a further two months but the end was inevitable and Boufflers eventually capitulated on 10 December that year by which time the Allies had suffered a further 4,000 casualties.[17]

While the Siege of the Lille citadel was taking place there had also been several small — albeit bloody — actions near the Harlebeck River during which the French were defeated by Marlborough and Count Carl Philipp von Wylich und Lottum, (von Lottum) clearing the way for the relief of Brussels which the Duke of Bavaria then had under siege with some 17,000 men. This siege was also a costly and bloody affray with many hundreds being killed on both sides.

Christian wrote:

> The Siege of Brussels, which the Duke of Bavaria undertook the 23rd November with a body of about sixteen thousand [French] men drawn from the garrison towns on the Scheld [Scheldt] and the Maes. The garrison consisted of five thousand men, under the command of Monsieur de Paseal, who, being summoned [to surrender],

made the necessary dispositions for a vigorous defence, and by a letter acquainted the Duke of Marlborough with the danger he was in. His grace, [the duke] on the 14th, [December] at the head of a hundred squadrons and fifty battalions, and Prince Eugene with nineteen battalions and fifty squadrons, marched to the Scheld. ... This march was so secret that the French had not notice of the allies directing towards the Scheld, though they had received advice of their crossing the Lis. The Count de Lottum, on the 17th, about four in the morning, arrived with the vanguard near to Harlebeck river, and instantly laid two bridges, led over his troops, and drew up in order of battle. The Duke of Marlborough, who had found means to pass the river at Kirkhoven, attacked the enemy so briskly at Berchem, that two hundred were slain, six hundred made prisoners, and the rest, with Monsieur Souternon, their commander, put to flight. The other French troops, posted near Oudenard [Oudenaarde] under the command of Monsieur Hautefort, soon followed the example of their companions. Thus were rendered fruitless these intrenchments, [sic] which had cost the French so much care and fatigue; and the allies, beside a great quantity of stores, provisions and baggage, with two standards and a pair of kettle-drums, which fell into their hands, had a free passage to march to the relief of Brussels. ...

The trenches ... [had been] opened before it [Brussels] on the 13th; [December] on the 15th the Duke of Bavaria began to batter the town with great fury, between the gates of Namur and Louvain: at ten o'clock at night five or six thousand men attacked the covered way. The regiment of Dodignies, and the hussars, who defended it, resolutely stood the assault, which was repeated no less than nine times, and the fight having lasted till six in the morning,

> they left the covered way, and in their turn, falling in [hand-to-hand combat] with the besiegers, retook all the posts they had lost, and made a prodigious slaughter of the [French] enemy, whom they drove almost to their trenches.
>
> It was reported as a certainty, that the besiegers lost in this action two thousand five hundred men, and the besieged eight hundred. The next day the elector did nothing farther than batter the town; but all the spies agreed in their account of his being resolved to give a general assault the night following, and to cannonade the town with red balls [heated cannonballs to destroy much of the city with fire — author's note] to make an insurrection of the burghers. Necessary dispositions were immediately made to repel the enemy, and to prevent the threatened conflagration. About eleven at night, when every one expected the signal for the assault, news was brought that the whole camp of the enemy was in motion; and soon after that, they having had advice of the passing the Scheld by the allies, decamped with such precipitation that they left behind them their wounded, to the number of eight hundred men, sixteen pieces of cannon, four mortars and a great deal of baggage to retreat to Namur.[18]

After the relief of Brussels, Marlborough ordered his men to encamp at the small town of Aalst (French: Alost), some thirty kilometres from Brussels on the Dender River (where the oldest surviving town hall in Belgium now stands and where the famous Southern Netherlands printer, Dick Martens, lived and worked. Martens published books by various authors including Christopher Columbus).[19]

It was at Aalst that Christian claimed she observed an officer, '... who, by his laced clothes I conjectured to be one of the guards,' walking back and forth along the lines of horses. Christian later wrote:

> I fancied he had a mind to steal some of the horses, and for that reason watched him narrowly. At length I saw him head off a mare, belonging to a poor woman, into a ditch, and with her commit ... the most detestable sin that one can enter into the thoughts of man. Colonel Irwin and another officer, both of Ingoldsby's regiment, happened at that instant to pass by, caught him in the act and gave him into the custody of the provost where he remained until the duke ... returned, when he was tried, condemned to the gallows, and executed accordingly.[20]

The provost's office of Marlborough's army, of which Christian Davies wrote, was staffed by a cadre of particularly harsh military police who marched with the army, controlled all prisoners and were instrumental in carrying out the functions of the field courts martial. During the various marches they would select the sturdiest house near the main army's encampment for use as a temporary prison. Christian recalled that prisoners convicted of relatively minor offences were handcuffed and marched in the centre of a guard, but more notorious prisoners were chained hand-and-foot and placed in the bread wagons.[21]

With the capture of Lille, and the relief of Brussels, the French presence in northern Flanders virtually crumbled. The Allies moved quickly against Ghent which the French had captured in July that year, and on 18 December, 1708, Marlborough opened a siege on the city which he was determined to recapture. The French surrendered on 29 December and once again Ghent came under Allied control. This defeat so demoralised the French that they evacuated Brugge, Plassendael and Leffinghe.[22]

During the Siege of Ghent, Richard Welsh had been one of a party of men under the command of a lieutenant detailed to lay guide ropes for the assault group which was to cut into the

French trenches. Later reports claimed:

> Mrs Davies as usual accompanied him in this dangerous service but, being stopped by Colonel Hamilton, who would have persuaded her not to run such hazards, she lost sight of her husband, for, having laid the ropes, he and his companions were retiring into a turnip-field and lay flat on their bellies 'til the workmen had thrown up a trench to cover them. After seeking him some time, Major Irwin told her where he was and both major and Lieutenant Stretton begged hard of her for some beer, which she refused them, for having but three flasks and fearing her husband might want, she had no pity for anyone else. As the night was very cold and the ground wet, she had also provided herself with a bottle of brandy and another of gin for her dear Richard's refreshment. Leaving these officers she met a lieutenant. ... A musket shot had grazed on and scratched his forehead which his fright magnified to a cannon ball. In his panic he lost his hat and wig, but they being found and restored to him, and he at length assured his wound was no way dangerous, recovered his small share of spirits but never his reputation, for he was soon after broke as a coward. Mrs Davies now proceeded to the turnip-field where she found her husband in the front rank, to whom her liquors were comfortable. The next morning, as she was standing by Colonel Gossedge, he received a shot through the body upon which she gave him some beer and a dram and carried him through, though it was very dangerous, to Colonel Folke's quarters, for which piece of service the gentleman was extremely thankful and promised if he recovered to reward her handsomely, but he died in three days.
>
> The next day the drum [drummer-boy] of their regiment went into a very dangerous place to ease nature,

notwithstanding he was cautioned against it, and as he was buttoning up his breeches, both his arms were taken off by a cannon ball. The place where he rashly exposed himself was so very dangerous that not a man would venture to go to his assistance. Mrs Davies therefore ran and carried him off to a surgeon, under whose care he was in a fair way of doing well, but a cold he got killed him.

A mile from the town [of Ghent] and out of reach of any shot from thence ... Mrs Davies pitched her tent and took possession of a neighbouring garden from whence she had so stored her tent with potatoes, turnips and etc. that she had left but just room sufficient to sit down close by the door. One day a ... shot went through the tent into the garden where it killed an officer's horse that was grazing there. Mrs Davies happened to be out foraging, or she must inevitably have lost her life, as she always sat directly fronting the door of the tent. This obliged her to remove her tent farther off that she might be out of danger. When the two gates [of the town] were given up before the signing of the capitulation, Mrs Davies got leave to go into the town where she sold her garden stuff, of which there was then a scarcity, for fifty shillings. The [French] garrison, to the number of 14,000, marched out with military honours.[23]

The fall of Lille, the relief of Brussels and capture of Ghent had now opened up a corridor for the invasion of France the following year and would lead directly to one of the most horrific events of that period, the Battle of Malplaquet.

CHAPTER 6

1709 — Malplaquet and the Death of Richard

During the savage winter of 1708/09, with the British Whigs and Tories at each others throats over the costly European war, a full Whig government was formed and parliament was determined to pursue the war with all the forces under its power.

King Louis XIV was all but ready to concede in order to bring hostilities to an end. He was prevented from doing so by intrigue in Spain, the principal cause of the war, and through assurances from Marshal Claude Louis Hector de Villars that the French Army was still strong enough to defend the monarchy. Negotiations carried on through the Hague were at first promising, but these talks quickly broke down, Louis refusing to agree to the Allied demands which were so harsh that he and his people vowed to continue fighting to the bitter end. An Allied ultimatum delivered from Marlborough to Louis was flatly rejected, and, as winter turned to spring, the vast armies once again awoke from hibernation and prepared themselves for what was to be the bloodiest campaign of the entire war.

King Louis realised that an Allied advance deep into French territory towards Paris was imminent but he was determined to recover the vitally important city and fortress of Lille. He took extraordinary measures in order to field an army of some 150,000 men in Flanders and placed Marshal Villars in command. It was an almost impossible task to raise such a force. The 1708/09 winter had been bitter and destructive; livestock had died in the fields, grains and seedlings had failed to survive, leading to widespread starvation.

The war had ravaged the European countryside, and, as Winston Churchill, a direct descendant of the Duke of Marlborough, later pointed out, savage frosts had gripped Europe that winter which caused the seeds to freeze in the ground. Cattle froze or starved to death in the fields, as did the wildlife such as rabbits — often a source of nourishment for both the military and civilian populations. The French people were sick of war and death; all they wanted was a return to peace and prosperity. The will to fight had drained from them.[1]

Added to this problem was the Allied sea blockade which prevented the importation of goods, leaving much of the population to starve. Tenant farmers were unable to grow a significant quantity of crops and when they failed to pay their rents they were evicted from their properties. Starving, embittered by the long war, the European population dreaded the coming of the new offensives which were guaranteed to wreak even more carnage, starvation and misery in their lives.

Christian Davies wrote:

> ... a very great frost immediately followed the [December 1708] taking of Ghent, and ... two of our sentinels were found frozen to death. This frost continued and was so terribly severe, that a number of people, fruit-trees, and sown seed, perished by the cold. This hard winter occasioned a very great scarcity, and excessively raised the price of all manner of provisions, especially in France, where most of the vines were frost-nipped to the very roots: so that of many years before, that kingdom had not been in so deplorable a situation. The treasury was exhausted by the expense of the war, trade was interrupted by the number of ships the two maritime powers kept constantly cruising in all parts of the seas to prevent the importation of goods, the farmer was not only incapable of paying his rent, but even of supplying the towns with necessary provisions; in a word they were

> in the utmost desolation. ... The king [Louis XIV] gave his people to understand that he was sensibly touched with their sufferings, and declared that he was inclined to give them peace, whatever it cost him. In effect, he sent Messieurs Voisin and Rouillé to Holland, in appearance upon the affairs of the fishery; but in earnest, to set on foot a negotiation with the allies. The secret was so closely kept all the time the conferences were held at the Hague, that no one had any certain knowledge of what was upon the carpet.[2]

Richard and Christian were stationed for the 1708/09 winter at Ghent, Christian earned a modest living by cooking and making beer for the soldiers, brewing being one of her stocks-in-trade. Richard had obtained a little leave and together he and Christian left Ghent for a short time to see some of the countryside. During this journey they came upon a woman who was crying bitterly. Christian asked the woman if she could help and the woman said that she had three small children to support and the only way she could do this was to smuggle geneva into Ghent and avoid paying the spirit tax which was due for any liquor taken within the limits of a fortified town. The excise officers had recently confiscated a consignment of spirits which had almost bankrupt the woman. The woman explained that if her next consignment was also seized, she and her children would starve.

They took the woman to a nearby public house and Christian immediately offered to run the geneva into Ghent, promising that no one would take the spirits from her. The woman readily agreed. She had ten bladders, nine of which were filled with geneva, but the last Christian filled with liquefied excrement taken from a pit where it was putrefying ready to be used as flax fertiliser. Christian gave three bladders to her husband, two to the woman, and took the others, plus the one filled with excrement, herself. The bladder of manure she carried in her left hand, only partially concealed from view. She told her two accomplices that when they were challenged she would cause a commotion with one of the excise officers and while the diversion was occurring they were to run swiftly into the town.

The plan worked perfectly. As the three approached the gates, several excise officers came forward and demanded to know what the bladders contained. Christian fumed at them, pleaded poverty and told them that she had several children to feed and that if the bladders were confiscated they would all starve. While the altercation was in progress the woman and Richard sidled towards the town gate and slipped through. One of the excise officers laid a hand on one of Christian's bladders and demanded it from her. Christian stepped back, took out a pair of scissors, snipped the bladder open and stated: 'Since you must have it, then take it,' and threw the excrement in the face of the officer. Another officer ran forward to take control of the situation, however, Christian held up a second bladder, brandished her scissors, and the officer backed away leaving Christian free passage into the town.Christian later wrote:

> This success animated us to a second attempt. The exciseman saw me and cried out, 'There's the retailer of soil.' I answered, they should find I dealt by wholesale if ever they offered to disturb me.[3]

Christian conducted many other such forays into Ghent with spirits and was not again molested until a new officer was posted to the gate. However, in attempting to confiscate one of the bladders he too was showered with excrement and the smuggling operation continued unchecked. Christian became the recipient of the guards' foul language and she was particularly offended by this. She stated that they would not come near her for fear of being showered with excrement, but added:

> ... their language, however, was so provoking that I threatened for the future to carry a pistol and blow

> their brains out the first time they durst come within my reach. I did indeed arm myself as I had threatened, but I had neither powder nor ball. However, as they had been told my history, I was so terrible to these poltroons that I believe I might have kept them in awe with a black pudding.[4]

Emboldened by these successes, Christian also ventured into the smuggling of casks of spirits over the moat which bordered the town. Christian owned a large spaniel which she had reared from a puppy. It was a thickly coated animal and every six months she sold its fur to a hatter. The dog had been well trained to fetch and carry, its reward being an oily biscuit. Christian devised a method of getting the casks of spirits into the town by lying in wait for the smugglers' carts at the town side of the moat, and when they arrived she would send the dog over to meet them. Two or three small casks would be tied to a rope and the dog would swim back to Christian, the rope in its mouth, where it would receive its oily biscuit as a reward. This stratagem would be repeated until the entire consignment was stacked on the town side of the moat. The smugglers would pay Christian and Richard three crowns per night for this service.[5]

Here, Christian reportedly suffered an almost uncontrollable urge to eat eels. A man named Hugh Jones — who was to become Christian's second husband — went out of the town without leave in order to procure some for her — robbing the wicker eel-traps in the town's moat. Christian had always been a consummate lover of eel-flesh. However, Dr J. Wilson recorded that after Christian's later return to England she experienced an occurrence that was to put her off eels for life. The event allegedly developed while she was waiting for a boat at Westminster Ferry to cross over to Lambeth, when she saw a fisherman drag ashore the body of a Negro in one of his nets. The Negro had accidentally drowned some time previously. Wilson's report continued:

> She had the curiosity to observe what was doing, though she was obliged to stop her nose from the putrefaction of the corpse, and saw a large quantity of eels issuing out of the rotten carcass, and the fisherman very diligent in putting them into his ... boat in order for sale. This had such an effect upon her that she could never after endure the sight, much less the taste, of these foul feeders.[6]

During her time at Ghent Christian also became involved in a dispute with a young cadet who regarded her as being too familiar with the other officers. Christian was furious and later wrote that she told the cadet to take care to avoid her in the future. She then returned to her quarters, '... in a passion', dressed herself in one of her husband's two suits, both of which she had purchased for him from her own money, and went to visit a young girl whom the cadet was courting. Christian, again pretending that she was a man, said that she was in love with the girl, and would marry her if she would stop seeing the cadet. After a great deal of flattery and promises, the girl acceded. Christian later wrote:

> I stayed with her three hours, in which time I had promised her mountains; a life which should be but one continued round of pleasure, and an affection which no time should have force to alter. During my visit I had the satisfaction to hear her servant tell the cadet, who came to see his mistress, that she was not at home, and that she had left word, in case he came to the house in her absence, that she should take it as a favour, his giving over visiting her, which would beside save him a fruitless trouble. He said, 'I suppose she has some new favourite, I shall find him out,' and flung away in a rage, which gave me the most sensible pleasure. I took my leave soon after, and was going home to shift my dress [change], when I spied my cadet at a little distance,

> who watched his mistress's door. He hastened after me, and asked what business I had in that house, which he saw me come out of. 'Sir,' said I, 'by what authority do you ask me?'
>
> 'Here,' said he, 'is my commission to examine you,' laying his hand on his sword; and I, doing the like, replied, 'Here is my reason for not answering you.' We both drew, the moment my husband passed by, who, knowing me, also drew, and got between us, saying, 'My dear Kitty, what's the meaning of this?' At these words, the cadet, looking earnestly in my face, knew me, put up his sword, laughed heartily, and taking me by the hand, said, 'Let us be friends for the future; I am glad I have not a more dangerous rival ... I'll give you and your husband a bottle and bird for dinner.'
>
> 'You see,' said I, 'what it is to affront me; for I have made such a progress that you have been twice refused entrance.' An officer of our acquaintance coming by, he prevailed on him to keep us company. The cadet carried us to the Couronne Imperiale, where he ordered a handsome dinner, after which we drank a hearty bottle, were very merry with the manner of my revenge; he begged pardon for having affronted me, promised he would be no more guilty, and entreated me to undeceive his mistress, whom he could easily forgive agreeing to honourable and such alluring conditions as I had offered. I reconciled them and we were all good friends the little time he stayed in the Low Countries, which was but ten days after; for his elder brother dying by a hurt he received by a fall in hunting, his father sent for him over, and he carried his lady with him to England.[7]

Meanwhile, the political negotiations of the winter of 1708/09 aimed towards bringing about a peace had not in any way suspended the military preparations to carry on the fight after the thaw. The French Army had been severely depleted during the previous years' campaigns, but against all odds Louis had managed to instil the population with a new will to continue the fighting at whatever cost, particularly as it now appeared that the Allies were preparing to invade France. The Allies too, although tired of war, were determined to make one final effort with the capture of Paris as their objective. Marlborough's armies had been inflated considerably with fresh reinforcements, and, as hostilities commenced, each side threw themselves into the fighting with a previously unheard of ferocity and tenacity in a desperate attempt finally to bring the war to an end.

In Flanders the Allies could concentrate about 120,000 men, consisting of 152 battalions and 245 squadrons. The French Army, under the command of Marshal Villars, was concentrated behind very strong defensive positions blocking the route to Paris; there was a small French garrison at Ypres, another at Tournai and strong defensive position at Mons. It was evident, considering that the Allies held Lille, like an arrow pointing at the heart of Paris, and also considering the wide gap between Ypres and Tournai, that the French stood little chance of preventing an Allied march towards the capital. It was therefore necessary to throw up a far more formidable barrier across the proposed Allied line of advance. This line was drawn in front of La Bassee from St. Venant on the left flank to beyond Valenciennes on the right. Ypres, Lille (in Allied hands) Tournai and Mons stretched from left to right in the front of the French lines. The French positions blocking the route to Paris were to become known as 'the Lines of La Bassee'.[8]

On 14 June, 1709, Villars commenced throwing up earthworks along this line for the provision of a defensive camp between Hulluch and Cuinchy with the town of Lens just behind, and utilising the waterways and swamps in his front and to his right as natural defensive positions. Villars also threw up another line of earthworks to the front of Bethune and St. Venant so that his left flank would be protected in case he had to make a march to the left to turn any enemy advance in that direction. (Both Bethune and St. Venant would fall to siege the following year).[9]

The Allies had concentrated their forces south of Ghent and it was Marlborough's initial intention to strike directly at 'the Lines of La Bassee', destroying Villars' command and thus opening a line towards Paris. However, after a thorough reconnoitre of the French lines it was decided only to make a feint towards Villars' lines and then to concentrate the Allied effort on Tournai. As their feint the Allies moved their siege-train to Menen (Menin) making it appear that Ypres was their actual target. Villars, fooled by this manoeuvre, siphoned off about 3,000 troops from the garrison at Tournai in order to strengthen Ypres but Marlborough then suddenly turned to the south-east to invest Tournai.[10]

On the 27th the Dutch appeared at Tournai, as did Marlborough, and the following day Prince Eugene had focussed his own forces at Tournai and a bridge was thrown across the River Scheldt. By the evening of 28 June, Tournai was invested on every side with an army in excess of 100,000 men. Inside the fortress the position was defended by around 7,000 troops including a couple of Irish brigades, the whole coming under the command of Lieutenant-General le Marquis de Surville-Hautfois. The defenders were not short of food or other provisions and with rationing there was sufficient wheat to last for four months.[11]

Yet despite the disparity in troop numbers, the defences at Tournai were superb, having been created by the famous French fortifications designer and engineer Sébastien Le Prestre de Vauban. (Readers might be interested to know that Vauban had died at Paris of inflammation of the lungs two years earlier, 30 March, 1707. His remains were scattered during the

French Revolution but his heart was later discovered and Napoleon ordered that it be deposited in the Church of *Les Invalides*).[12]

The citadel of Tournai itself had been constructed by the French engineer Jean Mesgrigny who was now also at Tournai and his presence there would, of course, have been of considerable assistance to Surville-Hautfois. The French had been able to pre-dig a significant web of countermines emanating from the city and citadel and during the battle these would be used to dig further subterranean tunnels into which explosives could be packed to attack the besiegers' operations. It was to prove an effective countermeasure to the siege.

There was little doubt that the battle for Tournai was to be both bloody and difficult and by the time it ended the defenders would have held out for sixty-nine days of terrible fighting.

Marshal Villars was incapable of bringing his own forces into the battle to relieve Tournai by advancing towards the position and attacking the Allies from the rear. Villars was battling his own problems of supply and until the season's wheat had been harvested he was unable to move. He did not have more than four days' supply for his men at any one time and as the Siege of Tournai commenced the French were living literally 'from hand to mouth'.[13]

Trenches before Tournai were opened in three separate places along the line of the siege; these sections were commanded by three separate generals, Count Carl von Lottum, Count von der Schulembourg (also reported as Schulemberg and Schulenburg) and General Fagel.[14]

The Allied trenches were opened on the night of 7/8th July. There were three attacks made: the first would concentrate on the north-west of the town and two others would be pressed against the south of the town on either side of the river. The batteries against the fortification were steadily increased until

Marlborough could bring more than a hundred heavy cannons and seventy mortars to bear on the town.

On the night of 24/25 July the covered way on the right of the river was taken with heavy loss of life and forty-eight hours later the covered way on the left also fell. Within days breaches had been made in the walls and on the 28th Lieutenant General Surville-Hautfois demanded terms for the civilian population in exchange for the surrender of the town.

The capitulation of Tournai itself was signed on the 29th. On the 31st Surville-Hautfois with some 4,000 men — all that remained of his original force of 7,000 — retreated into the citadel to hold out for as long as possible. About 300 French wounded were also evacuated to Douai.

Marlborough now placed about 8,000 men into the town but as part of the terms of surrender it had been agreed that the defenders in the citadel would not fire upon the civilian part of the town nor would Marlborough fire on the citadel from that part of Tournai. However, the battle for the citadel was to prove far more difficult than that which had been waged for the town itself.[15]

There was now no longer any need for Marlborough to maintain such a massive force at Tournai and the majority of the Allied army was able to move back towards Villars' line to harass the French as much as possible and keep them at bay. Meanwhile at Tournai the fighting for the citadel was about to take a more bloody form — subterranean warfare. This had first emerged during the battle for the town itself when the French had been able to place a mine beneath one of the main Allied batteries, blowing it up. Now, however, this type of warfare would become a principal and very deadly feature in the defence of the citadel.

Massive earthworks were constructed under the lines of both sides and into these works hundreds of tons of gunpowder were placed in order to destroy the enemy positions. Christian Davies later wrote:

> ... the citadel was everywhere mined around, notwithstanding the industry and fatigue of the Allies to discover them ... we often saw hundreds of men at once fly into the air and fall down again piecemeal or buried alive, and if any were dug out living, they were miserably shattered in their limbs or half roasted.[16]

As these excavations were being dug deep underground the opposing factions often met each other and fought bitterly in the darkness. When these mines were detonated. Christian was often present with the men in their underground labyrinths of death, as Dr J. Wilson, later wrote:

> We have often said that Mrs Davies followed her husband wherever he was ordered upon duty, so that sometimes she went with him in the party employed to search for and draw the enemy's mines. Their engagements underground were very terrible, their weapons being spades and pick-axes and the men sometimes half suffocated with the smoke of straw which the French fired to drive them out. In short, as we have observed before, [an] abundance of mines was sprung by the besieged, most of which did great execution, and one in particular blew up four hundred men at once.[17]

Yet Christian had no fear of following her husband into these deep mines. She wrote:

> I always followed him and he was sometimes of the party that went to search for and draw the enemy's mines. I was often engaged with their party underground where our engagements were more terrible than in the field ... the fighting with pick-axes and spades, in my opinion, was more dangerous than with swords.[18]

During the Siege of Tournai, Lord Cobbam arrived at the trenches and ordered one of the regimental engineers to point a cannon at a windmill which was obstructing the view of the fort's inner citadel. Cobbam reportedly offered a guinea to whoever could bring down the windmill. Christian immediately stepped forward, took the match out of the hands of the engineer, placed the flame at the touch-hole and brought down the windmill, the recoil of the huge cannon throwing her off her feet. Cobbam made good his promise, in fact giving Christian two guineas. General Fagel gave her another, and several officers each gave her a ducat.[19]

Soon afterwards one of the officers, a Captain Brown, was shot in the leg with a musket ball. The leg was very badly injured and surgeons decided that it would have to be amputated. Nurses were almost non-existent and so Christian offered her services, although it seems that her role was confined to that of merely holding the surgeon's candle.[20]

All through these campaigns it seems clear that Christian worked diligently at one of her primary objectives — that of acquiring as much plunder as possible. She almost always carried a grappling iron with which she sounded the wells in the villages, having learnt from Dutch soldiers who had participated in King William III's campaigns in Ireland that the peasants would often place their valuables into sacks and tip them into the village well in order to hide them from the marauding troops of either army. Using this grappling hook Christian was frequently rewarded with silver or copperplate and other items of modest value. A sword she carried was designed not so much for fighting but for probing the ground around the cottages in search of buried plate.[21] 'I never lost an opportunity of marauding', Christian later claimed, '... with my grapple I searched all the wells I met with and got good booty.'[22]

During one of these scavenging forays Christian was fortunate not to have been at her camp, for, as Dr J. Wilson claimed:

> While she was one day busied in search of plunder, she heard behind her a great burst like a sudden clap of thunder, and turning nimbly around saw the air full of shattered limbs of men. This happened, as she was informed at her return, by a spark from a pipe of tobacco setting fire to a bomb by which fifty shells and twenty-four men were blown up, but luckily the magazine of powder, though near the same place, escaped.[23]

Meanwhile Marshal Villars' troops had not been idle. In addition to countering the fairly ineffective harassing strikes made at them by Allied forces, the French had been frantically harvesting the summer wheat and were now becoming better supplied every day. This enabled Villars to utilise his forces more effectively by continually extending 'the Lines of La Bassee', making a solid barrier from St. Venant on his left to Valenciennes on his right and strengthening this line to a considerable extent, making the best use of the natural barriers of a dyke, inundation of low regions and of the two large rivers. Yet Villars realised that once Tournai fell then Marlborough would be able to bring the whole of his force to bear on 'the Lines of La Bassee'.

By 30 August the capture of the citadel at Tournai was imminent; Villars had received intelligence from deserters or spies that the defenders of the citadel had at last run out of food and that the capitulation must come within days, if not hours. The next day, 31 August, Lieutenant General Surville-Hautfois proposed a capitulation. Marlborough demanded a complete surrender of all the troops but Surville-Hautfois declined, threatening to destroy the citadel completely. Marlborough conceded and finally agreed to Surville-Hautfois' demands that the officers and men should be allowed to march out with arms and colours and that they would receive safe conduct to Douai. In exchange for this courtesy Surville-Hautfois agreed that they would not take up arms against the Allies until they had been 'technically' exchanged for Allied prisoners. These terms having been agreed, the citadel at Tournai surrendered on 3 September, 1709. This victory freed up many Allied troops for the coming Battle of Malplaquet and also opened up a part of the Scheldt River for the transport of Allied supplies.[24]

With the successful completion of the first part of the Allied plan, it was now Marlborough's intention to press on towards Paris, but that meant breaking Villars' forces along 'the Lines of La Bassee'. Even with his superior numbers, Marlborough realised that a direct attack against Villars' fortified positions would be bloody and impractical, therefore it was decided to invest the small garrison at Mons while on the right of the French position an attempt should be made to break through the extreme extension of the French lines along the River Trouille near Mons. This was known as 'the Line of Trouille'.

The weather created enormous difficulties for Marlborough's men; incessant rain had turned the countryside into a quagmire and troop movements were sluggish and difficult. It was not until 7 September that Mons was finally invested.

Prior to the investment of Mons, and as the Allies were moving forward towards the French lines, Christian was marching with the camp colour-men — those who carried the regimental banners. This was a dangerous undertaking as the colour-men marched well in advance of the main body and were often first in the thick of the fighting; they were also prime targets as the capture of an enemy's colours was often one of the principal objectives. The survival rate amongst these men was not great. However, Christian perceived that the position — well forward of the front line — afforded the best opportunities for plunder. During this march Christian saw a large horse standing alone. Leaving her mare with a sergeant she took charge of the horse and rode forward. Soon afterwards she came upon twelve chickens with their legs already tied, a basket of pigeons and four sheep. She killed one of the sheep and yarded the other three while she was waiting for the sergeant to come up with her mare. When the sergeant arrived Christian placed the carcass of the dead sheep onto the mare and the sergeant helpfully hung the chickens around Christian's neck. Christian then drove the three sheep before her to the place designated for the army's camp. While the troops were setting up the camp, marking out each regimental space, Christian pitched her tent close to a deserted tavern which had been requisitioned for the regimental commander, Colonel Hamilton. Christian then turned out her sheep in a paddock and hung the carcass on a tree for it to cool. She then bribed the soldier on guard at the door of the former tavern, from where she took a large quantity of faggots, some hay and straw and a barrel of beer. Having conveyed these items to her tent she was in the process of boiling some of the mutton when the remainder of the army arrived, including the commanding officer and one of his staff who expressed great surprise at the volume of stores Christian had been able to procure in such a short space of time. They ordered a gallon of beer and instructed Christian to roast a shoulder of the mutton. Christian made twenty shillings from the sale of her mutton, disposed of the chickens and pigeons for a handsome profit and even sold the fat to a local candle-maker.[25]

On the same day that the Allies invested Mons, Villars moved the majority of his army to take advantage of a natural defensive feature behind the forested barrier of two great woods, the Forest of Sars (this was also known under several other names including the Wood of Sars and Wood of Taisnieres but in this publication will be referred to under the general title of the Forest of Sars) and the Wood of Lanières facing the Rivers Haine and Trouille.[26]

On Villars' left now lay the village of Montreuil and on his right was the village of Malplaquet, after which the famous battle would be named. Marlborough countered the move by bringing his forces over the River Trouille and stretching the men from the villages of Quevy to Quaregon. Meanwhile Prince Eugene brought up his forces and it was apparent that the Allies would have to attack Villars through the large gap between the Forest of Sars and the Wood of Lanières. On the morning of 9 September the centre of the French forces was drawn up at the village of Malplaquet, directly behind the gap between the forest and wood, and by noon that day the troops marched forward to the 2,000 yards gap which faced them. There they began constructing massive defensive redans (openworks of quite spectacular strength) and waited for the Allies to advance.

It was at about this moment that Marshal Louis François, duc de Boufflers arrived on the scene, giving the French a huge boost to their morale. Boufflers, as we have seen, was a highly experienced commander much loved by his troops and it has been recorded that upon his arrival the French camp was drowned in cheers which could be heard even from the Allied lines. Though he was older, and had greater military experience, Boufflers placed himself at Villars' disposal, telling Villars that he had come simply to assist in any way possible. Villars wisely appointed Boufflers as second-in-command and placed him in charge of the troops holding the French right, behind the Wood of Lanières, while Villars himself retained overall command and positioned himself on the left holding the Forest of Sars.[27]

It was quite clear to all the commanders present that a very large battle was about to be fought and that casualties would necessarily be heavy on both sides. In fact, as Winston Churchill later wrote, it was to be the largest and bloodiest battle of the eighteenth century.[28] Accurate casualty figures for this battle are not known; the French are believed to have lost somewhere in the region of 12,000 men and the Allied casualties may have reached as high as 20,000 or even 24,000, depending on the sources of information.

It was at this time that a body of Allied troopers, in company of a group of hussars, were instructed to reconnoitre a heavily wooded area which Christian Davies referred to as 'the woods of Taisnieres' (the Forest of Sars) with instructions to find where the French had entrenched themselves.

The soldiers were ordered to return from the woods at the sound of a single cannon-shot. Christian was determined to accompany this group, knowing that there would be recently abandoned cottages in the woods where fresh provisions and other valuables might be found. Christian rode her mare and led another packhorse which she had bought from a hussar. Before going into the depths of the forest Christian found a small orchard where she dug a hole in the ground and buried all her money. The group moved out and before long Christian saw a large house which looked promising. One of the men advised her that it might be dangerous, but despite this risk Christian urged her horse forward and entered the house alone. There she found a bed made up, two or three large tubs of flour, an oven full of hot bread, a large quantity of bacon and beef hanging in the chimney [where they were being smoked], a basket of chickens and two pots of butter. Christian was delighted with her discovery. She emptied the feathers from the mattress-tick to cover the mare's back, as the bread was still oven-hot and Christian did not want to burn the animal. She then emptied the bolster and filled it with bread, beef and bacon, tying the bolster at one end and roping it to the mare. She tied a pot of butter on each side of the mare, grasped the chickens in one hand and mounted the horse. No sooner was she ready to leave when she heard the single cannon-shot to tell her that the French Army was advancing towards her and the other men. (This apparently was at the moment the French advanced, as we have seen above, to take up positions between the Forest of Sars and the Wood of Lanières and to occupy the woodland and forest on both sides of the battlefield). The English troops immediately turned and, in panic, rode recklessly for their own lines. Christian, however, did not panic; she calmly dismounted, loaded a truss of hay onto her packhorse and left the scene minutes before the arrival of the French.[29]

Back at the Allied camp, Christian was surprised to discover that everyone was packing ready for a hasty move. She again did not panic, but unloaded her booty, killed her fowls, unearthed the money she had buried in the orchard, struck her tent, and loaded everything onto her horses. Only then did she follow the army. Soon afterwards she found her husband dragging his heels in the last ranks and Christian had time to speak with him. Richard, however, was now filled with fears and foreboding. He told Christian that he felt sure the Malplaquet battle would be the last he would ever fight, and that he was certain he was marked for death. Christian tried to dispel his gloom, telling him of the loot she had found and that when the battle was over they would enjoy a royal feast. Yet nothing she could say would cheer her husband.[30]

It was raining heavily as they marched and the ground for miles around was a muddy morass. As Christian and Richard moved slowly forward, Christian came upon a lost child whom she recognised as belonging to one of her husband's friends. Fearing that the child would be drowned in the deep mud and water, Christian took the child upon her shoulders as she continued her march.[31]

That evening the opposing armies were in sight of each other, the ruddy glow of their campfires reflecting in the low, rain-heavy clouds. The Allied army camped that night in a fallow field, the ground was sodden, and anyone who could find a dung-heap to sleep on considered himself fortunate. Christian left the main body of the army and rode to a large house in the rear of the lines so that she could prepare the provisions she had found. She took her horses into the house and unloaded them with the aid of the regimental butcher and a French baker. Christian made a fire, laid the lost child on a bed of straw, and went looking for some forage for her horses. Having found a quantity of hay she locked the animals in the parlour of the house and began to prepare her food. She went to the well for a bucket of water but when the bucket was lowered it struck against a metal object. Christian brought her grappling hook and went fishing for loot in the well. Almost immediately she brought up a kettle and then a brass pail in which there was a silver quarter-mug in a fish-skin case. More loot! Christian was well pleased with her day's work.[32]

Returning to the house, Christian sliced bacon and beef into her pot, added sprouts from the garden and, leaving the rest of the cooking in the care of the butcher and baker, she scoured the remainder of the house for plunder. In the cellar she found a barrel of strong beer and leaning against an inner cellar door were two quart-bottles of vinegar and two quarts of brandy. Christian happily confiscated everything and placed the booty in the parlour with her horses. She then shared a portion of her earlier gains with the butcher and baker, placed the remaining provisions and some flasks of beer on her mare, took the lost child in her arms, and went in search of Richard. She soon found the child's father, gave him some food, deposited her charge and continued in search of her husband. The evening mist lay thickly over the ground and in the mass of confused humanity, with thousands of soldiers trying to sleep prior to the coming battle, Christian had great difficulty in finding Richard. Eventually, however, she discovered him in a field with his head resting on a friend's back. Christian awakened him and asked what officers and friends he would like to have as his guests for dinner. Richard was amazed at the suggestion. Rations at this time were so rare that men were offering a guinea for a loaf of bread.[33]

The food was eventually shared among many of Richard's friends, several officers and a few raw recruits who were later described as, '... not [being] immured to hardships, were ready to perish with hunger.'[34] Christian reserved a few pullets and some eggs for the general officers and then went in search of the regimental commanding officer whom she found in conference with three generals. Pushing her way into the tent she placed before them some fowls, bacon, sprouts and hung beef. The senior officers were amazed at the unexpected bounty. A later report claimed:

> ... this was a very agreeable surprise to them all who did not imagine there had been so much victuals in the whole army of the Allies. They tore the meat with their fingers and ate very heartily, and, wanting water to mix with their wine, Mrs Davies went to the well within musket shot of the enemy and fetched them some which several of the soldiers had refused to do.[35]

The atmosphere generally in the Allied camp that night was, however, tense. Everyone knew that on the following day there would be a huge fight to the death and that casualties would be high. Some men spoke darkly of the safety the senior officers enjoyed, claiming that many of them not only remained well clear of the fighting but that they also had light armour concealed beneath their uniforms to protect their chests from musket balls. Hearing this, the Duke of Argyll went to his men and, opening his coat and shirt, exposed his chest to the troops telling them that he was as unprotected as they and asked them to behave as Englishmen. He reportedly said:

> You see, brothers, I have no concealed armour, I am equally as exposed as you and I require none to go where I shall refuse to venture. Remember you fight for the liberties of all Europe and the glory of your nation, which shall never suffer by my behaviour, and I hope the character of a Briton is as dear to every one of you.[36]

Marlborough knew that the French were not about to come out of their defensive positions to meet him; his superiority in numbers and the strength of the French positions assured him of that. Therefore he had several alternatives before him. He could attack on his right towards the Forest of Sars and attempt to turn Villars' left flank; he could do the same on his left, attacking Boufflers at the Wood of Lanières, or he could attempt to do both, turning both French flanks, forcing the collapse of the centre and thus folding up Villars' army. His superiority in numbers almost guaranteed successes on these lines. He could also attack in the centre, right through the gap in the woodlands, driving a stake right through the heart of Villars' army and forcing the flanks to retreat or perish. The other problem facing Marlborough was the construction of earthworks which Villars had wasted no time in throwing up. The two armies had come face-to-face on 9 September but Marlborough had delayed his attack, waiting for the troops from Tournai to come up, which had allowed Villars time to construct his earthworks. Two whole days were to pass before Marlborough attacked and this delay would cost him dearly.[37]

Villars spent all day on the Monday and all Monday night constructing his line of defence. When Marlborough and Prince Eugene rode out to look at the opposing lines they were astonished to find that within just twenty-four hours Villars had been able to construct no fewer than nine redans which now stretched almost right across the 2,000 yards gap between the wood and forest. The remainder of the gap had been fortified with a continuous line of entrenchments. Marlborough and Eugene had no idea what similar lines of defences might have been constructed within the forest and wood, but it was now evident that any attack on the French lines was going to be bloody. Behind these defences Villars had also thrown up a second line of earthworks and even the village of Malplaquet itself was strongly defended. The work of improving all these defences continued through Tuesday and Tuesday night utilising relays of men. By the time Marlborough had reached his decision as to where and how to attack, his superiority in numbers had largely been negated through the construction of these immensely effective French defences.[38]

The battle that was to change the life of Christian Davies and take the life of her husband commenced on 11 September, 1709.

Long before dawn the Allied troops had been preparing for the day which, for many of them, would be their last on earth. It was damp and misty after a wet night; the sun rose to a grey, bleak morning and it was impossible for the drawn up forces to see each other. The heavy mist prevented the artillery gunners from estimating range, thus postponing commencement of the battle. The order of battle had been ranged since about four o'clock but hours were to pass before the mist lifted.

In the stillness of that cool morning, approximately 200,000 men sombrely faced each other as they waited for the signal for the battle to commence. Ministers of various religions had gone among them, praying for deliverance, giving Communion and easing fears. Facing the Allies, although inferior in numbers, was one of the most efficient fighting forces then on earth, a nation immured to war and bloodshed, a nation raised to become an empire. The French troops were no ordinary foe; battle-hardened by years of war, they now had the additional incentive of facing an enemy who wished to invade their very homelands. United in their Catholic faith, they were almost fanatically determined that the forces of Protestantism would never take a step into France.

On the other side the troops of the various Allied commands were well aware that they were superior in numbers and believed (as did the French) that God was on their side. They had eaten breakfast, had enjoyed a tot of rum or brandy, and were in good spirits. They believed that a mighty victory was at hand which would open the road to Paris and end the war allowing all of them to return to their homes and families.

Marlborough, Prince Eugene and the then Prince of Orange (Johan Willem Friso, commanding the Dutch troops, who had become the titular Prince of Orange in 1702), had agreed to launch their attacks right across the entire front, but staggering their timing. They would strike at the centre where the French had constructed their highly effective earthworks but not until attacks had been made on both flanks, right through the forest and woods. It was, as one writer has described, a 'hammer and tongs' assault upon strongly defended positions. Within the wooded areas Villars had constructed a series of barricades comprising earthworks and felled trees. Behind these lines stood a mass of French cavalry, ready to press forward at any moment.

On the Allied lines the Prince of Orange was on the left flank, facing the Wood of Lanières, with his Dutch troops and also the Scottish Brigade, a corps of Highlanders who had been specially enrolled in the Dutch Army. Behind them was a corps of cavalry — a formidable force of some 10,000 sabres commanded by the Prince of Hesse-Cassel.

At the other end of the Allied line (the Allied right flank) were two major infantry forces. The first under Count von der Schulembourg which was tasked to attack the outer line of the two salient angles of the French defences at the Forest of Sars. In these there were no English troops but its strength amounted to some 20,000 men. The second arm of infantry, commanded by Count von Lottum, contained a small number of English and was only about half the strength of its associated force of infantry. Lottum would attack the inner side of the French salient. A smaller force under the English officer General Withers would make a turning movement through the woods with orders to turn the French extreme left. These forces would be facing some of the cream of the French Army including the regiments of Picardie and Champagne, two of the oldest, most experienced and famous in the French forces. In addition to their experience, they, like all the other French troops facing the

Allies that day, were stiffened in their determination to resist any invasion of their homelands.

In the centre of the Allied lines were about 6,000 English troops under the command of Lord Orkney. These were spread out and linked with their Allies on the right and left flanks. Before Orkney's men stood a battery of forty Allied cannons. The general command on the Allied left and centre, including the Prince of Orange's men on the extreme left, Lord Orkney's men in the centre and Count von Lottum's men on the inside salient of the Allied right, fell under Marlborough's overall control. The command on the Allied right, Schulembourg's men and his massed cavalry tasked with taking the French outer salient came under the control of Prince Eugene.[39]

By 7.30 that fateful morning the sun had sufficiently dissipated the mists for the Allied gunners to commence firing on the French positions in the centre. By this time Marlborough and Eugene had decided to attack firstly through the Forest of Sars (the Allied right flank) which was teeming with French troops, and after this assault had proceeded for about half an hour to launch the second attack on the Allied left flank through the Wood of Lanières towards Boufflers' sector. It was anticipated that with both flanks under very powerful attack the French would be required to draw reinforcements from the centre to one or both flanks, thus weakening the centre. Lord Orkney and detachments drawn from both Allied flanks could then launch an attack at the heavily defended redans and entrenchments facing the gap between the two forested areas. Marlborough and Eugene firmly believed (correctly as it transpired) that this would sufficiently weaken the centre, thus making Orkney's job easier. With a weakened centre, Orkney and his backup cavalry should be able to plough through the French centre and both French flanks would then begin to fall apart.

By the time all troops were in position it was nine o'clock. Marlborough had placed himself right at the forefront of the attack being carried out by Count von Lottum's men on the inside arm of the right flank into the Forest of Sars. The huge Allied battery at the centre commenced a massive barrage and this was the signal for the general attack to commence.

Eighty-five Allied battalions were launched simultaneously against both sides of the French salient at the Forest of Sars. With the Allies outnumbering the French in this sector by about four to one, Marlborough was confident that he would have a speedy result.

Schulembourg's force managed to penetrate the forest on the outside of the salient but got no farther, the French resistance being too great. Meanwhile Marlborough, at the head of Count von Lottum's inside salient advanced under heavy fire and reached the French entrenchments which had been constructed just inside the line of trees. However, this attack also failed.

A second attack faired little better although by this time a British brigade under the Duke of Argyll had joined in the affray. The fighting in the forest was bloody and brutal. Lottum's corps was brought to a standstill, 'torn and exhausted', and the situation was critical. However, Lord Orkney, himself still at the centre of the battlefield and not actually engaged, sent a further two battalions to the forest as reinforcements. One battalion was of the Guards and the other of the Royal Scots Greys.

The Scots Greys were ordered to attack through the forest where they encountered a line of French cavalry. These, while quickly being dispersed, were, however, replaced by some of the cream of the French forces including the French household cavalry who, clad in armour, advanced stolidly and in good order. The English troops met the French with notable courage but were finally driven back by superiority in numbers. The English were, however, quickly joined by several corps of horse and were able to rally. They charged the French once again but were unable to break their lines. Yet a third charge was successful in driving back the enemy. In this fairly brief action the Royal Scots Greys lost about thirty men.[40]

Meanwhile, events on the other side of the battlefield (the Allied left) were not progressing as well as Marlborough would have wanted. As planned that morning the Prince of Orange had launched his attack utilising thirty battalions of Dutch troops and the Scottish Brigade against the French holding positions at the Wood of Lanières. The mass of Allied infantry moved confidently against the wood but their line of advance was divided by a small coppice known as the Wood of Tiry. As the troops began to skirt or penetrate into the Wood of Lanières they came under withering fire from the French. The Prince of Orange was in the thick of the fighting and most of his staff were either wounded or killed around him. The prince's horse was shot and collapsed so the prince continued to advance on foot. The trenches and redoubts before him were held by some of the best troops in the French Army, including the French Royal Marines — a formidable fighting force. On this wing of the battle the numerical superiority lay with the French. Thirty Dutch battalions were attacking a well entrenched force of sixty French battalions. It was to be a two-to-one battle where the outcome should have been predicted long in advance.

The Dutch and Highlanders advanced in magnificent order, despite the firepower that was being brought against them. However, beyond the Wood of Tiry lay a long shallow trough of ground some 200 yards wide and into this depression the French had hidden a battery of about twenty cannons. As the Dutch and Scots approached, these cannons opened up a murderously raking fire on the Allied left flank, utilising both grapeshot and cannonballs which scythed through the ranks of the Dutch and Scots like summer wheat. Thousands of men were wounded or killed as the ranks continued to move forward with unshaken discipline and resolution. Soon the ground was littered with dead and dying, the brave Highlanders in their blue uniforms were splashed colourfully across the killing ground as the surviving Dutch moved on and over them towards their goal. They came up close to the French entrenchments under a hail of musket-balls fired at close range, volley after volley of French fire that tore bloodily into their ranks. Finally the ragged lines of Dutch reached the French entrenchments, stormed the parapets and captured the works. However, the remnants of the Dutch and Highlanders were now few, too many thousands had been left dead and dying behind them. The French reserves counterattacked, not only directly upon the front but also from the side at the Wood of Lanières. The French were so superior in numbers and the ranks of the Allies so depleted by casualties that the Dutch were forced to retreat in good order. The entire Allied left began to fall back, still taking terrible punishment from the French, retreating over the bodies of their own dead, the wounded crying for help which could not be given. The French were exultant in their victory and pursued the Allies as they retreated. There would have been a complete slaughter had not the Prince of Hesse-Cassel, with twenty-one squadrons of cavalry, made preparations to charge the French. This gave courage to the retreating Allies and seeing that their cavalry was in readiness to back them, the Dutch and Highlanders were able to halt their retreat, face about, and prepare to take the French on their bayonets.

The first attack had taken about half an hour and about 5,000 men had been lost to the Allies. Now, however, the Prince of Orange was determined to try again. Having lost his first horse he had found another but this too had been shot from beneath him. He now ordered a second attack and moved forward into the fray on foot at the head of his troops. Once more the Dutch and remnants of the Highlanders came under the withering fire of the French batteries. Once again they took the French entrenchments at massive loss of life where the prince planted his standard upon the parapet. However, the French remained strong enough to be able to counterattack and again drive the Allies from their hard-won positions. The Allies retreated but now in complete disorder, and it was only the cavalry of Hesse-Cassel that prevented total annihilation.[41]

Boufflers, the commander of the French right flank, would later come under severe criticism for not now advancing his troops and attacking the Allies all along their left flank. Had he done so it would have been likely that the Allies would have folded back towards their centre and the battle could have been won by the French. Boufflers did not do so, however, as he was reluctant to make any changes to Villars' overall plans. There was no chance to consult with Villars so the opportunity was quickly lost.[42]

The Allied left flank along the Wood of Lanières was now in almost complete disarray, despite the heroism of the Dutch and Highlander troops and the personal leadership and bravery of the Prince of Orange. Facing such superior enemy numbers and troops who had dug themselves into strong defences, the resolute determination and bravery of the Allied soldiers in carrying out two attacks under such murderous fire can only be applauded. However, the fact remained that heavy pressure on the French at the Wood of Lanières was vital to Marlborough's overall plan to ensure that reinforcements had to be drawn from the French centre and now that was not happening.

Marlborough and Prince Eugene were desperately summoned and they rode quickly over the battlefield to the far left Allied flank where they were appalled to witness the death and destruction that had been wrought on the Dutch and Scottish troops. About 2,000 corpses were scattered across the fields for half a mile, stretching back from the French defences to the original starting position of the Allies. Clearly, any further attacks against the Wood of Lanières would be murderous and futile. However, when Marlborough and Eugene arrived they found, despite the carnage, that the irrepressible Prince of Orange was planning yet a third attack against the French. Marlborough was both impressed and mortified. He and Eugene rode through the streams of Dutch and Scottish wounded, many of whom were preparing for the next attack, despite their wounds. The two

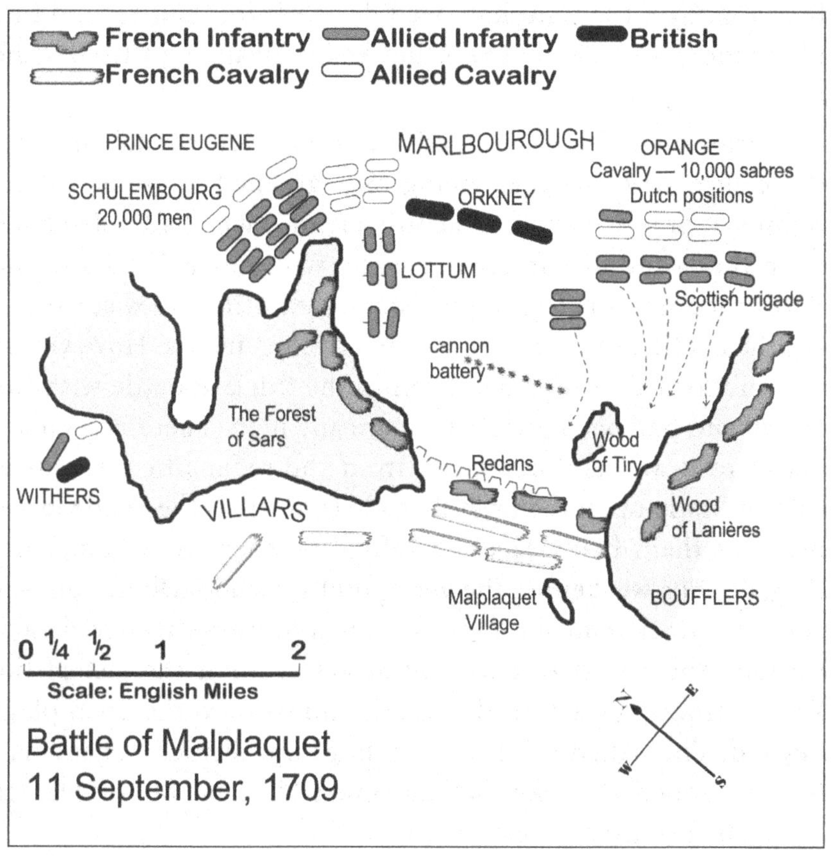

Battle of Malplaquet
11 September, 1709

commanders arrived at the point where the few survivors of the Dutch command were situated. There Marlborough forbade the prince to carry out any further attacks and ordered him to hold his position under the protection of the cavalry commanded by the Prince of Hesse-Cassel. Marlborough and Prince Eugene then returned quickly to their respective positions; Eugene at the Forest of Sars and Marlborough behind the massed grand battery in the centre. It was now about 11.30 a.m. on that fateful morning and there were still another three and a half hours of bloody fighting ahead of them.

When he returned to his position at the Forest of Sars on the Allied right, Prince Eugene discovered that his troops were making good progress. Unlike the position on the Allied left, the French on the right had been driven from their second line of defences and slowly the Allies were advancing through the forest.

Marlborough now ordered Lord Orkney to advance on the centre with his men being strengthened by some of the remnants of the Dutch and Scottish troops who had fallen back from the Wood of Lanières. It was a wise move. Villars in the Forest of Sars, was fighting desperately as the Allies advanced and had called upon Boufflers for reinforcements. However, at that moment Boufflers had been in the thick of battle with the Dutch and had been unable to spare any men. Therefore Villars began to draw reinforcements from the redans in the centre, calling firstly upon the Irish Brigade (known as the Wild Geese, many of them being Jacobite refugees), then the Champagne Brigade thus weakening the very point which Marlborough was about to attack. Foot-by-foot the French were being driven back through the Forest of Sars and at about noon the last of the French troops were forced from the forest onto the open plain beyond. The Allied toll had been huge and Prince Eugene had been wounded, a musket-ball had grazed him behind his left ear but he had refused to leave the field.[43]

Lord Orkney was now ordered to attack the French centre with his British troops and several Prussian battalions. Marlborough rearranged his grand battery of cannons so that they could bring a heavy crossfire on the French redans. The British and Prussians in the centre had previously withstood some quite severe French cannon-fire but now they were ready to advance. Orkney led them forward as a single line of thirteen battalions and the troops were quickly successful. The depletion of the redans to reinforce the French in the Forest of Sars enabled the French positions to be taken easily. By one o'clock Orkney's men arrived at the redans and the French who remained there gave way without much of a fight. Orkney later admitted that while this movement effectively gave the Allies a huge advantage, it was not his, but Marlborough's brilliance as a tactical military commander who had made it possible. 'It was the gift of Marlborough's genius dominating at last the confusion of battle,' he later wrote.[44]

The French were, however, preparing to counterattack. The two opposing armies were facing each other in the open plains, dead and dying were all around. This is when one single event caused massive problems for the French. Marshal Villars and his senior staff were riding forward when they were caught in a blast of musket-fire. Villars' horse fell dead and a musket-ball smashed into Villars' leg just below the knee. Two other senior officers were also casualties; one wounded and the other killed. Some of Villars' aides-de-camp rushed up with a surgeon but Villars refused to leave the field. He was unable to stand so a chair was found in a nearby farm cottage and seated in this Villars continued to conduct the French defence. However, he was in severe pain; he fell unconscious and had to be carried away. He remained unconscious until recovering in hospital at Quesnoy. It was the last he knew of the Battle of Malplaquet.[45]

There appears to be little doubt that the fall of their commander-in-chief, plus the loss of two senior commanders, created great confusion in the French lines just at the moment when they were preparing to launch a vital counterattack. A staff officer, General Puységur, who had attained an excellent reputation at the Battle of Oudenaarde, now assumed command of the French left wing and organised an ordered retreat. Marshal Boufflers meanwhile, as Villars' second-in-command, took control of the entire French operation. Some French regiments, realising that by pulling back, any hope for winning the day would be lost to them, marched forward to within about twenty yards of the Allied lines and loosed off a final vituperative volley. Yet within fifteen minutes or so some fifty French battalions had retired from the field.

However, now facing the Allies were the long lines of French cavalry. To counter this very serious threat the Allied cavalry moved through the lines of its infantry and commenced deployment to attack but as they were doing so the French cavalry pre-empted them and attacked in force. The English cavalry were forced back in confusion and it was this manoeuvre which ultimately was to save the French Army from complete defeat. However, the British cannon battery which had been held in the centre was now split in two, one moving to the right and the other the left so that their cannons could be brought to bear on the French cavalry without danger to the British troops. The barrage was extremely effective and as the French cavalry was almost broken by this fire another charge was made by the British cavalry. This was led by Marlborough in person and included both British and Prussian units. The battle now became one largely conducted on horseback. Boufflers was able to bring up the French household cavalry from before Malplaquet village and these men attacked Marlborough's troops, breaking them up. Prince Eugene came forward with another body of horse and charged, then total confusion ensued. The Battle of Malplaquet ended with two battered but undefeated lines of infantry and cavalry slowly retiring from the field to lick their wounds.[46]

The battle was undecided but both sides were incapable of taking it any further. The French fortifications remained in Allied hands but the troops of both sides were exhausted, having been fighting continuously from midmorning to about three in the afternoon. Some 24,000 Allied troops lay wounded or dead and at least half that number of French. Neither side had the strength to do more. Malplaquet was one of the most murderous battles in European history and little, if anything, had been achieved, although the French had claimed a tactical victory. If nothing else, Villars had inflicted massive damage on the Allies, and had prevented them from invading France and marching on Paris.

Both sides spent the next few days evacuating the field, recovering their wounded and burying their dead. Marlborough, for his part, continued with the Siege of Mons which finally capitulated on 9 October. Thus Marlborough's dreams of invading France and penetrating to Paris in 1709 were over.[47]

As stated earlier, Richard Welsh was to be killed during this battle. As the hostilities had commenced, Christian, determined to find her husband amid the confusion which then reigned in the mass of battle amid what she termed as Taisnieres woods (the Forest of Sars), walked into the forest carrying flasks of cool beer for Richard. Fighting is thirsty work and the men's most common complaint was the lack of water during the thick of battle. A later report claimed:

> When the engagement was begun she entered the wood to carry small beer to her husband, where the shot and bark of the trees flew about so thick as to give her some uneasiness, several pieces of the latter falling on her neck and getting down her stays. The dog, [Spaniel] which we have spoken of before, at the entrance of the woods, howled in a pitiful manner, which surprised her as it was unusual. A man who was easing nature, hearing him, said, 'Poor creature he would feign tell you that his master is dead.'
>
> 'How', said Mrs Davies, 'is he dead?'
>
> 'I know not', replied he, 'but I am sure he is very much wounded.'[48]

Christian was immediately reminded of the premonition of death Richard had felt prior to the battle. That scene came hauntingly back to her now: the two of them walking through the misted forests with the rain weeping down and Richard's words of doom, his profound fears. Christian had derided him; she was convinced that they would both see the end of the war.

Yet despite this her fears now quickly grew and she ran among the dead and dying, desperately searching for Richard. She later wrote, 'I was almost out of my wits, but though I feared the worst, my hopes of finding him alive supported me.'[49]

Christian turned over almost 200 corpses, among them several officers she had highly respected, Brigadier Lallo, (also recorded as Lalo), Sir Thomas Pendergrass, and a large number of her best friends.[50]

Finally Christian found Richard lying dead and crumpled in the mud. Dr J. Wilson's account claimed:

> At last she espied a stranger stripping her husband's body, but on Mrs Davies's approach he went off and left his booty, fearing the effects of her rage, which indeed was so great that she would certainly have killed him could she have laid hands on him. Her grief on this occasion was inexpressible, she bit out a great piece of her right arm, tore her hair, threw herself upon the corpse, and should have put a period [end] to her life had she had any instruments of death. At length she vented her sorrow in a flood of tears which gave her some relief. While she was thus deploring her loss, Captain Ross came by, who, seeing her agony could not forebear sympathising with her, and dropped some tears, protesting that the poor woman's grief touched him nearer than the loss of so many brave men. This compassion from the captain gave her the nickname of Mother Ross, by which she was afterwards commonly known. After her tears were abated, she dug a grave for the corpse, buried it, and would have thrown herself in with it, had she not been prevented by some of her husband's comrades. She then mounted her mare, notwithstanding she had no arms, and pushed into the wood with design to wreak her vengeance on the French whom the Allies were then pursuing, and to tear in pieces whoever fell into her hands. Nay, if she

> had strength and opportunity, she would have given no quarter to any man in the French Army. She was riding full speed after them when Captain Usher laid hold of her mare and forced her back, or she [would] have inevitably been either killed or taken. The former she would not have thought a misfortune, for her distraction rendered her incapable of minding her business, her whole being employed in running to her husband's grave and endeavouring to remove the earth with her hands in order to have another view of the man whom she loved with greater tenderness than herself, and for whose safety she would willingly have sacrificed her own life. The poor dog was always found lying on his master's grave, and for several days could not be persuaded to eat anything. Mrs Davies herself, although often opportuned, touched nothing of sustenance herself for a whole week.[51]

The Prince of Orange*, whose field quarters were situated close to the spot where Christian had pitched her tent, could hear her crying through the long night, and upon enquiring was informed of the death of Richard and of Christian's profound grief. The prince ordered that meals be taken to her and that she be watched, stating, '... the poor woman weeps night and day and I fear will kill herself, which would grieve me.'[52]

* Johan Willem Friso, the Prince of Orange who, as we have seen, had displayed such gallantry at the head of his Dutch and Scottish troops during the Battle of Malplaquet, then had just two years to live. He was drowned in 1711 when the ferry in which he was travelling sank during a heavy storm in the Hollands Diep. The prince was en route from the Belgian front to the Hague at the time of the accident. The prince's son, William IV, Prince of Orange, was born six weeks after J.W. Friso's death.[53]

The servants took meals to Christian, tempting dishes prepared for the prince from his own supplies, but she would eat none of them, however, she enjoyed sitting before the prince's fire and was allowed to take coals from it to make one of her own near her tent. Colonel Hamilton's wife, for whom Christian had often provided meals, sent for her and ordered that she be given light vegetarian meals. She told her of the sin she would be committing if she killed herself, adding that the grief would eventually ease, that another man would one day capture her heart and that he would be in need of the love and protection she had showered upon Richard. Within six weeks Christian's grief was indeed easing, but she remained morose and bitter for many months afterwards.

She later wrote:

> The first who prevailed on me to touch meat was a Scotch Cameronian who forced me to a tent where he had got a breast of mutton, but I was so weak that I could not support the smell of the meat but fainted away with the first bit between my teeth, lay a long time as dead, and was brought to my senses by very slow degrees.[54]

During the period of her grief Christian had wandered alone through the ranks of the army, sleeping wherever she found herself at dark and leaving her tent and provisions in the care of a drummer and his wife. When Christian finally returned to her tent she discovered that the man and woman had eaten all her provisions and neglected to look after her horses. The animals, however, had been well cared for by Hugh Jones, the grenadier who had stolen eels from the wicker traps in the Ghent moat some months previously.[55]

Hugh Jones had been in love with Christian for many years but had refrained from speaking of his feelings while Richard had been alive. Now, however, that Richard was dead, Hugh could not restrain himself any longer. He waited what he considered a decent time and then went to Christian, professing his love for her. Christian was so moved with his tenderness that she accepted his proposal and they were married in the camp almost three months after Richard's death. Christian's only condition to the marriage was that Hugh should not live with her or sleep with her until they were in garrison in winter quarters. Yet the affair was not without its critics, one sergeant laconically stating, '... the cow that lows most after her calf goes soonest to bull.' Hugh Jones, on hearing of the comment, went immediately to the sergeant and challenged him to a duel, however, the fight was prevented by several of the sergeant's friends who insisted that the sergeant should apologise for his indiscretion or face death at Hugh's hands. The sergeant saw reason and apologised.[56]

Christian and Hugh Jones' were garrisoned for the winter of 1709/10 at Ghent where nothing of any great importance occurred to the couple. 'We spent the winter without any event worthy of notice,' as Christian later wrote.[57] Indeed, the couple would need their rest, for the following year, 1710, would be another season of bitter warfare and bloodshed. Douai would successfully be besieged, as would Bethune, St. Venant and Aire.

CHAPTER 7

1710 — *Ne Plus Ultra*

At the end of the 1709 campaigns Marlborough once again returned to England to build support with the government for the following season's fighting. In fact he knew that he would be facing mounting political opposition and hostility from Queen Anne. Marlborough's wife, Lady Sarah Churchill, the Duchess of Marlborough, had once been a favourite of the queen but the two women had disagreed bitterly. Anne's natural inclinations lay with the Tories but Sarah was a Whig supporter and an enemy of the Tories who wished to destroy her husband. Despite the fact that Anne and Sarah had been extremely close friends, almost inseparable, it was Sarah's continual campaign against the Tories that finally alienated the two women and Sarah was now *persona non grata*. She had been dismissed from the Queen's offices and banished from the royal court.[1]

The England Marlborough had left behind in 1709 had changed dramatically by 1710. Queen Anne was facing a mounting political crisis that would later lead to elections (October 1710) and the subsequent forming of a very strong Tory government in complete opposition to the war.

Meanwhile Marlborough's massive losses at Malplaquet were strongly condemned by the Tories (then still in opposition) who were energetically in favour of finding a peace with Louis XIV. They were quite willing to sacrifice Marlborough in order to obtain their aims. However, the Tories soon realised the danger of such an action; the fall of a particularly able commander such as Marlborough could have meant the possible elevation of the French King to a position where he would be able to control virtually all of Europe.

Terms were eventually agreed upon for a continuance of hostilities while secret Tory negotiations were made with the French in an effort to end the war. When Marlborough returned to France in April 1710, amid all these hostile political machinations, he arrived with a heavy heart. Financial and political backing was lacking for any heavy campaigns and personally he too felt that the savage carnage of Malplaquet had been a price too high. During Marlborough's long career he had rarely failed to prosecute the war to its full measure, but after the Battle of Malplaquet his attitude, and that of Prince Eugene, changed dramatically. The two commanders now hesitated in sending large numbers of men to their deaths; their tactics, rather than being based upon brute strength, became ones of move and balanced countermove, a carefully thought out chess game with the enemy designed to lose ground at minimum cost to the Allies.

King Louis XIV was willing to negotiate a peace; he fully realised that the Allied plans to invade France and take Paris would again be Marlborough's objective for 1710 and was preparing for heavy fighting. However, he hoped that the coalition of Allied forces would fall apart due to political intrigue before he was forced either to negotiate any deals or lose masses of more troops defending the country. Peace negotiations took place at Geertruidenberg, opening in March 1710. However, these failed for a variety of reasons and it is believed that one of these reasons was the fact that Louis believed English politics would do more to end the war than any negotiated deal which might be struck at Geertruidenberg. Louis would not concede to Whig demands that he should force his grandson, Philip V, from the Spanish throne, believing that it would be a completely dishonourable thing to do.[2]

Marlborough, meanwhile, was planning to recommence where he had broken off hostilities in 1709. French forces opposing Marlborough included some 204 battalions and 308 squadrons.

The Allies could muster 155 battalions and 268 squadrons which were concentrated near Ghent.

At the beginning of the 1710 campaigns, Marshal Villars was entrenched with his army behind a series of strongly fortified lines termed the *Ne Plus Ultra* (variously translated from the Latin as 'Perfection' or: 'no more beyond' or: 'the highest point capable of being attained.' [First known use 1637]).

The *Ne Plus Ultra* was a massive series of fieldworks extending from the sea along the River Canche, east to Arras, along the Sensee River to Bouchain, and even beyond, as far east as Namur, although Marlborough was not interested in the lines farther east as there was virtually nothing below them of any real military significance.

At first, Marlborough seemed to hesitate and the month of June was filled with rumours and counter-rumours over the extent and tactics of the forthcoming campaigns. In the ranks there was considerable fear and discontent, many of the soldiers believing that after the difficulties Marlborough had faced at the hands of the English Parliament, especially the Tories, his judgment would be rash and he would lead them into battles that had been unwisely planned and for which the costs in lives would be extraordinarily high. In truth, Marlborough, facing the might of Villars' forces — many of whom had been hardened at the Battle of Malplaquet and were now supported by large numbers of recruits — was hesitating more from his reluctance to commit himself against such formidable strength rather than indecision.

Meanwhile Marshal Villars was content to maintain his *Ne Plus Ultra* line, without coming out to attack Marlborough. If the line could be held effectively then Marlborough's dreams of forging a passage through to Paris would again be thwarted, probably forever. Marlborough realised that it would need considerable strength and willingness to accept massive losses by taking on Villars' entrenched army and he was being cautious due to his sinking popularity with the English Parliament. This was to be a year characterised by significant and carefully planned military movements, counter-movements, and siege.

It must have been an agonising decision for Marlborough to make at the beginning of the 1710 campaigns. Marshal Villars' fortifications, constructed at huge cost, were to prove a highly effective barrier and Marlborough was left with few choices. Attack in force; attempt to go around the *Ne Plus Ultra*, or to lay siege to one or more of the significant French held positions in an attempt to drive a wedge into France. There was the possibility of marching up the Lys River to the coast, or marching up the Scarpe River, laying siege to Douai, and having achieved a success there to march on Arras. It was decided to lay siege to Douai which was then under the command of Marshal d'Artagnan, duc de Montesquiou with a garrison of 8,000 men in twenty battalions. It was to be a fairly brief but bloody conflict.[3]

The siege of the ancient university town of Douai was carried out by two princes, the Prince of Orange and Leopold I, the Prince of Anhalt-Dessau, Douai's powerful fort, a small distance from the town, being completely surrounded. The city had been sealed off by 28 April that year while Marlborough and Prince Eugene covered the siege troops.

On 10 May the French sallied out from Fort Scarpe to attack the bread-wagons of the Allies. However, reaching Pont-a-Nache they were halted in their tracks by a squadron of Royal Scots Greys and two squadrons of Royal Irish Dragoons who, at full gallop, put the enemy to flight, inflicting heavy losses. The commander of the Irish Dragoons, Lieutenant Colonel Caldwell, was wounded during this action.

The siege guns trained on Douai commenced firing the following day, 11 May, 1710.

Meanwhile, as the Allied armies were digging their trenches and preparing their assault weapons, Marshal Villars brought out every man he could from winter quarters, marched quickly to Douai and drew lines opposing Marlborough's forces.

Christian Davies later wrote of this siege:

> This town, in which Philip the Second, King of Spain, founded a university in 1560, was taken by Lewis [sic] XIV in 1667, five days after the trenches were opened, since when that monarch had it regularly fortified, and raised a fort on the Scarpe half a quarter of a league distant from the town. We opened the trenches in two places on the north side of the river ... at night. While we carried on our works, Marshal Villars, having reinforced his army with all the men he could draw out of the garrisons, gave out that he would march to the succour of the town.[4]

Seeing this massive French support, the garrison at Douai put up a very stiff resistance when the two princes carried out their attack, but it was a resistance that was futile against such powerful forces and the garrison surrendered on 26 June, 1710. Marshal d'Artagnan retreated with honour to Cambray taking with him some 4,500 of his men. Marlborough had lost approximately 8,000, many of them to disease.[5]

During the Siege of Douai a man named Morgan Jones stole one of Christian's horses and, needing the animals to carry her provisions and plunder, Christian was forced to purchase another. A hussar offered her a strong mare and Christian immediately bought her. However, this horse had been stolen from a peasant farmer who later found the animal in Christian's possession. The horse had been disguised, by Christian herself, so she evidently realised that it had been stolen. Christian later wrote that she had, '... docked, trimmed and endeavoured to disguise her.'[6] However, despite this disguise the peasant readily recognised his horse. Christian stated that she had purchased the animal in good faith, that it was rightfully hers and she refused to part with it. The peasant complained to the regimental commander, Lord Orrery (Charles Boyle — the 4th Earl of Orrery, commanding his Regiment of Foot, later the 5th Royals), who ordered that Christian should return the animal to its rightful owner. Christian attempted to get her money from the hussar who had sold her the horse, but — rather surprisingly considering her renowned temper — without any reported success. Later Christian was said to have got back her original horse and the man who had stolen it, Morgan Jones, had been '... heartily drubbed' by Christian's husband (Hugh Jones) as punishment for his crime.[7]

Following the successful Siege of Douai, Marlborough's armies besieged Bethune. Bethune was under the command of Monsieur du Puy Vauban, nephew of the famous French fortifications engineer, Sébastien Le Prestre de Vauban, who had died three years earlier. Bethune had been strongly fortified with deep trenches, a large number of underground mines filled with explosives, double protective outworks and all the ground surrounding the centre had been swamped with water. The citadel itself had been fully provisioned so that the defenders could withstand a lengthy siege. However, Marlborough's engineers managed to drain off the water and an attack was carefully prepared so that the underground mines could either be by-passed or rendered ineffective. Despite the elaborate precautions the town resisted the Allies for only a relatively brief period. The siege commenced in early July and by late August after much bloody fighting, the counterscarp had been taken by the Allies, 'sword in hand'. Vauban opened negotiations for a surrender on 'honourable terms' beating the chamade and hanging out the white flag. What remained of the French garrison was then allowed to march out of the citadel with two pieces of cannon and full honours.[8]

Christian and her husband were part of Marlborough's force covering the Siege of Bethune and so took no part in the actual event, although Christian was involved in a bloody affray and came close to being captured by several detached squadrons of French troops.

Finding little to attract her in the way of profit at the siege, Christian volunteered to go out with mounted foragers. It was a risky business, French cavalry roamed the region and the chances of being cut off from the main Allied army and then being either captured or killed were very great. Indeed, Marshal Villars had despatched several squadrons of horse with orders to attack the foraging parties. When these squadrons found the foragers they obeyed their orders and immediately attacked, but did not realise the ferocity of the roaming Allied troops. They were beaten back, '... with great slaughter', and only stood their ground when they were reinforced with extra squadrons of French cavalry. The foragers were then forced to retreat to a small village where they expected to meet some Allied reinforcements from the main body of the army. The French surrounded the village and ordered them to surrender. When this request was refused the French launched a bloody attack against the foragers' positions, but were beaten back when the Allied reinforcements arrived at the last moment. Christian was jubilant. As the French rode off in defeat she climbed into a barn where she found a bolster filled with wheat, two pots of butter and a large number of fresh apples. She loaded the provisions onto her horses and carried them safely to her tent. She wrote of this event, '... the wheat I got ground at a mill the enemy had deserted and made pies which I sold in the camp. Of the bran I made starch.'[9]

Following the surrender of Bethune the town was garrisoned by Allied troops and its defences repaired.

Finding that Villars was still not prepared to come from behind his entrenched positions to confront the Allies, both Marlborough and Prince Eugene decided to lay simultaneous siege to St. Venant and Aire

Soon afterwards (6 September) St. Venant was besieged by the Prince of Orange, while Aire was surrounded by Leopold I, the Prince of Anhalt-Dessau. Leopold was an interesting character who, however, possessed only modest abilities as a military commander. He served as field marshal of the Prussian Army, which he modernised. Born in Dessau, the eldest son of John George II, Prince of Anhalt-Dessau and his wife, the Dowager Princess Henriette Katharina, Leopold I devoted his life to military service and had been present at the Siege of Namur. (He later married an apothecary's daughter [much against his mother's wishes] and sired ten children with her and two illegitimate sons by a mistress).[10] Under his command at Aire, Leopold had no fewer than four lieutenant-generals, eight major-generals and eight brigadiers.[11]

St. Venant fell on 30 September followed by the surrender of Aire on 9 November. This brought military actions for 1710 to an end.

Christian and her husband, Hugh Jones, had been present at the Siege of St. Venant, and during one of the attacks against the counterscarp, while kneeling in the front rank ready to discharge his own musket, Hugh was shot in the thigh with a musket-ball. Christian immediately arranged for him to be carried from the battlefield on a stretcher. She was not unduly concerned over the wound; it looked ugly but she was rather more worried about him catching a fever which, added to the wound, could have proved fatal. Christian took off some of her own clothing and wrapped Hugh warmly before arranging for him to be taken to a trench where one of the army doctors had set up a temporary surgery. The doctor examined Hugh's leg and stated that the wound was slight, however, the following day he again examined the wound, saw that the leg was broken, and told Christian that the injury was dangerous. After the capitulation of St. Venant the wounded were taken to Aire which had also recently surrendered to the Allies. After the surrender of Aire the army was ordered into winter quarters. The wounded were carried to Lille where Hugh was placed in hospital. Here, however, the wound became infected and had to be opened frequently. Hugh became progressively weaker and soon afterwards he died.[12]

Christian again moved into a period or mourning. She had been married to Hugh for only about twelve months but had grown very fond of him and felt his loss greatly. She knew few people in Lille and had no work, but Brigadier Preston, the only officer she knew, awarded her a crown a week from the army coffers and a dinner each Tuesday. Additionally, whenever the brigadier entertained, Christian was employed as an assistant cook, her payment being the privilege of taking enough provisions from the larder to last her for three or four days. Preston's generosity was primarily due to gratitude. Having been wounded at Ramillies, Christian had cared for him, virtually saving his life.[13]

CHAPTER 8

1711 — The Final Struggle

The year 1711 was to prove a highly successful one for Marlborough, it was also the last year of his campaigns. Politically, however, the year began badly. The Tories were now in power and Marlborough was very much in their sights. Yet to sack the duke would have caused huge problems with the alliance of powers in Europe. It was possible that the Dutch would make a separate peace with the French and the Prussians seemed likely to withdraw completely from the alliance. This and other political decisions saw Marlborough once again sent to Europe to take command of the Allied armies for 1711. Meanwhile the English Parliament secretly continued to negotiate with the French for peace, but it was a peace that could come only through the iron anvil of military might and the Dutch were convinced that any peace deal which might be struck with the French should come only after Louis XIV's forces had received such a massive blow that they would be unable, afterwards, to renege on any deals that might have been struck. Previous peace treaties with King Louis had quickly and notoriously been broken by the French monarch.[1]

During this year Marlborough was determined to defeat the French defensive stratagem, the *Ne Plus Ultra*, the fortifications that stretched from the sea at Etaples through the huge fortresses of Arras and Bouchain, all the way west towards Namur, and then snaking north-east and later north-west ending at Antwerp, a massive swath of land effectively enclosing the Allied armies in the Spanish Netherlands.

With an army of some 90,000 men, an army weakened because Prince Eugene had been forced, following the death of Emperor Joseph, to withdraw his forces to cover the Upper Rhine, Marlborough made it seem to Marshal Villars that he was planning to attack the French, then some 120,000 strong, on a massive scale south of Arras.

After a careful study of the French defensive lines, Marlborough decided that he would attempt to drive his army through them between Arras and Bouchain. He had chosen difficult ground because the Sensee Valley contained significant swamps and waterways. However, there were two major causeways through the valley: one at Arleux and another at Aubanchoeil-au-Bac (also given as Aubencheul-au-Bac).

The campaigns commenced with Marlborough, then camped on the Plain of Lens, sending a strong detachment to capture Arleux. This was an important part of his overall plan as it would deny its use to the French and also secure a water supply to Douai which could have been cut off by raising a dam across the canal that supplied the town. Christian was sent with the piquet guard that went forward in support of the main attacking force. This force quickly took Arleux (6 July, 1711) and, knowing that the French would soon attempt to recapture it, the Allies set about repairing the defences. Another large body of troops was also sent as reinforcements. However, one night shortly afterwards the French unexpectedly attacked, catching the men in their undershirts. Despite this the Allied defenders mounted the barricades, swords in hand and the French were driven back. The following morning Christian set out on one of her innumerable sorties in search of plunder. In a neighbouring wood she discovered a horse tethered to a tree. On the animal's back was tied an almost new tent which Christian considered as being a perfect war trophy.[2]

On the night of 4/5 August Marlborough ordered his men to force-march quickly and secretly towards Aubanchoeil-au-Bac. Leaving their campfires burning to deceive the French, the army crossed the Scarpe and intensified the pace of their march.

It was an arduous and deadly march, the men being pressed on by their non-commissioned officers as the columns wended their way through a watery moonlight. Many men fell out, unable to keep up the pace, some even died of exhaustion.

By daybreak it seemed clear that the French, having received their intelligence reports, had realised Marlborough's intentions and were also moving rapidly on a parallel course on the opposite side of the River Scarpe. But the French were trailing well behind and had little chance of countering Marlborough's brilliant move. During that day (5 August) the Allies crossed the Scarpe on pontoons and drew up ready for battle inside the enemy's lines. Villars' troops were tired and in disarray when they arrived and were unable to attack Marlborough's well positioned men. However, rather than force a battle that must have resulted in the loss of tens of thousands of lives, Marlborough moved quickly and besieged the fortress of Bouchain. Villars, frustrated by Marlborough's incisive move, was determined that Bouchain should not fall to the Allied forces. He raised a fortified entrenchment near Marquion, extending it through to the Morass of Bouchain, placing within the position a total of twenty battalions. Yet the move proved highly ineffective and did not prevent Marlborough from completing his besieging operations. Using some 6,000 conscripted workers obtained in Flanders, Marlborough constructed his lines of circumvallation all around Bouchain and dug double entrenchments to protect his lines of communication and supply to the Scheldt. Soon afterwards Marlborough's army began the bombardment of the fortress while Villars, in turn, bombarded Marlborough's besieging forces.

Bouchain was then under the command of Governor de Ravignau with some 5,000 men facing a besieging army of 30,000 — one third of Marlborough's total force. Bouchain was then one of the strongest fortresses left to the French, its defences naturally strengthened because it was surrounded by marshy grounds in the confluence of the Rivers Sensee and Scheldt. Villars' army now lay to the west of the Allies and he was able to establish a brief link with those who were besieged in Bouchain. Along this line of communications Villars no doubt was able to supply provisions and armaments but Marlborough was subsequently able, through the use of an assault force and the guns placed in an earthworks battery, to close Villars' line of communications with the fortress.

Marlborough was also able to establish a protective corridor from the siege-camp to his own supply base at the port of Marchiennes on the Scarpe. Villars made frequent raids on the Allied supply convoys but failed to make any impression on the siege.[3]

Bouchain capitulated on 13 September, 1711, and Villars' forces could do nothing while the garrison marched out to become prisoners-of-war. Breaking through Louis XIV's seemingly impregnable defensive barrier and the capture of the important fortress at Bouchain, elevated Marlborough to an almost demigod status in the eyes of the English public, although in some quarters Marlborough was criticised for not having attacked Villars' forces when they were in such disarray.

While the fortress was under siege, Christian Davies had been employed by Lord Stair in his kitchen as an under-cook. While working in the kitchen she was assaulted by a colonel, and Christian had to defend herself with a kitchen knife. The assault and defence was interrupted by the arrival of Lord Forrester who demanded to know what the commotion was about. Christian explained, and the colonel somewhat sheepishly stated that he had only wanted to kiss Christian. The colonel was sent away with a reprimand and Lord Forrester rewarded Christian, 'for her virtue', with a piece of gold. Several days later one of the colonel's heels was shot off with a musket ball. At about this time Christian was foraging close to the besieged town; she found a basket of fowls and pigeons which she later gave to the wounded colonel. It was a fine gift as such provisions were rare commodities. The colonel reciprocated Christian's kindness, making her a present of three barrels of strong beer.[4]

As the siege had continued the staff officers decided that they would have a great dinner and General Meinhardt Schomberg's[5] cook was borrowed to help in the kitchens. After the dinner this cook was allowed to take some of the leftover provisions, however, while returning to his quarters he met a corporal who had been on duty for two full days without food or rest, and, taking pity on him, he gave the man the food he was carrying. The incident was witnessed by one of the quartermasters who approached the cook and asked for any extra provisions that may have come from the officers' kitchens. The cook said that he had no more food and the quartermaster lost his temper. Angry words quickly followed and these finally came to blows, the cook giving the quartermaster a sound thrashing. The quartermaster took his grievance to his commanding officer who ordered that the cook should be arrested by the provost and gaoled for twenty-four hours. The following day this officer and several others again dined together with Lord Stair.

It was later reported:

> When they were all seated Mrs Davies entered the room with her usual freedom, and looking upon Lord Stair full in the face, opened the case in the following manner. 'May it please your Lordship, I have heard of persons put into confinement for theft, but never yet of one imprisoned for not stealing. I beg your Lordship therefore to prevail on the general to release his cook for not filching from your Lordship's table ... if it is a Dutch custom, I desire that it may be, for once, overlooked.'[6]

The general immediately acceded to Christian's request and ordered that the cook be released. The meal then progressed and a short time afterwards the cook came to the kitchen to thank Christian. Christian went into the dining room and told the officers that she had come personally to thank the general by giving him a kiss. The general was aghast. Here before him stood the decidedly unappetising but powerful figure of Christian Davies, dressed for the kitchen, the perspiration running down her face and her lips covered from the grease of the meat she had recently eaten. However, Lord Stair laughingly urged her on and with a determined stride Christian closed with her objective. The general, finding that he was trapped, rose from his chair and bolted around the table with Christian hot on his heels. Finally, seeing that he was trapped, he stopped and allowed Christian to kiss him wetly on the lips, later stating that, '... if he had not had a very good stomach, the greasy bitch would have spoiled it.'[7]

~~~~

At about this time a staff footmen caught a venereal disease, almost certainly from one of the many prostitutes who regularly followed the army. Dr J. Wilson later reported:

> One of my Lord's footmen had been playing the game of up-tails-all, and he had the ill luck to meet with a fire-ship. The poor fellow was in a desperate condition. ... At last my Lord's gentleman [possibly his valet] found it out, and having a smattering of physic, [medical knowledge] undertook the cure. Mrs Davies, being of an inquisitive nature, soon came to the truth and was barbarous enough to plague the poor wretch about it, but he still denied the affair, telling her he feared he was in a consumption and frequently borrowed saucepans etc. to prepare medicines by order of his 'physician'. One day, unknown to Mrs Davies, he had taken a stew pan to boil his ingredients for a poultice, and when she wanted it, it was nowhere to be found. She searched every place
~~~~

> she could think of and all to no purpose, so, hearing people whisper in a little room where the lumber was generally put, she peeped through the keyhole and soon perceived that the use the gentleman and the footman made of the stew-pan. She had not patience to call to them, but broke the door open with her knee, which so much surprised the doctor and patient that they both rushed out of the door, the footman with his breeches down and twenty yards of roller [bandage] at his heels. She called after them, threatening to tell my Lord the use he had made of the stew-pan, and was as good as her word, although her motive was not ill nature, for she knew my Lord would order a proper surgeon to take care of the poor fellow. One day at dinner she told the story to the company whilst the footman was waiting at the table just as he had been ordered to take away the first dish, which he did in such confusion that he threw down what broth was left over the Duke of A...E, this increased the poor wretch's disorder, who, running with precipitation out of the door, met full but three servants coming in with the rest of the dinner. He threw down the first, the first the second, the second the third, dishes and all, and never made his appearance all night. The fellow, by his Lordship's order, was put under the care of the surgeon of the regiment, and that in good time ... by the surgeon's skill ... he became a found man again, returning thanks to Mrs Davies for the 'lucky accident' as he called it.[8]

The Siege of Bouchain was Marlborough's final military campaign; as we will see in the next chapter he would be stripped infamously of his position as captain-general, and of all his other official offices. The command of the Allied army would be handed for 1712 to James Butler, the Duke of Ormonde, who would be given strict instructions not to engage the French in battle because peace talks were by that time well advanced.

Marlborough, undoubtedly one of the greatest military geniuses of all time, disgusted with the way he had been treated by Queen Anne and her parliament, would subsequently retire to live in Holland.

CHAPTER 9

1712 — Return Home

As we have seen, the year 1711 was, militarily at least, to be Marlborough's swan-song. During the winter quartering of 1711/1712 he returned to England to find the English Parliament divided over the war. The Whigs controlled the House of Lords, but the Tory Party controlled the Commons. In an effort to bring about successful peace negotiations, the Tory Party accused Marlborough of peculation, claiming that he had used for his own private purposes, certain funding that was supposed to have been set aside for financing the operations of his secret service. Additionally, Marlborough was accused of having illegally received money from the bread and transport contractors in the Netherlands. The first case allegedly amounted to a sum of £280,000 and the second to about £63,000; combined, this was a fantastic amount of money at that time. Marlborough defended his actions stating that receiving funds from the bread and transport contractors was an old and traditional custom while the seconding of money for the secret service had been approved by the queen. He even produced a warrant, signed by the queen in 1702, authorising him to do so. Despite this and before the charges could be examined properly, Queen Anne sent a letter to Marlborough dismissing him from his posts. Marlborough, who had been responsible for giving the queen most of her major victories in Europe, was so disgusted by the letter that he is reputed to have thrown it on the fire.[1]

In Marlborough's place parliament appointed James Butler, the Duke of Ormonde, to continue the campaigns through 1712, but, as we have seen, Ormonde was warned not to make any military decisions that might jeopardise the ongoing peace negotiations.

Prince Eugene, Marlborough's friend and confidant, rallied to Marlborough's cause but his alliance was in vain. (Interestingly Ormonde was given the same allowances that had been the basis of the criminal charges brought against Marlborough).[2]

In Flanders the Allies were able to muster about 122,000 men for the campaigns of 1712. The French, who remained under the command of Marshal Villars, were able to muster around 100,000 men. These were indeed vast armies for those times. It is not intended within this publication to delve into the political and even treasonable machinations that were taking place behind the scenes, but Prince Eugene now decided to lay siege to Quesnoy.

When he laid siege to Quesnoy and asked Ormonde to aid him, Ormonde was instructed by the Tory government not to take part in the siege. The British Army was ordered to Dunkirk, leaving Eugene to fend for himself. Sensing that final victory was at hand, Marshal Villars advanced quickly, destroyed Eugene's magazines at Denain and drove many of his troops into the Scheldt where they were drowned. Villars' army then surged forward recapturing Douai, Quesnoy and Bouchain. All the fighting and deaths of the previous years had been in vain. The British had sought a separate peace, had deserted their allies, and the French were left to dictate terms to what remained of the shattered Allied forces.

At the later Treaty of Utrecht, in the Spring of 1713, the terms of the cessation were hammered out. England's reward for deserting its allies included some of the great prizes. France agreed to demolish the fortifications at Dunkirk and ceded territories in South America and the West Indies. Spain agreed that England should hold both Minorca and Gibraltar, and so with its vastly superior sea forces, England held total control of the Mediterranean. The English also won the sole right, for a period of thirty years, to import African Negroes as slaves into the New World. The Dutch gained a line of defence through

Furnes, Fort Knocke, Ypres, Menen, Tournai, Mons, Charleroi and Namur — along the lines where many of the bloody battles of the First World War were to be fought more than 200 years later. Prussia was awarded Guelderland, but all the other fortresses and defensive positions that had cost so much during the terrible battles of the preceding eleven years, were restored to France.

Many of the veterans of Marlborough's campaigns were bitter that they had been forced to desert their former allies, some of the paid mercenaries who had formed a proportion of the Allied armies remained to fight with them; others were simply glad that the war was at last over and they could return home.

With the troops at Dunkirk, Christian Davies remained for a while at Ghent where she requested of the Duke of Ormonde that she be allowed a passage back to England. Being a civilian she was not technically allowed free passage aboard one of the many troopships that were now ferrying the remains of the English Army across the English Channel. However, Ormonde granted Christian her request and gave her a purse of money to help with the costs of her passage. She left Ghent soon afterwards and travelled to Dunkirk where she again rejoined members of her old regiment. While she was awaiting the arrival of the ship that was to take her to England, she visited the governor, General Hill, so that her pass for the ship could be countersigned. Hill, although ill and confined to his bed, graciously made it clear on the pass that she was to be treated as an officer's wife, and gave her two pistols. Christian soon afterwards met another officer who invited her to dine with several of his colleagues, and these men too contributed to her passage.

The ship that was to take Christian to England arrived at Dunkirk within the week and a few days later she landed at London. Christian wasted no time in seeking out the Duke of Marlborough in order to obtain some kind of pension for her service and for the loss of two husbands during Marlborough's campaigns. At this time the duke was under considerable pressure from parliament over the charges ranged against him, yet he received Christian with great dignity. However, he was obliged to advise her that his own career lay in ruins and he no longer had the ear of Queen Anne. Parliament was against him and he was in no position to press for a pension in Christian's favour. Before she left, however, Marlborough gave Christian a guinea and wished her well.[3]

Christian decided to approach the Duke of Argyll who was still in the Queen's favour. The following day she set off towards the duke's house but met him on the road before she could reach her destination. Seeing her first, the duke stopped his chair and asked his footman if the figure hurrying towards him was indeed the now famous 'Mother Ross', as she was becoming widely known. The footman confirmed it and the duke called Christian to him. He asked her several questions and Christian told him of the pension she was attempting to obtain for her services. The duke gave her a guinea and told her to wait for him at his house where they would later discuss the situation. Accordingly, Christian walked to the impressive house and was shown into the housekeeper's room. One of the servants informed the duchess that Christian was in the house and the duchess sent for her, ordered breakfast for them both and asked Christian to tell her the story of her life, which she did. The duchess was so delighted with Christian's adventures that she gave her a guinea and a half. Within a few hours the duke returned and proceeded to tease his wife for allowing a 'rough dragoon' into her bedchamber. Christian dined with the servants that evening, declining an offer to dine with the duke and a small group of his colleagues, which included two of his former *aides-de-camp* who had served during Marlborough's campaigns. Later, however, she joined the dinner company and the duke asked her to form a petition to present to the Duke of Hamilton who might present it to Queen Anne. Christian agreed to do as he advised, and as she left, the duke gave her another guinea and the *aides-de-camp* each thrust three crowns into her hand. For Christian it had been a very profitable evening.[4]

Dr J. Wilson later wrote:

> According to the duke's advice she got a petition drawn up representing that she had served twelve years in the Earl of Orkney's regiment as a man, that she had received several wounds and lost two husbands in the service. With this she waited on [the 4th] Duke of Hamilton [soon to be killed in a duel (see below)], who, at first, made some scruple as if she was an impostor, but Mrs Davies appealed to any officer in the army for the truth of what she said. The duke went into a parlour, where, as it afterwards appeared, he had two officers belonging to the regiment wherein Mrs Davies had served. They confirmed all she had advanced in her petition, upon which the duke gave her a crown to get a new petition drawn up to present herself to the Queen next morning. He intended to present the other that night. She thanked his grace and was very punctual in following his directions, having got a petition finely written out, she dressed herself next day in the best she could and went to court. She placed herself at the bottom of the great stairs where she had not waited long when Her Majesty came down, supported by the Duke of Argyll. Upon this she fell on her right knee, as she had been instructed to do, and delivered her petition which the Queen received with a smile, helped her up and promised to provide for her, and perceiving her with child added, 'If you are delivered of a boy I will give him a commission as soon as he is born,' but to her sorrow it proved a girl who afterwards caused her great trouble and vexation. Her Majesty was farther pleased to give her an order to the Earl of Oxford* for fifty pounds to defray the charge of her lying in (during her pregnancy).[5]

* The 1st Earl of Oxford was Robert Harley, one of the Tories who had campaigned for a peace and who had largely been responsible for

> Marlborough's impeachment. He had commenced his political career as a Whig, the principles of Whiggism having been learned at an early age, but he subsequently defected to the Tory ministry. He served as first lord of the Treasury and in effect was Queen Anne's chief minister. Upon the accession of George I he retired to Herefordshire but was later impeached and imprisoned in the Tower of London [16 July, 1715]. He was subsequently acquitted of the charges of high treason and high crimes and died on 21 May, 1724.[6]

Christian was delighted by the Queen's generosity and went immediately to see the treasurer, Lord Oxford, who vacillated and finally refused to pay the money to Christian. Christian then returned to petition the queen who gave her a second order to approach Sir William Windham who soon afterwards gave her the money.[7]

Additionally, the queen made provision for Christian to be given a pension of one shilling per day for life. However Oxford, without the Queen's knowledge, later reduced this pension to fivepence.

Shortly after this event Christian gave birth to her child. She was later visited by Lord Forrester who asked her to appear at the King's Arms tavern in Pall Mall where he was to dine with a number of nobleman and other officers of the army. Forrester said that a collection would be made during the dinner to help her with immediate support. Accordingly Christian appeared at the tavern on the date allocated, and as none of the diners had appeared she waited at the door of the tavern, her new-born daughter in her arms.

A soldier approached her, and thinking she was a prostitute began to abuse her, using a torrent of foul language, finally hitting her across the breasts with his stick. It was more than Christian's well known temper could bear. Christian later claimed:

> The language he had given me was provocation sufficient to inflame me, but a blow was an indignity never put upon me and enraged me to such a degree that not considering I had a child in one arm I flew upon him and began to belabour him with my right fist.[8]

A passer-by, seeing the predicament Christian was in, took the child from her, and now having both hands free, Christian returned to the fray with renewed fury. Dr J. Wilson's book claimed that:

> ... she beat her aggressor in such a manner that he cried for quarter, begged pardon most submissively and promised to show her the greatest respect for the future. This insult and the consequential battle proved very lucky for Mrs Davies, for it happened as the quality [noblemen] were returning from [Queen Anne's] court, who stopped their chariots [coaches] to be spectators of the fray in which she received neither hurt nor loss but that of tearing her sarsenet hood which however was aptly repaired by money thrown by Lord Harvey and the Marquis of Winchester.[9]

In addition to this, Christian received the sum of about £9 from a collection made during the subsequent dinner and was allowed to take away a large quantity of untouched provisions that had been provided for the meal.

On the morning of 15 November, 1712, Christian had the misfortune to see a number of her benefactors fight in a duel, during which two of them were killed. This was one of the most infamous duels in London's rather sordid history and details of the fight are still legendary, even today, more than 300 years later.

That fateful morning Christian was walking through Hyde Park when she noticed four well dressed men, whom she thought she recognised. The men, all armed with swords, jumped over a ditch and walked into the thickets of the nursery. This led Christian to believe, quite accurately, that a duel was about to be fought. She hurried forward with the intention of preventing the fight, but was too late; by the time she arrived the four men were already engaged in a savage sword fight. Moments later Charles Mohun, the 4th Baron Mohun, and James Hamilton, the 4th Duke of Hamilton, were fatally wounded and fell together.

Both men soon afterwards died. The other two were both slightly wounded: Colonel Hamilton, one of the seconds (with whom Christian had fought in Marlborough's campaigns) had received a slight wound in the instep of his foot, and General George MacCartney (also reported as Macartney and McCartney), a second for Mohun, who walked quickly away as several park-keepers approached. Christian also walked away, not wanting to become involved as her evidence would have been damaging to the very men and their families who had become her benefactors.[10]

Christian later wrote:

> Had I been examined as a witness in this affair, my affidavit might possibly have left no doubt, but it was very happy for me I was not thought of, as my evidence would, in all probability, have made enemies of my friends, having experienced the charity of several noblemen, intimates of the deceased lords, and I must have disobliged one side, as I should have sworn to the truth of what my eyes had witnessed.[11]

But why was the duel being fought and why did two men have to die from what one writer has termed 'testosterone poisoning'? To answer this question we must step back a little in time and examine the lives of the principal antagonists.

Charles Mohun was an English politician and 'rake' — a person who would have been dubbed a 'cad and a bounder' in the England of the early twentieth century, a bit of 'rotter' in the public school jargon of the same period and a completely useless 'plonker' in today's rather interesting television-driven vernacular. He was infamous for fighting duels and one may suppose that despite his failings and the fact that he is reported to have killed three men in such duels he was, at least, courageous and would not back away from a fight, especially when his principles were involved. Indeed Charles Mohun's father had died, shortly after the child's birth, the cause of death being a duel, so such aggression apparently ran in the family. Following the death of the father, the Mohun family had been left destitute and Charles Mohun had later become an avid gambler — a calling that did little if anything to endear him to polite society or earn him any respect whatever. Like so many profligate characters of his era, Charles married for money. His first wife was a member of one of Britian's more influential families and Mohun hoped that the match would help to provide sufficient funds to clear his mountainous and mounting debts. However, the marriage brought no dowry and soon afterwards the couple parted company forever. [12]

Mohun now became even more reckless and in 1692 an argument over a gambling debt resulted in his first duel with John Kennedy, the 7th Earl of Cassillis, (also reported as Cassilis) a Scottish peer whose first wife had been none other than Lady Susannah Hamilton, the daughter of James Hamilton, the 1st Duke of Hamilton and a close relative of James Hamilton the 4th Duke of Hamilton with whom Mohun would fight the duel in 1712.[13]

Yet Charles Mohun really came to infamous prominence on 9 December of the same year (1692). At that time Mohun's friend, Richard Hill, an officer, was deeply in love with an actress named Anne Bracegirdle (*c.* 1671-12 September, 1748).

In fact many people were, apparently, in love with Anne. She was no ravishing beauty but had become well known for her excellent performances in numerous plays including the roles of Lady Anne in Shakespeare's *Richard II* and Desdemona in *Othello.*[14]

However, despite his amorous intentions towards Anne, Hill believed that her true affections lay with a competitive suitor named William Mountfort (*c.* 1664-1692).

Mountfort was another quite well known English actor and also a dramatic writer. He usually played roles depicting a 'fine gentleman' and had written a number of plays. In 1686 he had married another actress, Susanna Percival, but Mountfort was clearly intoxicated with Anne Bracegirdle.

Believing that the best way to deal with the presumed relationship between Mountfort and Anne Bracegirdle, Hill and Mohun planned to ambush Mountfort after a performance and murder him. The story then becomes a little confused but it is believed that on 9 December, 1692, the two antagonists met with the unfortunate Mountfort in Howard Street, the Strand, and while Mohun held him (or at least just watched) Hill stabbed Mountfort in the chest. Mountfort died of his wounds the following day. Richard Hill was able to flee the country but Charles Mohun was arrested and charged with murder. The trial was carried out by the House of Lords and on 6 February, 1693, Mohun was infamously acquitted. It was a verdict that created a great deal of public anger.[15]

Charles Mohun now joined the army in which he served in France under Charles Gerard, the 2nd Earl of Macclesfield, (1659-1701).[16]

In 1699 Mohun was again arraigned before the House of Lords charged with murder, this time following a duel that had taken place in Leicester Square. Mohun was acquitted but his friend, Edward Rich, then the 6th Earl of Warwick, was convicted of manslaughter yet escaped punishment by pleading the 'privilege of peerage'. Once again it was a classic case of one law for the rich and another for the poor. (Edward Rich died two years later in 1701).[17]

Following this case Mohun took his seat in the House of Lords.

In 1701 Charles Mohun went on a diplomatic mission to Hanover accompanying the Earl of Macclesfield. Later that year when the earl died he left a major portion of his estate to Mohun. For the following few years Mohun was forced to defend his inheritance against other claimants, including James Hamilton, the 4th Duke of Hamilton, with whom he would later fight his final duel.

Yet Mohun was now rich. In 1707 he commenced the construction of a new house in the country, *Gawsworth New Hall*, situated in the village of Gawsworth, Cheshire. (The construction of the hall would be abandoned following Mohun's death but the building would subsequently be completed).[18]

Five years later came major political events described earlier in this history when Mohun's Whigs lost government to the Tories. James Hamilton, the 4th Duke of Hamilton, a prominent Tory, was appointed special envoy to Paris. This was at a time when the dispute between Mohun and James Hamilton over the inheritance was at a very low and dangerous ebb. The dispute led to Mohun challenging James Hamilton to a duel and, accordingly, seconds were selected.

The contest that Christian Davies witnessed in Hyde Park on 15 November, 1712, was particularly savage and brutal. Christian would have been used to bloodshed, inured as she was by years of heavy fighting in the Low Countries, but the sight of four men frenziedly hacking at each other with little or no finesse must have been terrible indeed.

The seconds selected for the duel were General George MacCartney (on behalf of Charles Mohun) and Colonel Hamilton (on behalf of the James Hamilton, the 4th Duke of Hamilton). Normally it was the task of the seconds not to take part in the actual duelling but to ensure that the duel was conducted fairly and in the accepted manner, that no cheating took place and that honour was properly bestowed on both the winner and the loser of the duel. However, in this instance, the bitter enmity between the two parties must have been running particularly high as all four men drew swords and quickly came to blows.[19]

The well known contemporary publication *The Book of Days*, subsequently published a report of the event:

> On 15 November, 1712, a singularly ferocious and sanguinary duel was fought in Kensington Gardens. The keepers of Hyde Park, on the morning of that day, were alarmed by the clashing of swords, and rushing to the spot whence the sound proceeded, found two noblemen weltering in their blood. These were Lord Mohun, who was already dead, and the Duke of Hamilton, who expired in the course of a few minutes. Nor had the combat been limited to the principals alone. The seconds, Colonel Hamilton, on the part of the duke, and General McCartney on that of Lord Mohun, had also crossed swords, and fought with desperate rancour. The former of these remained in the field, and was taken prisoner, but McCartney fled to the Continent, from which, however, he afterwards returned and submitted to trial.
>
> A prodigious ferment was occasioned by this duel, owing to the circumstance of the Duke of Hamilton being regarded as the head of the Jacobite party both in North and South Britain, whilst Lord Mohun was a zealous champion of the Whig interest. Neither of the men could lay claim to great admiration on the score of integrity or principle, and it is difficult, at the present day, to pronounce any decisive verdict in their case. What, however, seems to have originated merely in personal animosity was represented by the Tory party as a dastardly attempt on the part of their political opponents to inflict a vital wound on the Jacobite cause, then in the ascendant, by removing its great prop, who had just been appointed ambassador to the court of France, and was expected to leave London for Paris in the course of a few days. It was maintained that the duke had met foul play

> at the hands of McCartney, by whose sword, and not that of Lord Mohun, he had been slain. But this allegation was never established by sufficient evidence, and the truth of the matter seems to be that both sets of antagonists, principals as well as seconds, were so transported by the virulence of personal enmity to neglect all the laws both of the gladiatorial art and the duelling code, and engage each other with the fury of savages or wild animals.[20]

The injuries suffered by both the victims of this duel were so terrible that thereafter pistols largely became the 'weapons of choice' for such events as they resulted in briefer fights that could often prove less bloody and fatal. (A nervously shaking hand at fifteen feet was usually far less deadly than a nervously shaking hand at two).

Both the seconds, General George MacCartney and Colonel Hamilton, were charged with manslaughter and murder. They gave different accounts of the duel and it is a pity that Christian Davies had not remained at the scene so that she could have been brought up to give evidence. At least justice might have prevailed. However, as with those cases when Mohun had been brought up on similar charges, the trial proved to be a farce and resulted in a complete debacle.[21]

~~~~

Christian was later filled with a longing to see her mother again, and wrote to her to say that she would soon be arriving in Dublin. Upon her arrival her mother, then almost 100 years of age, walked ten miles to see the daughter she had not seen for many years.

Dr J. Wilson later wrote:

> The poor old woman, who had long given her [Christian] over for dead, having in so many years heard nothing of her, wept for joy and in such an excessive manner
~~~~

> when she embraced her that the daughter could not refrain mingling her tears with those of her mother. Upon enquiry after her children she learned that the elder of them died at the age of eighteen and that the younger was in the workhouse. The nurse, with whom, at her departure she had left the best of her goods, together with her child, soon threw him upon the parish [charity]. Indeed, [only] ... one of those with whom she had instructed her effects was honest enough to give any account of them, and that was Mr Howel, father of the person who [had] ruined her virgin innocence. All the others, like the nurse, converted the goods to their own use, and looked upon her as an unreasonable woman to expect a return. ... She was equally unfortunate with regard to her house [tavern] for the person dying whom she left in it, one [person named] Bennett claimed it as his freehold and, having got possession of it, Mrs Davies could not eject him, nor contest his title, her writings [deeds of ownership] being lost or destroyed, and indeed, not having money sufficient to carry on a law suit without which it is in vain to expect justice, she was compelled to sit down with the loss and think on some method to get an honest living.[22]

The child who had been sent to a Dublin workhouse would certainly have suffered a degrading and difficult life and Christian would surely have been aware of the conditions at such institutions. The workhouses of England and Ireland at that time were harsh places where children often fought like animals for food. It was not uncommon for the children to be given sour milk while fresh milk was given to the pigs. Food was regularly plundered and sold by the workhouse managers or employees. The tables at dinner were sometimes covered with rotten potatoes; bread was half-baked, the soup was made from just peas, frequently rotten, and the tea was watery. Children and adults would fight with the pigs for scraps of meat and milk. Some inmates later reported that the Irish stew was so thin it could be squirted through a syringe. There were no potatoes in the potato soup which, in one Dublin workhouse, the children derisively termed, 'bluewater'.[23]

However, it was now far too late for Christian to do anything about the child she had left behind and who had eventually been placed into such an institution as the child would have left the workhouse by the time Christian returned to Ireland. She eventually decided that as she had previously run a tavern she would rent another house and also open it as a tavern. Christian was well experienced in the production of beer and with a growing trade in homemade pies she was able to earn a modest living.

Some time afterwards Christian met — probably at the tavern — a soldier named Davies, a man who had served in the First Regiment of Foot Guards during Marlborough's campaigns in the Low Countries and had much in common with Christian.

Davies had been in Flanders when his father had died, and, requesting a discharge, this had been granted. He had travelled to Chester where his father had left him a small amount of land. However, his brother had contested the will and kept the land for himself. Davies soon afterwards re-enlisted in the army, joining the Welch Fusiliers, and was sent to Dublin where he met Christian.[24]

Christian and Davies married and the couple lived in Dublin until Davies was transferred to Hereford in 1714, the year the Hanoverian King George I ascended to the throne following the rather ghastly death of Queen Anne. (Anne died of suppressed gout, ending in erysipelas at seven o'clock on 1 August, 1714. [Erysipelas is an acute febrile infectious disease due to streptococcus which is characterised by deep red inflammation of the skin or mucous membranes]. Anne's body was so grotesquely swollen that it had to be carried to the Henry VII Chapel at Westminster Abbey in a coffin that was almost square).[25]

Christian remained in Dublin, probably until the following year, while she sold her possessions, and then took ship for England, meeting her husband at Hereford. She then travelled with his regiment to Gloucester, and finally to London. Still embittered over the reduction of her pension from one shilling per day to fivepence, and now having a different administration to deal with, Christian tackled the ministry and was successful in persuading the new king to agree to having her original pension restored to her. Christian Davies was to enjoy the correct amount for the remainder of her life.[26]

Christian's husband was one of the troops sent to Preston to crush the Jacobite rebellion of 1715. The Jacobites led by Thomas Forster, a Northumberland squire, moved south from Scotland and by the time they reached Preston in Lancashire their numbers had grown to around 4,000. Their horse-troops entered Preston on the evening of 9 November that year. General Charles Wills was ordered to halt their advance and left Manchester with six regiments on 11 November. When he arrived at Preston he found that the Jacobites had barricaded most of the main streets. Preston was then virtually besieged by English troops and although a government attack was repulsed with heavy loss of life, Wills had many houses set on fire so that the fires would spread to the Jacobite positions. The Jacobites were finally forced to surrender (14 November, 1715) and 1,468 of them were taken prisoner, 463 of these being English. Many were executed, some of them suffering death by beheading or being 'hung, drawn and quartered' — a particularly hideous form of capital punishment. Most of the captured rebels were, however, transported to the Americas.[27]

While her husband was fighting the Jacobite rebels, Christian settled in a small house at Willow Walk, Tothill Fields, Westminster, where she earned a modest living by making pies and selling them for a farthing each. She also sold 'strong liquors' and was so successful in business that, after the Jacobite insurrection had been forcibly put down, she was able to purchase 'at large expense' her husband's discharge from the army.[28]

However, Christian's husband must have been something of a reprobate for soon after his discharge, being drunk, he again enlisted in the Guards.[29] Yet they were not parted, Davies still lived in Willow Walk with Christian. One night while they were both in bed they heard a commotion in the street. Rushing downstairs, almost naked, Christian, her husband and a lodger, saw that some ruffians were in the process of destroying the site where Christian sold her pies. Christian rushed them, took one of the men in her strong hands and beat him with her fists until he cried for mercy and promised to make good the damage he and his friends had caused. Christian's own account of the confrontation clearly portrays that even now, in her advancing years, she was more than prepared to tackle any man who wronged her. She wrote:

> ... some frolicsome sparks, thinking they show a great deal of humour in being sillily [sic] mischievous, took it into their heads to tear up the pitching place which I had made for the porters to ease themselves by resting their burdens upon, and to throw that, and the board on which I exposed my pies, into the ditch. No doubt they would have done further mischief had I not run down, followed by my husband and a lodger, all three almost naked, and put a stop to their career. I gave the worthy gentleman whom I first laid hold on such a thorough rib-roasting that he was glad to cry quarter and to promise that he would make good the damage.[30]

The house in Willow Walk in which Christian was living, and two others adjoining it, were rented by her for £8 per year. This was the equivalent of 7,680 pies at a farthing each. Christian would have had to make and sell about 148 pies every week of the year just to pay the rent and that is not taking into consideration the costs of the raw materials such as flour and meat. Christian would have had quite a job to meet her £8 yearly commitment. However, the landlord, needing money to pay a fine, let the houses on a long lease to a bailiff who soon afterwards instructed Christian that he was now her new landlord and that the rent would be increased for the following quarter.

Unsurprisingly, Christian was furious. She later claimed:

> I used all the rhetoric I was capable of to divert him from so great cruelty, as I termed the raising my rent; but finding he had no bowels, and that entreaties and submission only flattered his pride and made him more obdurate, as is the nature of these low-bred upstarts, who are purse-proud, I resolved to vent my passion, which with much difficulty I had hitherto curbed, and changing my dialect, I treated him with all the opprobrious terms I could think of.[31]

Christian had earlier purchased a stand of willow trees which grew before the houses. When the bailiff arrived the following day with a carpenter and began to cut down the trees, Christian's famous temper once again flared. Bringing her husband from the house to act as a witness and to prove that she had not struck the first blow, she berated the landlord, claiming that she had paid for the trees and they were her property. Harsh words followed; the landlord attempted to wrest a branch from Christian's strong hands and when he failed in this he struck her a blow. His sudden violence was his greatest mistake, as Dr J. Wilson later recorded:

> This was the first [blow] she ever received with pleasure, as it afforded her an opportunity of drubbing the rascal with impunity, which indeed she did unmercifully, being far superior to him in strength. The carpenter, seeing his comrade so roughly handled, came down to his assistance, and endeavouring to take her off him, tore her head cloths. This so enraged her that she left the bailiff,

> who took the opportunity to make a precipitous retreat, and having seized the carpenter, [she] struck up his heels and fell upon him with her knee in his stomach, then let him rise, knocked him down again, and in short beat him until he was quite weary, so that at last he got clear of her and followed the example of the bailiff.[32]

Christian's original landlord, the man who had leased the house to the bailiff, was so heavily in debt that with the prospect of a long period in debtors' gaol he later committed suicide by cutting his wrists. What became of the bailiff is not known, Christian only recorded that he, '... met with a just reward of his rogueries.'[33]

The year was now 1722, a decade since Christian had returned from the fighting in Europe. By this time Christian had made London her permanent home and was running a sutler's tent in Hyde Park. As the king, George I, was due to inspect a regiment of troops there, Lord Cadogan, the 1st Earl of Oudenaarde, with whom Christian had fought in Flanders, invited Christian to act as a guard at the king's tent. Christian was delighted with the honour but had to refuse as she had no-one to look after her business, her husband being on duty at the time. However, despite this she decided that she would see the king and went to a tent adjoining that of the king's where she met several staff officers who plied her with fortified wines. Their reception of her was so welcoming that Christian almost forgot her objective. After the officers had given her a shilling each in exchange for a kiss, Christian went to see the king but was too late as he was about to leave in his carriage. Christian rushed over to apologise but George's only comment was that he had thought to, 'have seen the old dragoon sooner,' and then drove off in his carriage leaving Christian bitterly disappointed. Her disappointment was easily assuaged, however, when the staff officers each gave her a guinea.

While she was working at the park Christian contracted a fever and was forced to leave the camp the following day. During the period Christian was away her husband sold her tent and all her possessions for £2 and spent the entire amount on drink. According to Christian the tent alone had been worth fifty shillings (£2/10/-. It was during her illness that Christian heard of the death of the Duke of Marlborough (16 June, 1722). The death of the former army commander was a serious blow to Christian who had fought through almost all of Marlborough's campaigns and had greatly respected him. Despite her illness Christian raised herself from her bed and marched beside her husband at the duke's funeral, '... with a very heavy heart and streaming eyes,' as she later wrote.[34]

Unable to come to any agreement with her landlord, Christian moved to another house and later moved once more to Paddington where she continued selling pies and beer for a living. She seemed reasonably contented although many of her old friends and benefactors — those with whom she had fought in the Low Countries — were now dying of advanced age. By now, Christian herself was fifty-six years of age, a significant achievement when few people lived to see sixty and even more remarkable when one considers the wounds she had survived and the harsh conditions under which she had lived during her years in the army.

One of Christian's benefactors at this time was a 'noble-lady' who made her a gift of a hoop-petticoat, a type of garment that Christian had never before worn, or, as Christian herself so characteristically admitted, '... a machine I knew not how to manage, and no wonder for I never had one on before and I believe it requires as much dexterity to exercise as a musket.'[35] However, as the gift had been in good faith Christian was determined to use the petticoat and put it on beneath her dress before venturing out into the street. Dr J. Wilson, wrote of the event:

> Being in a street where the footpath was narrow, she thrust against a post which made the other side of her

> hoop fly up. Imagining it was some rude fellow thrusting his hand up her coats, and thinking fully to be revenged on him, she threw her stick back without looking behind her and gave herself such a blow that she could not help crying out. She turned about but nobody appeared except some apprentices who laughed heartily at her roaring and her awkward management of her hoop. On this she walked off vexed and ashamed at becoming the sport of boys and cursing the hoop and its inventor.[36]

~~~~

Yet Christian herself loved a joke, especially at the cost of others, and she often participated in trickery and practical joking in company with her friends.

Shortly after the episode with the hoop-petticoat she was asked by some of her friends if she would be willing to play a practical joke on Sir James Baker, known affectionately to them as Lord Lateran. The friends invited Baker to dinner at the Thatched House, a local tavern. However, when Baker arrived he was told by the waiter that the others had already eaten and left, but that some very delicious soup, of which Baker was particularly fond, and some meats had been left for him. Shrugging, Baker sat down to dinner while in the next room his friends, and Christian, to whom he was not known, waited patiently for Baker's meal to commence. As soon as Baker was eating the first course, Christian knocked on the door and when the waiter answered it she demanded to be shown to Baker's table. The waiter, who was in on the joke, made a brief protest at the intrusion but Christian imperiously swept him aside and walked across the room to seat herself at the table opposite Baker. As this was happening the other conspirators slipped silently into the room and hid behind a screen that had been erected between the table and the door. Baker, surprised at the sudden appearance of this particularly forward woman,
~~~~

asked Christian what the devil she wanted, stating that she should be quick with her explanations as he had only just sat down for his dinner. Christian looked at him coolly and replied, 'My dear, I do not design to interrupt you, as I came on purpose to dine with you, though this pretended ignorance of me causes both my grief and astonishment. Since you cannot but know that I had more regard to your solicitations than to my own interest, having entirely disobliged all my friends by becoming your wife.'

'Wife ... wife!' Baker cried, quite astonished. 'Why woman I never was married.' (One can almost hear the stifled tittering coming from behind the screen).

'Is it possible, my Lord,' Christian replied, 'a man of your quality and good sense can bring a blemish on his honour by denying ... what can be so easily proved? It is happy for me and my two babies that I have three witnesses of our marriage, or I find you would ruin my character and bastardise your poor innocent children.'

'Children too!' cried Baker. 'Very fine, truly, I have a wife and two children without knowing anything of the matter.'

'Look ye,' Christian said, pretending to become annoyed, 'I am not a woman to be trifled with. Your simple denial will avail you nothing against the oaths of three creditable witnesses, though it has given me such a contempt for your person that I can part with you and not break my heart. But I expect you will immediately furnish me with money for my own and your children's support.'

By this time Baker was almost apoplectic. 'Why thou thorough-paced impostor,' he shouted, 'thou notorious abominable liar!'

'Go on, my Lord,' Christian replied, 'money I must and will have. This mean, foul language does not affect me or make me less your wife.'

'So I find,' he replied hotly. 'You will swear I am married to extort money from me!'

Baker then turned to the waiter and protested his innocence but the waiter stated that Christian seemed to have witnesses to prove her case and if it could be proved then Baker himself must be in the wrong.

'This is some old jade,' Baker protested angrily, 'who can no longer get money by whoring and would now exhort it by swearing a sham marriage upon me. I don't question her being prepared with false witnesses.'

'Come, my dear Lord,' Christian replied, 'fall to your soup, and after dinner I will give you incontestable proof of our marriage.'

Baker decided that it might be better to listen to such nonsense on a full stomach and quickly returned to his soup. When he had finished Christian told the waiter also to lay a table setting before her.

'Why sure,' Baker asked with some incredulity, 'you don't intend to dine with me?'

'Indeed I do,' Christian replied, 'and bed with you too. Do you think I married to have only the bare name of a wife?'

'Prithee woman be quiet,' Baker stated. 'I protest. If I had my sword here I would run you through the body.'

Christian ignored the threat and when the roast ducks and beef were laid on the table she offered to serve her 'husband' who, however, now lapsed into a sullen silence. Christian, in characteristic style, then helped herself to a generous serving of the meal. Afterwards she stated that she would now take her leave of Baker, adding that she hoped she would find him in a better mood the next time they met. She leaned forward, asked for a parting kiss and Baker angrily replied, 'No ... no woman, I kiss you, kiss the devils.'

'Kiss the devils, damn,' Christian shouted at him. 'I will have a kiss before you go,' and standing, she lunged at him. Terrified, Baker leapt from the table and ran around the room, hotly pursued by Christian who, being lighter and faster, quickly caught him around the neck and roughly kissed him. Baker attempted to break away but using her legendary strength Christian easily held him while those behind the partition made good their escape. She then released Baker and he scrambled downstairs where he threatened the owner of the tavern, claiming that a man of quality should not have to put up with such an 'insolent jade'.[37]

Christian, however, was the first to admit that Baker had almost certainly seen through the whole hoax. He could hardly not have heard the stifled tittering coming from behind the screen and Christian's accusations certainly had no effect on Baker's prodigious appetite.

~~~~

Some time after this event Christian again purchased her husband's discharge from the army, however, the man was of little use in the business and indeed was such a profligate that Christian was forced to sell her business and move to Charles Street, Westminster. While she was living at Charles Street she was summoned to appear before the Chelsea College Board in order that her pension rights could be discussed. After the examination she met two other pensioners, one of whom claimed that Christian was not entitled to the money. Christian was outraged; she told him of her service in the army of Marlborough, and, never being short of words, ended by calling him a, 'faggot and a cowardly dog'.[38]

The pensioner was aghast at these words, and so incensed at Christian's accusations that, despite his apparent age, he drew his sword and made a thrust at her. Christian, however, was armed with only a stick, but using this she fended the thrust, closed with her aggressor, took the sword from his hand and threw it over a fence. She then used her stick to good effect, breaking his head in two places. Two bystanders who had watched the event offered her ten shillings in payment for their enjoyment of the fun, but Christian — somewhat uncharacteristically — refused their offer.[39]

~~~~

Christian finally returned to Dublin, taking a humble wagon from London as she could not afford the coach-fare. She shared the wagon with several other women. Once in conversation she told them of her adventures in the two wars, however, her stories were treated with the utmost scepticism until an old soldier, with whom Christian had fought in Flanders, boarded the wagon and confirmed Christian's statements. Five miles before Coventry the wagon was suddenly halted by a mounted highwayman who ordered the wagon-driver to stop or die. The driver quickly pulled up the horses and the wagon rolled to a halt. The robber then urged his horse forward, pointed a pistol at the passengers and demanded their money. Most of the women immediately started crying, however, Christian looked at the robber calmly and told him to put away his pistol as it was frightening the passengers, adding, '... they will give you what they can spare immediately.'

'Everything they can spare', the highwayman was alleged to have replied, 'damn you I'll have all, and this moment too.'[40]

While the women were taking their valuables and money from their purses and pockets, Christian saw that the robber had a brace of pistols in a belt at his waist. She had not seen them when the man had first approached the wagon as the pistols had then been hidden by his coat. The highwayman was off his guard, believing that he had only to deal with a terrified driver, a cart full of semi-hysterical women and one old soldier. As he leaned forward, his hat in his hand, to receive the women's valuables, Christian snatched one of the pistols from his belt, quickly cocked it and shot him through the chest. She then reversed the weapon and using its butt, hammered him to the ground where he died within a few seconds. It was later reported:

> All this was done so quick that the waggoner and the women could not believe their eyes for some time till they saw Mrs Davies jump out like an old campaigner, seize his horse and begin to rifle his [the robber's] pockets,

> but finding nothing but bullets and a small horn of powder she was disappointed of her booty. However, when they came to Coventry the mayor of the town gave her his horse and accoutrements which she sold for eleven guineas. She received the thanks of the whole city for ridding them of this troublesome infester [sic] of the road who made the entrance of the town dangerous to travellers. The inn where they put up was crowded with the inhabitants to see the woman who had done them such a signal service, but their visits gave her little satisfaction till one among them posed a collection for her and solicited so warmly in her behalf that before her departure she received upwards of sixteen pounds beside the eleven guineas for the horse etc. The sight of so much money gave her new spirit and she pursued her journey with a cheerful heart. Her companions also were extremely joyful on having so unexpectedly saved their money. For fear there might be more of the [robber] fraternity upon the road, Mrs Davies reserved a brace of pistols with powder and ball, giving orders to the waggoner that if he saw any person that he suspected, to stop the wagon, and promised in such case to alight to defend her charge and his passengers. But they arrived safe at Chester without any other incident by the way, where the news of Mrs Davies killing the highwayman had got before them. In the city she received a farther collection of eleven pounds fourteen shillings which gave her such spirits that she wished to meet the highwayman every week.[41]

So widely known did Christian (Mother Ross) become because of her killing of the highwayman that an anonymous poet wrote of her:

> *All hail great Ross, thou glory of the age,*
> *Such deeds as thine are subjects for the stage*

The amazon race begins again,
And females toil for Empire o'er the men,
Go on bold heroine like Hercules,
And punish monsters both by land and seas,
Spread round thy actions by the mouth of fame,
Till tyrants tremble at thy glorious name,
England can boast a greater Joan than France,
To use the pistol as she did the lance,
Grant us kind heaven thy fate be not the same,
With Joan of Arc that famous Gallic dame,
The Frenchmen called her saint, the English witch,
And safely clapped a flambeau to her breech,
'Tis oft the fate of devils here at home,
To rise up virtuous and be saints in Rome.[42]

Once she had arrived in Dublin, Christian rented a house close to the castle and again set up a small tavern and pie-shop. While in Dublin she saw Thomas Howel, the man who had raped her when she was a teenager. Howel was now a church minister. He attempted to talk to her but she avoided him by turning suddenly into a coffee-house. In his 1742 'biography' Dr J Wilson, recorded that when Howel returned home that day he was, 'very melancholy', and that his family and friends had tried to discover the reason for his sadness, but he would speak only to his sister. To this woman he confessed the sin he had committed some forty years previously, adding that ever since that time he had known no real peace and that at times he had thought he was going insane. The following day, hoping to flee from those bitter memories, he left Dublin, taking his wife and eleven children with him. Yet the guilt evidently continued to haunt him and soon afterwards Mrs Howel sent one of their children to Howel's study to tell him that breakfast was ready. When the child opened the door he saw his father hanging by a rope from the window-sash. Mrs Howel's sister later told Christian of the event, adding that the warning signs had been evident, Howel himself had previously written to his brother, warning him that he was in a state of despair and not to be surprised if he, '... laid violent hands on himself.'[43]

~~~~

Christian had been only a year in her home country when she was again filled with a longing to travel. She sent a message to her husband asking him to rent a house in Chester. She was given passage aboard a yacht which was to take her to England and she went immediately to live in Chester.

Her memoirs, completed shortly before her death, end with the following rather sad paragraph which summed up the difficulties of the aged and infirm then living in the England of the 1730s.

> I lived for three years in Chester and then returned to Chelsea where I have remained ever since without anything happening of notice. I got my husband into the [Chelsea] College where he is a [pensioner] sergeant, and have been hitherto subsisted by the benevolence of the quality and gentry of the court, wither I go twice a week, but the expense of coach hire, as both my lameness and age increase, for I cannot walk ten yards without help, is a terrible tax upon their charity ... my former subsistence is greatly diminished from what it was.[44]

Age was now creeping inexorably upon Christian and her health quickly failing. It is difficult to reconcile the figure of the once vibrant young woman who marched earnestly to war dressed in her husband's clothing, to the pathetic but patriotic old woman of the 1730s with shuffling legs, hardly able to take more than a few steps at a time. By now Christian was suffering from, '... distempers, dropsy and scurvy', and was obviously in an extremely frail condition. She was poor, begging for funds from her friends among the gentry and collecting the pitiably small
~~~~

pension awarded to her by Queen Anne. Yet when her husband, also in his old age, was taken seriously ill, Christian lovingly tended to him, sitting with him through the long nights until she finally contracted a cold that quickly deepened into fever. Several days later, on 7 July, 1739, Christian died at the age of seventy-two years.

Christian Davies was buried with full military honours, reportedly at the cemetery of the Chelsea Hospital, a line of soldiers firing a final musket salute over her grave. It was a sad ending for a woman who had given so much of her life to others, who had risked her life on so many occasions just to be with her husband and who had thought nothing of the dangers she faced during those long years of bitter warfare.

Christian Davies was an enigma, one of the most unusual and unpredictable people of her age. She made enemies but cherished the many friends who shared her life. She was never to enjoy the comforts and safety of a home life, surrounded, as most people are, by their families; Christian gave up those precious elements of her life in an almost insane attempt to be reunited with her husband. To give up one's children, to take up arms in two of the bloodiest wars in Europe's history, to face years of uncertainty, discomforts, pain and probable death, were the benchmarks by which Christian measured her love for Richard Welsh. There is no doubt that Christian Davies was a rough, tough woman, but her undying love for her lost husband was the driving passion of her life. One has to ask, how many of us would risk so much, suffer so greatly, and give up such treasures as one's own children, just to be with the person we love?

Some people feared her; some loved her; others cherished their memories of her, but everyone, friend or foe, respected Christian Davies.

POSTSCRIPT

Readers might also find some interest in the experiences of several other women who, for a variety of reasons, have elected to dress as men and live their lives under difficult and sometimes particularly dangerous circumstances. Some even married, their wives steadfastly keeping their secret. Their assumed roles were various, and included soldiers, ship's pursers, clerks, barmen, factory hands, doctors, naval seamen and exchange brokers.

One of these, a woman named Margaret Bale, came originally from Colchester, England, and emigrated to Western Australia where she became a teacher. The press later reported of her:

> While her friends feared that she had been murdered and while the detectives were at their wits' end to trace her movements, Miss Margaret Bale, the young schoolteacher who mysteriously disappeared in Perth on December 22 last, [1909] was having her first experience as a young 'man' and was following various masculine occupations in Fremantle. On the day of her disappearance she had her hair cut at Cottesloe and afterwards discarded her female attire for a youth's suit and blue serge which she purchased from Messrs S. Freedmen and Co's stores in Hay Street. From that time she successfully carried out her masquerade until yesterday morning [4 August, 1910 — author's note] when Detective Dempsey found her acting as [a] clerk with a number of youths in the office of a city catering establishment. She was very crestfallen when she found that her identity had been discovered but consented to return to her friends in the city and resume her proper position in society.

The case is the most extraordinary of its kind that has ever been brought under notice in Western Australia and the story of the young lady's doings during the past seven months reads more like a romance than a narrative of what has actually taken place. Miss Bale was a school teacher at Kalgoorlie until the beginning of last December, when she came to Perth with the intention, it was thought, of returning to her family in England. Her passage had been booked by a White Star boat which was to leave Albany early the following month for Liverpool and it was arranged that she should reside with friends in West Perth until the time arrived for her departure for Albany. From what has subsequently transpired it now appears that she had no intention of returning to her family in England, although apparently as a subterfuge she allowed most of her baggage to be despatched to the southern port.

On December 22 for some extraordinary reason, she conceived the idea of eluding the vigilance of her friends by adopting male attire, and once having made up her mind it did not take her long to act. She accordingly left her residence with a small handbag, ostensibly to do some shopping in the city, and, as already stated, she did not return. On reaching the city she purchased a youth's blue serge suit ... and caught the next train to Cottesloe where, in order to alter her appearance, she had her hair cut short at a local barber's shop and parted on the left side. The same afternoon she discarded her female attire and appeared in Fremantle as a slim 'young man' in the serge suit. ...

Her next move was to secure lodgings at a Fremantle restaurant, [hotel] where she remained about two weeks, none of the inmates noting anything peculiar in her appearance except that they observed that her voice was distinctly feminine. She had a considerable sum of money at the time — quite sufficient to have paid her passage to the Eastern States or even further — but for some unexplained reason she preferred to remain in Fremantle and continue her masquerade which, up to that time, had been successful above her expectations.

Enquiries made at Fremantle show that she could adapt herself to almost any occupation as a means of earning a livelihood, and appears to have become so taken up with the daring role she had adopted that she was prepared to take up almost any position. Being only 25 years of age she had no difficulty in securing a situation as a steward at the Fremantle Club where she pleased the members considerably and was regarded as a very aristocratic 'boy' with many unexpected qualities as a steward. In consequence of some 'difference' with the other employees, she left this situation at the end of a fortnight.

After her experience at the club she felt qualified to answer an advertisement in the newspaper for a 'good strong boy to act as cellarman and handyman at the Oddfellows' Hotel, Fremantle.' She applied personally for the post, and despite her fragile stature, she was readily engaged. Here she appears to have acted her part particularly well, for she became a general favourite and in order to keep up her disguise she occasionally smoked a cigarette and conversed with a few youths whose acquaintance she made. She became an expert 'barman,' and the proprietor of the hotel was loath to lose her services when she found that the cellar work was too laborious. Up to this time, despite her effeminate voice, Miss Bale's masquerading had escaped detection. Having a fair sum of money, and being tired of bar work she determined to strike out on a new course and start a business in Fremantle. She accordingly rented a shop in High Street, stocked it with pictures, pictorial post-cards, stationery, general artistic works etc. and opened it under the name of Martin Able. It will be noted that the letters in the word 'Able' are a transportation of those in her surname, Bale. Though she was regarded as a very refined young 'man,' this venture proved a failure, and residents of the Port were surprised one morning about a month ago to read in the window of the closed shop that the proprietor had 'gone up country.'

During the time Miss Bale was in this business she was measured by a Fremantle firm of tailors for a suit of clothes, containing a greenish tint which would delight some of the youthful Beau Brummels of Perth. She also instructed a firm of city solicitors to proceed against a business establishment for breach of contract, and found, like many others, that the law is a thing to be avoided, for she lost the case and had to pay costs amounting to £6

After closing the business at Fremantle Miss Bale came to the city [Perth] and had no difficulty in securing a position as clerk at the catering establishment where she was found yesterday by Detective Dempsey. She was much perturbed when she discovered that her masquerading had come to an end. She explained, it is understood, that she always endeavoured to do things thoroughly and had determined not to be discovered. The youths, who had occupied stools in the same office as Miss Bale, were staggered when they heard of the denouncement. The only explanation Miss Bale offered for her extraordinary conduct was that she had determined not to go back to England, and resolved to sink her identity by adopting male attire and living as a man.

She is a cultured, pleasant-mannered young lady, speaks several languages fluently and is generally of an artistic temperament. Though not very communicative, she endeavoured yesterday to make no secret of the fact that she had enjoyed her many novel experiences of the past seven months.

Miss Bale would probably still be acting as clerk but for a message which Inspector Connell of the Criminal Investigation Department received from Fremantle yesterday morning to the effect that 'a decidedly effeminate young man had been conducting an art business in High Street, Fremantle.' Detective Dempsey, who had been engaged for the past three months investigating Miss Bale's disappearance, left for Fremantle by the next train, and as a result of enquiries, he traced the young woman's movements from the time she secured the situation at the Fremantle Club until she was engaged as a clerk in the city. He then returned to the city, and hurried to the office where Miss Bale was employed, and immediately recognised in the neatly-dressed 'Martin Able' the young lady for whom he had been searching for so long. Miss Bale, at his request, accompanied him to the Detective Office where, after a conversation with Inspector Connell, she promised never to again masquerade as a man. ... During the past seven months she had invariably worn a blue serge suit, a boater hat, a quiet tie and black boots, and [was] described as having been regarded as a 'retiring young man.'[1]

~~~~

Another woman to assume the mantle of a man was Nadezhda Durova, the 'lady cavalier' who, mirroring Christian Davies' experiences, served very successfully and bravely in the army of the Tzars. The daughter of a Russian major, Nadezhda had been born in Kiev and her father had placed her into the care of his soldiers after her abusive mother had almost killed the child by
~~~~

throwing her out of the window of a moving carriage. Nadezhda grew up with the army and her favourite toy was, apparently, a loaded gun. Following her father's retirement Nadezhda continued to play with weapons and was even reputed to have broken-in a stallion which was said to have been unbreakable. In this respect she shared an equine talent to match that of Christian Davies. In 1801 Nadezhda married V.S. Chernov and gave birth to a son in 1803. However, at the age of twenty-four she disguised herself as a young man, deserted her husband and son, and with her horse, 'Alkid', enlisted in a Cossack regiment under the name of Alexander Sokolov. Why she left her husband and son is not known although in her memoirs she later wrote of an unhappy relationship with her mother, a warmth towards her father but nothing whatever of her married life.

Nadezhda was accepted by the Cossacks and became inured to all the difficulties and hardships of camp life. She fought in many battles including the 1806-1807 Prussian campaign during which she saved the lives of two Russian soldiers. One was a private to whom Nadezhda courageously gave first aid under heavy fire. The second was an officer who had been unhorsed. Using a lance, Nadezhda is said to have scattered three French dragoons who were closing in for the kill and then given the officer her horse so that he could retreat safely.

Meanwhile, members of Nadezhda's family were attempting to find what had become of her and it was soon rumoured that she was fighting in the Tsar's army. Nadezhda was a slim, attractive woman and it did not take long for rumours about her gender to become widespread. Soon she and the rumours were linked. Nadezhda's officers reported that she was a courageous soldier and interest in the case reached the ears of the Tzar himself, (Aleksander I) the Emperor of Russia (Aleksander Pavlovich [reign: 1801-1825 also the King of Poland from 1815 to 1825]) who summoned Nadezhda to St. Petersberg. There Nadezhda so impressed the Tzar that he awarded her the Cross of St. George and promoted her to the rank of lieutenant in a hussar regiment.

Yet Nadezhda's youth and beauty prevented rapid promotion. At a time when officers were expected to be manly, virile and to grow expansive moustaches, Nadezhda looked like a boy of sixteen with a smooth hairless complexion. So attractive was she that the regimental colonel's daughter fell in love with her and as a result Nadezhda was transferred to a Lithuanian regiment.

Nadezhda fought in the Napoleonic wars. During the Battle of Borodino she was wounded in the leg by a cannonball but continued fighting for days afterwards until ordered away to recuperate. In 1816 she retired from the army with the rank of captain.

Returning to civilian life, Nadezhda met the famous Russian writer Aleksandr Pushkin who encouraged her to write her autobiography from a diary she had kept during her war service. The autobiography was released in 1836 under the title: *The Cavalry Maiden*. Nadezhda went on to write four novels and continued to wear men's clothing for the remainder of her life. She died at Yelabuga and was interred with full military honours.[2]

~~~~

Another famous male 'impersonator' (as they were then described) was Marie le Roy. In June 1911 the people of Enfield Lock, the famous small-arms factory district in Middlesex, England, were shocked by the announcement that a popular local figure known as Harry Lloyd had died and that it had subsequently been discovered that Harry had actually been a woman.

Harry Lloyd was a French woman named Marie le Roy who, until about 1880, had been a teacher of French and an assistant to Mr Austin Holyoake at the Hall of Science in London.

Her precise motives for disguising her gender are not known but around the year 1881 Marie decided that she wished to live and work as a man. For a while she worked at an electric-lighting station and later, after she had enrolled sufficient pupils to begin a
~~~~

profitable class in French, she abandoned her rather more manual work. She later began courting a widow who had a baby girl, and after marrying the widow the couple went to live at Enfield Lock. There they lived as Mr and Mrs Harry Lloyd and child.

Besides teaching French, Marie also ran a newsagency and was very well known throughout the region. She wore an eyeglass and the men at the small-arms factory, who knew her well, called her, Joey Chamberlain. She was a keen liberal politician and an advocate of votes for women.

The stone on Marie le Roy's grave carries the inscription: 'Harry Lloyd died June 18, 1910, aged 74 years.'[3]

~~~~

Another famous woman who lived as a man was Theodora Grahn, the only daughter of a Bayreuth architect. Theodora was reputed to have been brilliant, even during her early childhood. At just eighteen years of age she could speak French, Italian and English as well as her native German.

Before she turned twenty-one Theodora inherited a legacy that enabled her to start in business as an exchange broker in Berlin. Several years later she disappeared, for no known reason, and adopted men's clothing. She took the somewhat pretentious name of Baron de Verdion and bought a small estate near Berlin where, as a man, she became prominent in educational reform.

However, Theodora was also quite an attractive woman who found it difficult to hide the alluring contours of her body. Rumours as to her gender finally drove her to London where she took the name of Doctor John de Verdion. She established herself as an exchange broker dealing in pictures, coins and precious metals. Theodora was reported as having worn, '... elegant costumes and sported a handsome sword when attending ceremonial functions.'[4] On one occasion at a coffee-house named Furnivals Inn, Theodora was challenged as to her gender. However, she brazened it out with
~~~~

strong words and quickly left the premises. Theodora died in lodgings at Hatton Garden in July 1802, aged sixty-two years, and was buried in the churchyard of St. Andrews, Hordorn. The first inscription on the tombstone recorded the death of John de Verdion; a second revised inscription read simply 'Miss Verdion'.[5]

~~~~

Other remarkable stories of women who dressed as men include that of a woman we know only as Dr James Barry who, for forty years, up until the time of her death in 1865 — successfully concealed her gender. As a man she attained high offices in the army medical appointments and became well known as a social reformer in South Africa.[6]

~~~~

However, one of the most remarkable cases was that of Amy Bock, who was something of a rogue and who also succeeded in marrying another woman. In order to disguise her past and gender Amy changed her name many times; her aliases included Shannon, Vallane, Skevington and Percy Redwood. Yet these aliases may have been more to elude the police than to conceal her true gender. In Dunedin Amy obtained work with a family named Roy. When the family went on holidays they left Amy in charge of the house and she quickly took advantage of the situation. She forged her employer's signature to a receipt and claimed that the employer had sold all the furniture in the house to her. She then sold the furniture for £30 and fled the scene of her crime. The press later reported:

> She was next heard of when she took up her residence at the boarding house kept by Mr and Mrs George Ottaway as Percy Carol Redwood, nephew of an archbishop. With hair cut short, and dressed in the latest fashion, Percy soon became a favourite. The impostor found in

> Miss Ottaway, daughter of the boarding housekeeper a most desirable acquaintance. 'He' forthwith made advances, and a friendship sprang up, which unfortunately ripened and finally ended with disastrous results for the young lady.[7]

~~~~

Another extraordinary story was that of an Irish woman who masqueraded as a man for twenty years under the name of Michael Minch. 'Michael' married a young woman in County Kildare, Ireland, and afterwards emigrated to the United States. She worked as a gardener, employed at Mount Kisco, while her 'wife' was employed as housekeeper. Their married life was always regarded as extremely happy, and relatives later claimed:

> ... Aunt Margaret and ... 'Uncle Michael' had known each other from childhood. They have always been known as Mr and Mrs Minch and have always had the highest reputation. No one has ever suspected 'Uncle Michael' is a woman; nothing will ever separate them; they are so devoted to each other.[8]

~~~~

Another woman was Frances Lamonche who, at just twenty years of age, on her deathbed in hospital, told a nurse of her remarkable story. Wearing the clothes of a young man she had been admitted to the hospital as Frank Williams; her brown hair had been closely cut and there seemed nothing in her manner to indicate that she was, in fact, a female. When the nurse discovered that Frances was a woman she was taken immediately to the female ward where she admitted that she had been wearing men's clothing and doing the work of a male since she had been five years of age. With the aid of her mother she had attended several boys' schools in America. When her gender had been discovered at these schools her mother had taken her away and enrolled her as a boy in another school. Lamonche claimed that her mother was under the impression that boys succeeded in life better than girls. In Chicago she worked firstly as a newsboy, then a bookkeeper. She travelled to England where she learned to ride and later visited Paris where she became a race-jockey sponsored by a French nobleman. A report of her life later concluded:

> Finally, she returned to America with her mother, a Frenchwoman by birth, and a music-hall dancer. The mother died and Frances became a homeless wanderer, sleeping in barns and porches. After her death a package was found containing letters from a young Frenchman in New Orleans, begging to be permitted to come to her rescue, and take her back to France.[9]

~~~~

It seems evident that living as a man also brought the possibility of significant psychological problems, and the case of Captain John Tweed may well have been the result of such trauma.

The case came to light following a post-mortem examination of the body of Captain John Tweed on Staten Island and it was discovered that Tweed was a female. She had been the captain of cargo vessels on the Atlantic sea routes for many years and although she had been on friendly terms with her sailors, towards the end of her life she had become morose and sad, spending most of her days brooding. Tweed's body was found in the basement of a house. Her throat had been cut. The post mortem examination concluded that the injuries had been self-inflicted with a penknife. Prior to this examination her real gender had never been suspected, although her delicate features had sometimes been a matter of some comment, particularly amongst the rough, seafaring community.[10]
~~~~

Notes & Sources

Introduction

1. Admissions register, Royal Chelsea Hospital, http://royalhospitalchelsea.blogspot.com.au.

Chapter 1
Early Life and Marriage

1. Wilson, J. *The British Heroine, or An Abridgement of the Life and Adventures of Mrs Christian Davies, Commonly Called Mother Ross.*, (1742), p 2.
2. Ibid, pp 3-6.
3. Defoe, (attributed) *The Life and Adventures of Christian Davies, Commonly called Mother Ross*, (hereinafter referred to only as 'Davies') (1928), p 1.
4. Davies, p 1.
5. Wilson, pp 7-8.
6. Davies, p 1.
7. Ibid, p 2.
8. Wilson, p 8.
9. Callow, *The Making of King James II, the Formative Years of a King*, (2000), pp 143-4.
10. Miller, *James II*, (2000), pp 69-71.
11. Miller, p 87; Harris, *The Great Crisis of the British Monarchy, 1685-1720*, (2006), p 74.
12. Harris, p 88.
13. Miller, p 142.
14. Harris, pp 349-50.
15. Davies, p 4.
16. Wilson, p 9.
17. Davies, p 4.
18. Ibid, p 3.
19. *Gentleman's Magazine*, August 1739, reproduced in *Maryborough Chronicle* (Queensland), 21 January, 1893. Also in Davies, p 4-5.
20. Davies, p 5.
21. Szechi, *The Jacobites, Britain and Europe, 1688-1788*, (1994), p 48.
22. Davies, p 6.

23. Ibid.
24. http://enwikipedia.org/wiki/Battle_of_Aughrim p 2.
25. Waudchope, *Patrick Sarsfield and the Williamite War*, (1992).
26. Davies, p 7.
27. Ibid, pp 6-7.
28. Ibid, p 8.
29. Wilson, p 17.
30. Davies, p 9.
31. Ibid, p 10.
32. Ibid.
33. Ibid, pp 11-12.
34. Ibid, p 12.
35. Ibid, p 13.
36. Ibid, p 15.
37. Wilson, pp 19-20.

Chapter 2
The Nine Years War

1. Wilson, p 21.
2. Ibid, p 22.
3. Davies, p 21.
4. *Maryborough Chronicle* (Queensland), 21 January, 1893.
5. Davies, p 21.
6. Ibid, p 22.
7. Somerset, *The Affair of the Poisons*, (2003).
8. For additional particulars see: excerpts from Bastille trial records published in Paris, (1870s) www.angelfire.com
9. Childs, *The Nine Years War and the British Army*, (1991). http://en.wikipedia.org/wiki/Battle_of_Landen.
10. Davies, p 23.
11. Ibid, pp 23-5.
12. http://enwikipedia.org/wiki/Fran%C3%A7ois-Henri_de_Montmorrency, duc_de_Luxembourg. For details of the life of Louis Bourdaloue see: http://en.wikipedia.org/wiki/Louis_Bourdaloue.

13. Wilson, p 27; Davies, p 26.
14. Ibid.
15. Davies, p 26.
16. Ibid.
17. For details of James FitzJames' interesting career see: McFerran, *The Family of the Dukes of Beswick*, at www.jacobite.ca
18. Davies, p 27.
19. Wilson, p 28.
20. www.britannia.com/history/monachs/mon51.html.
21. Davies, p 27.
22. Ibid, p 28.
23. Wilson, pp 28-29.
24. Davies, p 29.
25. Wilson, pp 29-30.
26. Davies, p 30.
27. Wilson, p 31.
28. Ibid, pp 31-32.
29. Davies, p 33.
30. http://enwikipedia.org/wiki/Scots_Greys; www.royalscotsgreys.com/history/history.htm.
31. Aubrey, *The Defeat of James Stuart's Armada, 1692*, (1979), pp 118-21.
32. Chisholm, *Baron von Menno,* (1911).
33. Smyth, Sir James Carmichael, 1st baronet (1825) *Chronological Epitome of the Wars in the Low Countries*, http://books.google.ca/books?
34. Davies, pp 35 and 37.
35. Childs, *Warfare in the Seventeenth Century*, (2003), p 202. http://enwikipedia.org/wiki/Nine_Years'_War.
36. Davies, p 38.
37. Wilson, pp 36-37; Davies, pp 38-9.
38. Wilson, p 37; Davies, pp 39-42.
39. http://en.wikipedia.org/wiki/Scots_Greys, p 3.
40. Davies, p 42.
41. Ibid, pp 42-3.

Chapter 3
The War of the Spanish Succession

1. http://en.wikipedia.org/wiki/Scots Greys, p 3.
2. http://www.spanishsuccession.nl/kaiserswerth.html.
3. Ibid.
4. Ibid.
5. Ibid.
6. Wilson, p 42.
7. Davies, p 46.
8. Gregg, *Queen Anne,* (2001).
9. Ibid, p 153.
10. www.spanishsuccession.nl/1702.html.
11. Holmes, *Marlborough, England's Fragile Genius,* (2008) pp 192-93.
12. www.spanishsuccession/nl/1702.html.
13. Davies, p 46.
14. Wilson, p 43.
15. Davies, p 47.
16. Wilson, p 43.
17. Davies, p 48.
18. Wilson, p 43, and Davies, p 48.
19. Wilson, p 44-45.
20. Davies, p 49.
21. Ibid.
22. Ibid, p 50.
23. Hibbert, *The Marlboroughs*, (2001), p 115.
24. Davies, p 50.
25. http://en.wikipedia.org/wiki/Scots_Greys, p 3.
26. Davies, pp 52-3.
27. http://en.wikipedia.org/wiki/War_of_the_Spanish_Succession.
28. http://en.wikipedia.org/wiki/Scots_Greys, p 3.
29. For details of Thomas Blood's career see: *Colonel Thomas Blood*, www.clarelibrary.ie
30. The last will and testament of Holcroft Blood may be seen at: www.holcroftbloods.co.uk/holcroft.html.

31. Wilson, p 49.
32. Ibid, pp 49-50.
33. Ibid, pp 50-51; Davies, p 57.
34. Davies, p 57.
35. Wilson. p 51.
36. Davies, p 57.
37. Wilson, p 51.
38. Ibid, pp 53-54.
39. Davies, p 61.
40. http://en.wikipedia.org/wiki/Scots_Greys, p 3-4.
41. Chisholm, *Blenheim* (1911).
42. Ibid.
43. Churchill, *A History of the English Speaking Peoples: Age of Revolution*, Vol III, (2002), p 44.
44. http://en.wikipedia.org/wiki/Scots_Greys, p 3.
45. Wilson, p 54.
46. Davies, pp 62-63.
47. Wilson, pp 55-56.
48. Wilson, p 56; Davies, 64-65.
49. Wilson, p 66; Davies, p 65.
50. Davies, p 66.
51. Wilson, p 66.
52. Ibid.
53. Ibid, p 57.
54. Ibid, p 58.
55. Ibid.
56. Ibid, p 59.
57. Wilson, p 60; Davies, pp 69-70; http://en.wikipedia.org/wiki/Scots_Greys, p 4.
58. Davies, pp 72-3.
59. Ibid, pp 70-73.
60. Ibid, pp 73-7.
61. Wilson, p 65.

Chapter 4
1706 — Ramillies — Discovery and Discharge

1. www.spanishsuccession.nl/1706.html.
2. Barnett, *Marlborough* (1998).
3. http://en.wikipedia.org/wiki/Scots_Greys, p 3.
4. Trevelyan, *England Under Queen Anne: Ramillies and the Union with Scotland,* pp 132-35; http://enwikipedia.org/wiki/Battle_of_Ramillies.
5. Barnett, *Marlborough* (1998).
6. Chandler, *Marlborough as Military Commander*, (2003), p 179.
7. Wilson, p 67.
8. Davies, pp 79-80.
9. Wilson, pp 67-68.
10. Ibid, pp 68-69.
11. http://enwikipedia.org/wiki/Lord_John_Hay_(Scottish_Army_Officer.
12. Davies, pp 81-82.
13. Churchill, *A History of the English Speaking Peoples, The New World,* Vol. II, p 50.
14. Davies, pp 84-5; http://www.spanishsuccession.nl/1706.html.
15. Wilson, p 72.
16. Davies, pp 85-86.
17. Wilson, pp 72-73.
18. Davies, p 86.
19. Ibid.
20. Barnett, *Marlborough* (1998).
21. Davies, p 86.
22. Wilson, p 73. See also Davies, p 87.
23. Davies, p 88.
24. Ibid.
25. Ibid.
26. Wilson, pp 74-75.
27. Ibid, p 75.
28. Davies, pp 89-90.
29. Wilson, pp 75-77.
30. Churchill, *Marlborough: His Life and Times*, Vol II, (2002), p 313.

Chapter 5
1707–1708 — The Plundering Continues

1. www.battlefield anomalies.com/oudenarde/o1_hope_and_failure.htm.
2. http://www.spanishsuccession.nl/1707.html.
3. www.battlefield anomalies.com/oudenarde/o1_hope_and_failure.htm.
4. www.1911encyclopedia.org/James_III_(the_Old_Pretender).
5. Davies, pp 96-7.
6. www.1911encyclopedia.org/James_III_(the_Old_Pretender).
7. www.spanishsuccession.nl/1708.html.
8. Ibid.
9. Ibid.
10. Davies, pp 99-100.
11. www.spanishsuccession.nl/armies_uk/regiment_f1_orkney.html.
12. Davies, pp 102-3.
13. For a biography of Arnold Joost van Keppel see: www.thepeerage.com/pl684.htm.
14. Davies, p 103.
15. Lynn, *The Wars of Louis* XIV, 1667 - 1714. (1999), p 321.
16. Davies, pp 105-106.
17. Chandler, *The Oxford History of the British Army,* (1986) p 89; http://enwikipedia.org/Siege_of_Lille_(1708).
18. Davies, pp 107-8.
19. Ogrizek, *Belgium and Luxembourg, The World in Colour,* (article 1961) (World Heritage Encyclopedia [undated]; http://en.wikipedia.org/wiki/Aalst,_Belgium.
20. Davies, p 110.
21. Ibid.
22. www.spanishsuccession.nl/1708.html.
23. Wilson, pp 96-98.

Chapter 6
1709 — Malplaquet and the Death of Richard

1. http://en.wikipedia.org/Wiki/War_of_the_Spanish_Succession.
2. Davies, pp 122-3.
3. Ibid, p 117.

4. Davies, pp 117-118.
5. Wilson, pp 98-101.
6. Ibid, pp 101.
7. Davies, pp 120-122.
8. Belloc, *Malplaquet*, p 29.
9. Ibid, p 30.
10. www.fortified-places.com/sieges/tournai1709.html.
11. Belloc, *Malplaquet*, pp 32, 36-7.
12. http://en.wikipedia.org/wiki/S%C3%A9bastien_Le_Prestre_de_Vauban.
13. Belloc, *Malplaquet*, pp 37-8.
14. Wilson, p 107.
15. Belloc, *Malplaquet*, pp 39-40.
16. Davies, p 126.
17. Wilson, p 111.
18. Davies, p 128.
19. Wilson, pp 109-110.
20. Wilson, p 110; Davies, p 127.
21. Wilson, p 110.
22. Davies, p 127.
23. Wilson, p 110; Davies, p 128.
24. Belloc, *Malplaquet*, p 43; www.spanishsuccession.nl/1709. html, p 3.
25. Wilson, p 115; Davies, pp 131-33.
26. Belloc, *Malplaquet*, p 47.
27. Ibid, pp 53-5.
28. Churchill, *A History of the English Speaking Peoples: The Age of Revolution*, Vol. III, (2002), p 69.
29. Wilson, p 116; Davies, pp 123-34.
30. Davies, p 134.
31. Ibid.
32. Davies, p 135.
33. Wilson, p 118.
34. Ibid, p 119.
35. Ibid.

36. Ibid, p 120.
37. Belloc, *Malplaquet*, pp 61-2.
38. Ibid, p 63.
39. Ibid, pp 32-3
40. http://www.ebooksread.com/authors-eng/edward-almack/the-history-of-the-second-dragoons--royal-scots-greys-hci/page-6-the-history-of-the-second-dragoons--royal-scots-greys-hci.shtml.
41. Churchill, *Marlborough: His Life and Times*, Vol II, (2002), pp 601-609; Belloc, Hilaire, *Malplaquet*, pp 81-2 copy available at www.gutenberg.org/files/32257/32257-h/32257-h.htm.
42. Churchill, *Marlborough: His Life and Times*, Vol II, (2002), p 610.
43. Belloc, *Malplaquet*, p 83.
44. Letters of the First Lord Orkney, English Historical Review p xix (1904), copy in Churchill, *Marlborough: His Life and Times*, Vol II, (2002), p 610.
45. Churchill, *Marlborough: His Life and Times*, Vol II, (2002), p 623.
46. Belloc, *Malplaquet*, pp 87-88.
47. Ibid, p 90.
48. Wilson, p 121.
49. Davies, p 139.
50. Ibid.
51. Wilson, p 122.
52. Wilson, p 123; Davies, pp 140-41.
53. For details see: http://enwikipedia.org/wiki/John_William_Frisco_Prince_of_Orange.
54. Davies, p 141.
55. Wilson, p 123; Davies, pp 141-42.
56. Wilson, p 123 Davies, p 142.
57. Davies, p 142.

Chapter 7
1710 — *Ne Plus Ultra*

1. Gregg, *Queen Anne*, (2001), p 181; http://en.wikipedia.org/wiki/John_Churchill_1st_Duke_of_Marlborough.
2. Jones, *Marlborough*, (1993), p 215; http://en.wikipedia.org/wiki/John_Churchill_1st_Duke_of_Marlborough www.spanishsuccession.nl/1710. html.
3. www.spanishsuccession.nl/1710.html.

4. Davies, p 148.
5. http://www. britishbattles.com/spanish-succession/battle-malplaquet.htm.
6. Davies, p 150.
7. Wilson, p 131; Davies, pp 149-50.
8. Wilson, p 132; *Queen Anne's Reign*, http://books.google.com.au.
9. Davies, p 151.
10. http://en.wikipedia.org/wiki/Leopold_I_Prince_of_Anhalt-Dessau.
11. *Queen Anne's Reign*, http://books.google.com.au.
12. Davies, pp 152-153.
13. Wilson, p 134; Davies, pp 153-4.

Chapter 8
1711 — The Final Struggle

1. www.spanishsuccession.nl/1711.html.
2. Wilson, p 136.
3. http://en.wikipedia.org/wiki/Siege_of_Bouchain.
4. Wilson, pp 138-39.
5. General Meinhardt Schomberg, the 3rd Duke of Schomberg, had commanded the right wing of King William's army at the Battle of the Boyne in 1690 where he had fought with extraordinary vigour to avenge the death of his father Frederick Schomberg, the 1st Duke of Schomberg, who had been killed at the battle that same day. http://en.wikipedia.org/wiki.Meinhardt_Schomberg,_3rd_Duke_of_Schomberg.
6. Wilson, pp 140-41.
7. Ibid.
8. Ibid, pp 141-42.

Chapter 9
1712 — Return Home

1. Gregg, *Queen Anne*, (2001), p 349; http://en.wikipedia.org/wiki/John_Churchill_1st_Duke_of_Marlborough.
2. Ibid, p 356.
3. Wilson, p 152.
4. Ibid, pp 153-54.
5. Ibid, pp 154-55.

6. http://wikipedia.org/wiki/Robert_Harley,_1st_Earl_of_Oxford_and_Earl_Mortimer.

7. Davies, p 174.

8. Ibid, p 175.

9. Wilson, pp 155-56.

10. Wilson, pp 157-58; Davies, p 176.

11. Davies, pp 176-177.

12. http://en.wikipedia.org/wiki/Earl_of_Macclesfield.

13. http://www. cracroftspeerage.com.uk (Cassillis entry); http://enwikipedia.org/wiki/John_Kennedy,_7th_ Earl_of_Cassilis.

14. Chisholm, Hugh, (Ed), *Encyclopaedia Britannica*, 11th Edition, *Anne Bracegirdle,* (1911), pp 358-59.

15. Lee, *Dictionary of National Biography*, *William Mountfort,* Vol XXXIX (1894) pp 211-13.; http://en.wikipedia.org/wiki/William_Mountfort.

16. http://en.wikipedia.org/wiki/Earl_of_Macclesfield.

17. Doyle, James William Edward, *The Official Baronage of England* (1886) p 600; http://en.wikipedia.org/wiki/Edwards_Rich,_6th_Earl_of_Warwick.

18. http://en.wikipedia.org.wiki/Gawsworth_New_Hall.

19. Chisholm, *Encyclopaedia Britannica*, 11th Edition, *Charles Mohun*, (1911). http://en.wikipedia.org/wiki/Charles_Mohun_4th_Baron_Mohun.

20. www.thebookofdays.com/nov/15.htm.

21. www.elizabethhoyt.com/extras/research/dueling.php.

22. Wilson, pp 158-59.

23. *Maryborough Chronicle* (Queensland) 24 February, 1913.

24. Davies, pp 178-9.

25. Benians, *The Cambridge Modern History*, (1909), pp 97-106; http://en.wikipedia.org/wiki/Anne_of_Great_Britain.

26. Wilson, pp 159-160; Davies, p 179.

27. www.northumbrianjacobites.org.uk.

28. Davies, p 180.

29. Wilson, p 160.

30. Davies, p 180.

31. Ibid, p 181.

32. Wilson, p 162.

33. Davies, p 184.
34. Davies, p 184; Wilson, pp 162-63.
35. Davies, p 185.
36. Wilson, p 165.
37. Wilson, pp 166-69; Davies, p 180.
38. Davies, p 193.
39. Wilson, p 174; Davies, p 193.
40. Wilson, p 174.
41. Ibid, pp 175-76.
42. Ibid, p 176.
43. Wilson, pp 177-78; Davies, pp 194-5.
44. Davies, p 196.

Postscript

1. *The West Australian*, 5 August, 1910, p 5.
2. *Maryborough Chronicle* (Queensland), Saturday, 7 October, 1939, p 2; http://en.wikipedia.org/wiki/Nadezhda_Durova
3. *Maryborough Chronicle* (Queensland), Saturday, 7 October, 1939, p 2.
4. Ibid.
5. Ibid.
6. *Maryborough Chronicle* (Queensland), 4 October, 1919, p 5.
7. Ibid. For further details of Amy Bock's career see: http://en.wikipedia.org/wiki/Amy_Bock
8. *Maryborough Chronicle* (Queensland), 4 October, 1919, p 5.
9. Ibid.
10. Ibid.

BIBLIOGRAPHY

Aubrey, Philip, *The Defeat of James Stuart's Armada, 1692*, (Leicester: Leicester University Press, 1979).

Barnett, Correlli, *Marlborough* (Wordsworth Editions Ltd., 1998).

Belloc, Hilaire, *Malplaquet*, (copy available at www.gutenberg.org/files/32257/32257-h/32257-h.htm)

Benians, Ernest Alfred, *The Cambridge Modern History*, (London: MacMillan and Co. 1909).

Callow, John, *The Making of King James II, the Formative Years of a King*, (Gloucestershire: Sutton Publishing, Stroud, 2000).

Chandler, David G., *Marlborough as Military Commander*, (Staplehurst: Spellmount Ltd., 2003).

Chandler, David G., *The Oxford History of the British Army*, (Oxford: Oxford University Press, 1986).

Childs, John, *The Nine Years War and the British Army*, (Mancester: Manchester University Press, 1991).

Childs, John., *Warfare in the Seventeenth Century*, (London: Cassell, 2003).

Chisholm, Hugh (Ed), *Encyclopaedia Britannica*, 11th Edition, *Anne Bracegirdle*, (Cambridge: Cambridge University Press, 1911).

Chisholm, Hugh (Ed), *Encyclopaedia Britannica*, 11th Edition, *Baron von Menno*, (Cambridge: Cambridge University Press, 1911).

Chisholm, Hugh (Ed), *Encyclopaedia Britannica*, 11th Edition, *Blenheim*, (Cambridge: Cambridge University Press, 1911).

Chisholm, Hugh (Ed), *Encyclopaedia Britannica*, 11th Edition, *Charles Mohun*, (Cambridge: Cambridge University Press, 1911).

Churchill, Winston, *A History of the English Speaking Peoples: The Age of Revolution*, Vol. III, (London: Weidenfeld and Nicolson, 2002).

Churchill, Winston, *A History of the English Speaking Peoples, The New World*, Vol. II, (London: Weidenfeld and Nicolson, 2002).

Churchill, Winston, *Marlborough: His Life and Times*, Vol II, (Chicago: University of Chicago Press, 2002).

Defoe, Daniel, (attributed), *The Life and Adventures of Christian Davies, Commonly called Mother Ross,* (London: Peter Davies Ltd, 1928).

Doyle, James William Edward, *The Official Baronage of England* (London: Longmans Green, 1886).

Gregg, Edward, *Queen Anne,* (New Haven, Connecticut: Yale University Press, 2001).

Harris, Tim, *The Great Crisis of the British Monarchy, 1685-1720,* (London: Penguin Books, 2006).

Hibbert, Christopher, *The Marlboroughs,* (London: Penguin Books, 2001).

Holmes, Richard, *Marlborough, England's Fragile Genius,* (London: Harper Press, 2008).

Jones, James Ree, *Marlborough,* (Cambridge: Cambridge University Press, 1993).

Lee, Sidney, (Ed), *Dictionary of National Biography*, Vol XXXIX, *William Mountfort* (New York MacMillan & Co., London: Smith Elder & Co. 1894).

Lynn, John A. *The Wars of Louis* XIV, 1667 – 1714. (Longman, 1999).

Miller, John, *James II,* (New Haven, Connecticut: Yale University Press, 2000).

Smyth, Sir James Carmichael, *Chronological Epitome of the Wars in the Low Countries,* (http://books.google.ca/books?; http://en.wikipedia.org/wiki/Siege_of_Namur_(1695)

Somerset, Anne, *The Affair of the Poisons,* (Weidenfeld and Nicholson, 2003).

Szechi, Daniel, *The Jacobites, Britain and Europe, 1688-1788,* (Manchester: Manchester University Press, 1994).

Trevelyan, George Macaulay, *England Under Queen Anne: Ramillies and the Union with Scotland,* (Harlaw: Longman 1936).

Waudchope, Piers, *Patrick Sarsfield and the Williamite War,* (Dublin: Irish Academic Press 1992).

Wilson, J., *The British Heroine, or An Abridgement of the Life and Adventures of Mrs Christian Davies, Commonly Called Mother Ross.* (London: T. Cooper, 1742).

INDEX

A

Aalst
(French: Alost) 104
Abbey of Park 76
Abbey of Ulierbeek 76
Adda
Ferdinand d' (papal nuncio) 6
Aeth 84-85, 91
Aicha 60
Aire 145, 152-54
Albemarl (Albemarle) 99
Alegre
Monsieur d' 53
Amsterdam 69, 71
Antwerp 45, 155
Archbishop of Salzburg 60
Arco
Count d' 55-56, 59
Arleux 156
Armerdingen 56
Arras 148-49, 155-56
Artagnan
Marshal d' (duc de Montesquiou) 149-50
Ascham
Mr (..) 8
Athlone 12-13
Aubanchoeil-au-Bac
(also given as Aubencheul-au-Bac 156
Aubray
Antonine Dreux d' 27
Aubray
Marie-Madeleine-Marguerite d' (the Marquise de Brinvilliers) 27
Aughrim 12-15
Augsburg 21, 58, 60
Autre Eglise 79
Auverquerque
Lord 84-85

B

Baker
Sir James 183-86
Bale
Margaret 192-96
Ballinasloe 13
Barry
Dr James 200
Bastille
(Paris) 27-28
Battle of Aughrim 12, 14-15
Battle of Blenheim xi, 55, 57, 61, 64, 73
Battle of Borodino 198
Battle of Landen (also given as Lauden) xi, 26, 30, 32
Battle of Malplaquet xiii, 107, 122, 139-40, 143, 147-48
Battle of Nijmegen 46
Battle of Oudenaarde 95, 139
Battle of Ramillies 80
Battle of Schellenberg 55
Battle of Sedgemoor 6
Battle of the Boyne 7, 11-12, 15
Battle of Waterloo 38
Bavaria 40, 42, 44-45, 55, 58, 60-61, 69, 79, 102-03
Bayreuth 199
Bedburg 55
Beggs
John 71, 73
Belgium 25, 45, 104
Bembrick
Bryan (Christian's maternal grandfather) 3, 10

Berchem 103
Berg 56
Bethune 116, 145, 151-52
Bill of Rights 7
Black Forest 56
Blenheim xi, 55, 57, 61-64, 73, 93
Blood
  Colonel Holcroft 56-57, 63
Blood
  Colonel Thomas 56
Blood
  Elizabeth 57
Bloody Assizes 6
Bock
  Amy 200
Boer War 38
Bonn 40, 46, 52-53
Bonnie Prince Charlie 95
Boschberg Wood 56
Bost 41
Bouchain 148, 155-58, 161, 164
Boufflers
  Louis François de 40, 44, 49, 97-98, 102, 124, 129, 132, 136, 138-40
Bourbon
  Louis Joseph de (Duke of Vendôme) 44, 91
Bourdaloue
  Louis 32
Boyle
  Charles (Lord Orrery – the 4th Earl of Orrery 1674-1731) x, 24, 151
Brabant 25, 49, 78
Bracegirdle
  Anne 171-72
Breda 64-65
British Royal Navy 39
Brown
  Captain 100, 120
Brugge 84, 95, 105
Brussels 40, 57, 78, 91-92, 98, 102-05, 107
Brussels Gate of Namur 40
Bulau
  Monsieur de 54
Butler
  James (Duke of Ormonde) 161, 163
Byng
  Admiral George (1st Viscount Torrington) 93-94

C

Cadogan
  Lord (Earl of Oudenaarde) 181
Caldwell
  Lieutenant-Colonel 149
Cambray 150
Cambridge University 52
Campbell
  Archibald (the 9th Earl of Argyll) 6
Campbell
  Colonel 101
castle of Wang 75
Cavanagh
  Christian 'Kit' x
Chalmont
  General Charles (Marquis de St. Ruth) 12
Chamberlain
  Joey 199
Chambre Ardente
  (the burning court) 28
Champagne 131, 138
Charleroi 165
Charles
  Archduke 44
Charles I
  (executed by Cromwell in 1649) 7
Charles II 5-6, 34, 38, 45
Chelsea 2, 190
Chelsea College Board 186
Chelsea Hospital xiii, 191
Cherbourg 39
Cherbourg peninsula 39
Chernov
  V.S. 197

Chester 177, 188, 190
Chevalier de Luxembourg 100
Cholmondeley
Lord (also Colonel) 29, 97
Churchill
Arabella 34
Churchill
John (the first Duke of Marlborough) xii, xiii, 6-7, 47-49, 51-52
Churchill
Sarah 48, 52, 146
Churchill
Winston 109, 124
Church of England 5
Church of Les Invalides 117
Cobbam
Lord 120
Coehoorn
Baron Menno van 40
Cologne 45, 55
Columbus
Christopher 104
Connacht 12
Connell
Inspector 196
Cook
Dorothy 57
Cooper
T. xiv
Cottesloe 192-93
Couronne Imperiale 114
Courtray 97
Coventanters
(militant body of Scots) 38
Coventry 187-88
Crimean War 38
Cromwell
Oliver 7
Cronstrom
(..) governor 74
Cuinchy 115

D

Damper
Mr (..) 86
Davies
Christian vii-xv, 1-4, 7-22, 24-26, 29-30, 32-39, 41-44, 46-47, 49-53, 55-57, 59-61, 64-70, 73, 77, 79-82, 84-91, 93, 97, 99-02, 104-07, 109-13, 119-20, 122-23, 125-28, 130, 141-45, 150-54, 156, 158-61, 165-70, 173, 175-91, 196-97
Davies
Christian
(2nd husband, Hugh was shot in the thigh) 153
(accepted Hugh Jones proposal of marriage) 144
(accompanied Richard while laying guide ropes) 106
(again enlisted in the Scots Greys) 46
(again purchased her husband's discharge from the army) 186
(almost drowned while repairing the dykes) 33
(argument with corporal over pig) 51
(arrested for duelling, placed in prison-cell) 37
(assaulted by a colonel) 158
(a sutler – a camp-follower) 82
(attacks a lieutenant) 86
(attacks Richard's former mistress, cutting off her nose) 87
(Battle of Landen, her first battle) 26
(became involved with another woman) 41
(began a duel, wounded in right arm) 36
(began work as an army cook) 82

Davies
Christian
(began a romantic charade with Dutch girl) 70
(buried with full military honours) 191
(captured by a group of French soldiers) 100
(captured by the French) 33
(comes to mother's assistance) 10
(confronts excise officers) 111
(contracted a fever) 182
(cooking and making beer for the soldiers) 110
(died on 7 July 1739) 191
(disguised herself as a man) 24
(dismissed from the service) 81
(dispute with a young cadet) 113
(drafted to Captain Tichbourn's company of foot) 25
(employed as an assistant cook for Brigadier Preston) 154
(encounter with a mounted highwayman) 187
(enlisted under the name of Christopher Welsh) 24
(entered into service with the Royal Regiment of Scots Dragoons) 38
(falls pregnant) 82
(fifty pounds to defray the charge of her lying in (during her pregnancy) 167
(filled with a longing to see her mother again) 175
(finds long-lost husband, Richard) 64
(found Richard lying dead) 142
(fought during the thickest of the fighting during the Siege of Kaiserswerth) 47
(gave birth ... daughter) 168

Davies
Christian
(gave birth to her child) 86
(gift of a hoop-petticoat) 182
(given the nickname Mother Ross) 142
(has her original pension restored to her) 178
(Hugh Jones professing his love for her) 144
(husband, Hugh died) 154
(husband mysteriously missing) 22
(inherited aunt's public house) 17
(involved with a burgher's daughter) 35
(landed at London) 165
(leaves her eldest son with her mother and infant child with nurse) 24
(long-maintained subterfuge was now over) 80
(marched beside her husband at the duke's [Marlborough] funeral 182
(married soldier named Davies) 177
(met Richard) 18
(met ... soldier named Davies [her 3rd husband]) 177
(modest living by making pies) 178
(Morgan Jones stole one of Christian's horses) 150
(moved once more to Paddington) 182
(musket shot ... split her under-lip) 85
(obtained leave to visit the Hague) 70
(offered her services as a nurse) 120
(often present with the men in their underground labyrinths of death) 119
(pardoned, but discharged from the regiment) 37

Davies
Christian
(passage aboard a yacht which was to take her to England) 190
(petition drawn up [for a pension]) 167
(piece of shrapnel struck her on the back of her head) 80
(placed onto a turning stool and whirled around until she was sick) 87
(posted as a night guard) 29
(practical joke on Sir James Baker) 183
(present at the Battle of Nijmegen) 46
(prisioner exchanged) 34
(put off eels) 112
(queen made provision ... a pension of one shilling per day for life) 168
(raped by Howel) 17
(received a letter from Richard) 22
(returned to Chelsea) 190
(returned to Dublin) 187
(Richard asked for hand in marriage) 19
(risks her life to carry drummer-boy to surgeon) 106
(running a sutler's tent in Hyde Park) 181
(sees French bringing up a large number of cannon; reports to Duke of Argyll) 101
(sent to forage for food) 49
(sent to live with aunt) 17
(set out on one of her sorties in search of plunder) 156
(settled in a small house at Willow Walk) 178
(share in the plunder) 61
(shot highwayman through the chest 187
(shot in the hip with a musket-ball) 59

Davies
Christian
(smuggling of casks of spirits) 112
(stationed for the 1708/09 winter) 110
(suffering from, ... distempers, dropsy and scurvy) 190
(summoned to appear before the Chelsea College Board regarding her pension rights) 186
(takes part in the Battle of Blenheim) 61
(Thomas Howel offers her marriage) 15
(took part in a horse-race) 97
(took passage aboard ship for Dublin) 42
(trepanned by an army surgeon) 80
(under-cook for Lord Stair) 158
(volunteered to go out with mounted foragers) 152
(was born in Dublin in 1667) 3
(with child) 167
([witness to] a duel about to be fought) 169
(wounded by a musket ball in leg) 29
Davies
Peter xiv
Dedem
Lieutenant-General 76
Defoe
Daniel xiii-xiv
Delft 70-71
Dempsey
Detective 192, 195-196
Denain 164
Dendermonde 84, 91
Dender River 104
Dessau 153
Dijle 95
Dillingen 55

Dompre
  Major-General 47
Donauwörth 55, 59-60
Douai 118, 121, 145, 149-51, 156, 164
Drogheda 10
Dublin x, 3, 10-11, 14-15, 17, 22, 25, 42, 175-78, 187, 189
Duchess of Marlborough 146
Duchy of Savoy 44
Duke of Anjou
  (Philip) 45
Duke of Argyll 95, 101, 128, 133, 166-67
Duke of Bavaria 102-03
Duke of Burgundy
  (Louis XIV's eldest grandson) 95
Duke of Hamilton 98, 166-67, 169, 171, 173-74
Duke of Luneburg 59
Duke of Luxembourg 26, 28, 32, 39, 100
Duke of Marlborough xii-xiii, 6-7, 34, 40, 44, 46-47, 49, 52, 55-56, 58-59, 61-64, 73, 75-80, 83, 85, 90-93, 95-99, 102-05, 108-09, 115-16, 118, 121-23, 128-29, 131-34, 136-41, 146-52, 155-58, 161-66, 168, 170, 177, 182, 186
Duke of Ormonde 161, 163, 165
Duke of Vendôme 91
Duleek 10
Duncannon 11
Dunkirk 93-94, 164-65
Durham 3
Durova
  Nadezhda 196-98
  (awarded the Cross of St. George) 197

E

Earl of Argyll 6
Earl of Dumbarton 98
Earl of Macclesfield 172
Earl of Oudenaarde 181
Earl of Oxford 167
Earl of Warwick 172
Edinburgh Castle 39
Elector of Bavaria 42, 55, 58, 60
Elector of Hanover 29
Elissen 29
Enfield Lock 198-99
Etaples 155
Eugene
  Prince of Savoy 44, 55-56, 62-63, 73, 91, 95-97, 103, 116, 124, 129, 131-32, 136-38, 140, 147, 149, 152, 155, 164
Ewart
  Sergeant Charles 38

F

Fagel
  General 117, 120
Fairborne
  Admiral 83
First Regiment of Foot Guards 177
First World War 38, 165
Firth of Forth 93
FitzJames
  James (Duke of Berwick) 33, 205
Flanders 2, 24, 30, 51, 78, 91, 93-95, 105, 108, 115, 157, 164, 177, 181, 187
Fleuris 42
Flight of the Wild Geese 14
Folke
  Colonel 106
Forest of Sars
  (also known as Wood of Sars, Wood of Tasiniers) 123-25, 129, 131-33, 137-38, 141
Forrest
  Mr (..) 22
Forrester
  Lord 158, 168
Forster
  Thomas 178
Fort de Plasendaal 83
Fort Knocke 165

Fort Picard 54, 74
Fort Scarpe 149
Fort St. Joseph 54
France 11-12, 14, 21, 27, 40, 44-46, 61, 73, 79, 92, 94-97, 107, 109, 115, 130, 140-41, 147, 149, 164-65, 172, 174, 189, 202
Freedmen and Co 192
Fremantle 192-96
French Revolution 117
Friso
  Johan Willem 48, 131, 143
Furnes 165

G

Galway 13
Galway
  Lord 32
Gardener
  Ensign 33
Garrickfergus 10
Gawsworth New Hall 173
Geertruidenberg (in English 'Saint Gertrude's Mountain) 25, 32, 147
Genappe 92
George
  (Prince) 47-48
George I 95, 168, 177, 181
Gete 29-31
Gete River 29, 31
Ghent xii, 42, 85-88, 91, 95-97, 105, 107, 109-11, 113, 116, 144-45, 148, 165
Gibraltar 164
Ginkell
  General Godert de 12-15
Gloucester 178
Godfrey
  Brigadier 98
Golden Last
  (tavern) 24
Goor
  General Johan Wijnand van 57, 59
Gorcum (Gorinchem) 25
Gossedge
  Colonel 106
Gosselies 91
Grahn (used aliases: Verdion, Baron de & Verdion, Doctor John de)
  Theodora 199-200
Grand Alliance (referred to as the Allies within this text) 21, 25, 45-46, 48, 55, 61-62, 84, 96
Great Seal of the Realm 7
Great War (see First World War)
Groeningen 88
Guelderland 165
Guelders 51
Gustavus's Fort 56

H

Hague 48, 52, 69-70, 73, 77, 83, 93, 108, 110, 143
Hamilton
  Colonel 100, 106, 123, 144, 170
Hamilton
  George (Lord Orkney) 98, 166-67, 169, 173-75
Hamilton
  James 169, 171, 173
Hamilton
  Lady Susannah 171
Hanover 29, 172
Harlebeck River 102-03
Harley
  Robert (Lord Treasurer, 1st Earl of Oxford) xiii, 80, 85, 167
Harvey
  Lord (Marquis of Winchester) 169
Hatton Garden 200
Hautefort
  Monsieur 103
Hay
  John (2nd Marquess of Tweeddale [father of Lord Hay]) 82
Hay
  Lord John 79, 81-82

Heilisheim 75
Helvoetsluys (today Hellevoetsluis) 23
Henriette Katharina
  Dowager Princess 153
Henry VII Chapel
  Westminster Abbey 177
Hereford 177-78
Herefordshire 168
Herenthals 77
Hesse-Cassel
  Prince of 131, 135, 137
Hill
  General 165
Hill
  Richard 171-72
Holland x-xi, 25, 42, 45-46, 69, 71-72, 77, 84, 110, 162
Hollands Diep 143
Holloway 89
Holyoake
  Austin 198
Hooglede 99
Hoogleden (probably Hooglede) 99
Hordorn 200
House of Lords 163, 172
Howel
  Mrs Thomas 189
Howel (also reported as Howell)
  Thomas (later Reverend) 15-16, 176, 189-90
Hulluch 115
Huy 30, 40-41, 53, 73-75
Hyde
  Edward 5
Hyde
  Lady Anne (wife of James II) 5, 47, 169, 173-74, 181

I

Ingoldsby's regiment 105
Ireland xi, 4, 7, 10-12, 14-15, 17, 21, 24-25, 41, 69, 120, 176-77, 201
Irish Parliament 7, 14
Irwin
  Colonel 105
Irwin
  Major 106

J

James II x, 4, 6-7, 9-12, 15, 33-34, 39, 47, 92
James III
  (James Francis Edward Stuart 'The Old Pretender' [never formally recognized as sovereign]) 92
Jeffreys
  Judge 6
John George II
  Prince of Anhalt-Dessau 153
Jones
  Hugh (Christian's 2nd husband) 112, 144-45, 151, 153
Jones
  Morgan 150-51
Joseph
  Emperor 156

K

Kaiserswerth 46
Kalgoorlie 193
Kelly
  Mr (..) 15
Kennedy
  John (7th Earl of Cassillis also reported as Cassilis) 171, 213
Kensington Gardens 174
Kent 7
Keppel
  Arnold Joost van (1st Earl of Albermarle) 100
Kerr
  Lord Mark 101
Kiev 196
Kilcommadan Hill 13
Kirkhoven 103

L

Laar 29-31
La Bassee 115-16, 121-22
La Hogue 39
Lallo (also reported as Lalo)
  Brigadier 142
Lambeth 112
Lamonche
  Frances 201-02
Landen 25, 28, 30, 32
Landen Brook 29
Lateran
  Lord 183
Lauingen
  (Lawingen) 60
Lawrance
  Ensign Herbert 24
Léau 45, 79
Leffinghe 105
Leicester Square 172
Leopold
  Emperor 55
Leopold I
  Prince of Anhalt-Dessau 149, 153
Leslip 9
Leuven
  (French: Louvain) 78-80
Leuwe 76
Lewenstein-Worthem
  Count 61
Liége 27, 30, 50, 73-75
Lille 96-98, 100, 102, 105, 107-08, 115, 154, 209
Limbourg 53-54
Limerick 12-14
Line of Trouille 122
Lines of La Bassee 115-16, 121-22
Lloyd (alias)
  Harry 198-99
Lottum
  Count Carl [Karl] Philipp von Wylich und Lottum) 102-03, 117, 131-33
Louis XIV 12, 21, 26-28, 34, 39, 42, 45, 55, 61, 78-79, 85, 92-93, 95, 108, 110, 146-47, 150, 155, 158
Louvain 76, 78-80, 103
Low Countries x, 26, 42, 73-74, 114, 173, 177, 182
Lower Rhine 45
Lyme Regis 6
Lys River 149

M

Maastricht 27, 49-50, 73, 79, 84
MacCartney (also reported as Macartney and McCartney)
  General George 170, 173, 175
Maes 74, 102
Maestricht 73
Malary
  Reverend (..) 10
Malplaquet vii-viii, xiii, 107-08, 122-24, 129, 139-40, 143, 146-49, 151, 153
Manchester 25, 178
Marchiennes 158
Margrave of Baden 55
Marquette 99
Marquion 157
Marquis de Beuvron 27
Marquis de Pisare 25
Marquis de St. Ruth
  (General Charles Chalmont) 12-14
Marquis de Vauban 97
Marquise de Brinvilliers 27
Marquis of Blandford 52
Marquis of Winchester 169
Marsin
  Marshal Fredinand de 55, 62, 91
Martens
  Dick 104
Mary
  (princess royal) 7
Mary I 6

Mary II 47-48
(wife of William III) 5, 7, 21, 34
Mary of Modena
(second wife of James II) 5, 7, 34
Maximilian II
(of Bavaria) 40, 55, 79
McCartney
General 174
Mehaigne River 79
Meldert 80, 92
Menen
(French: Menin) 84, 99, 116, 165
Mesgrigny
Jean 117
Meuse 41, 45, 49-51
Middle East viii
Middlesex 198
Mildelheim 77
Millner
John 80
Minch
Michael 201
Minorca 164
Mohun
Charles (4th Baron Mohun) 169-75
Mons 45, 115, 122-23, 141, 165
Mont
Baron du 76
Montgomery
Mr (..) 97
Montmorency-Bouteville
Comte de 27
Montmorency-Bouteville
François Henri de (duc de Pincy)
(Duke of Luxembourg) 26, 28
Montreuil 123
Montrose 95
Monvoisin
Catherine Deshayes 28
Moore
J. R. xiv
Moselle 41, 73-75
Mother Ross xiv, 142, 166, 188
Motte
Monsieur la 99
Mountfort
William 171-72
Mount Kisco 201

N

Namur 39-41, 45, 76, 78, 103-04, 148, 155, 165
Namur siege 40
Napoleon 117
Nassau-Sarbruck
Prince (Veldt-marshal of the States) 42
Nassau-Woudenburg
Brigadier Count 99
Nederhespen 75
Neerlanden 29, 31
Neerwinden 29
Ne Plus Ultra 146, 148-49, 155
Neuburg 58
Neuss 46
Nijmegen 46
Nine Years War vii, x, 21, 43, 45
Nordlingen 58
North Brabant 25
Noyelles
Count 75

O

Oates
Titus 5
Old Pretender 92-93
Oostmalen 75
Orkney
Lord 98, 132-33, 138, 167
Ormonde
(James Butler) 161, 163-65
Orrery
Lord x, 23-24, 151
Ostend 83-84, 91, 94, 99, 102
Ottaway
George 200

Oudenaarde
(also known as Oudenarde or Oudenard) 88, 95, 103, 139, 181
Overhespen 75
Overkirk
Count 79
Oxford
Lord 168

P

Paddington 182
Paseal
Monsieur de 102
Pavlovich
Aleksander (Aleksander I) 197
Peace of Ryswick xi
Pendergrass
Sir Thomas 142
Percival
Susanna 172
Perth 192-93, 195
Peterhead 95
Philip II 150
Philip V 44-45, 147
Picardie 131
Plain of Lens 156
Plain of Ramillies 79
Plassendael 105
Pont-a-Nache 149
Pope 5, 95
Preston
Brigadier (..) xii, 80-81, 154, 178
Prince of Anhalt-Dessau 149, 153
Prince of Hesse-Cassel 131, 135, 137
Prince of Orange 7, 27, 131-32, 134-36, 143, 149, 153
Protestant Church 4
Pushkin
Aleksandr 198
Puységur
General 139

Q

Quaregon 124
Queen Anne xiii, 1, 47-48, 52, 92-93, 146, 162-63, 166, 168-69, 177, 191
Quesnoy 139, 164
Quevy 124

R

Rain 60
Ramillies xii, 78-80, 83, 90-91, 154
Rastatt 44
Ratisbon 58, 77
Ravignau
Governor de 157
Redwood (alias)
Percy 200
Regiment de Roi
(King's Regiment) 79
Rich
Edward (6th Earl of Warwick) 172
River Boyne 10
River Canche 148
River Haine 123
River Lech 58
River Nanny 10
River Scarpe 157-58
River Scheldt 158, 164
River Sensee 158
River Shannon 12-14
River Trouille 122-23
Roermond 49
Roman Catholic Church 4-5
Rooke
Admiral 39
Ross
Captain 142
Rotterdam 69-72
Rouillé
Monsieur 110
Roy
Marie le 198-99

Royal Hospital, Chelsea x
Royal Irish Dragoons 149
Royal North British Dragoons
(also known as the Royal Regiment of North British Dragoons) 38
Royal Regiment of Scots Dragoons 38
Royal Scots Dragoon Guards (Carabiniers and Greys) 39
Royal Scots Greys xi, 38, 42, 46, 53, 55, 57-58, 61, 64, 79, 82, 133, 149
Russell
Admiral 39

S

Sainte-Croix
Captain Godin de 27
Saint-Germain-en-Laye 11, 33, 92-93
Sanduliet 77
Scarpe River 149-50, 156
Scheldt River 102, 104, 116, 122, 157
(Dutch: Schelde River, French: Escaunt River) 95-96
Schellenberg xi, 55-56, 58-59, 64
Schlangenburg
General 76
Schomberg
General Meinhardt 159
Schulembourg (also reported as Schulemberg and Schulenburg)
Count von der 117, 131-33
Schultz
Lieutenant-General 75
Schwenningen 62
Scots Greys (see Royal Scots Greys)
Scott
James (1st Duke of Monmouth) 5-6
Second World War viii, 38
Seneffe 92
Sensee River 148
Sensee Valley 156
Siege of Aeth
(Ath) 84
Siege of Bethune 151
Siege of Bonn 40
Siege of Bouchain 161
Siege of Douai 150-51
Siege of Ghent xii, 105
Siege of Huy 40
Siege of Kaiserswerth 46
Siege of Landau 69
Siege of Lille 96-98, 100
Siege of Mons 141
Siege of Namur xi, 39, 153
Siege of Philippsburg 34
Siege of St. Venant 153
Siege of Tournai 117, 120
Siege of Turin 91
Sinzendorff
Count 54
Sligo 12
Sobieski
John 95
Sobieski
Maria 'Mary' Clementina 95
Soignies 91, 95
Sokolov
Alexander (see Durova: Nadezhda) 197
Son 46
Souternon
Monsieur 103
Stair
Lord x, 158-60
Stair's Dragoons x
St. Andrews
(Hordorn) 200
Staten Island 202
St. Denis 27
Stevensweert 49
St. Germain 7
St. James's Palace 47
St. Leger
Lieutenant 86
St. Margaret's Church, Westminster xiii

Stone
Mr (..) 86
Storey
George 14
St. Peter's Basilica 95
St. Petersberg 197
Stretton
Lieutenant 106
St. Tron 76
Stuart
Charles Edward 95
Stuart
Henry Benedict 95
Stuart
James Francis Edward (son of James II & Mary of Modena) 7, 92-93, 95
St. Venant 115-16, 121, 145, 152-53
Styrum
Count von 57
Surville-Hautfois
Lieutenant-General le Marquis de 116-18, 121
Swabian Jura 62

T

Tallard
Marshal Camille de 54-56, 60-62
Temple
Sir Richard 101
Test Act
(passed in 1673) 5-6
Tichbourn
Captain (..) 25
Tienen
(Tirlemont) 41-42, 73
Tirlemont 41-42, 73, 76-77
Tongeren 79
Torbay 7
Tothill Fields 178
Toulon 91
Tournai 32, 115-18, 120-22, 129, 165
Tourville
Admiral 39
Tower of London 6, 57, 168
Treaty of Limerick 14
Treaty of Rastatt 44
Treaty of Utrecht 44
Treves 45
Trogné
Baron de 54
Tweed
Captain John 202

U

Ulster 10, 13
Usher
Captain 143
Utrecht 27, 44, 164

V

Valenciennes 27, 115, 121
Val-Nôtre-Dame 74
Vauban
Monsieur du Puy 151
Vauban
Sébastien Le Prestre de (later the Marquis de Vauban) 97, 116, 151
Vaudemont
Prince 42
Vegnacourt 74
Vendôme
Marshal 91, 95-96, 98
Venlo 45, 49, 51
Verdion
Baron de 199
Doctor John de 199-200
Versailles 32, 95
Vienna 54-55, 61-62, 77
Vignamont 32
Villars
Marshal Claude Louis Hector de 44, 54, 91, 108, 115-18, 121-24, 129, 131, 136, 138-40, 148-50, 152, 156-58, 164

Villeroy (also known as Villeroi)
Marshal 42, 53, 60, 79-80
Villiers
Elizabeth 34
Voisin
Monsieur 110

W

War of Devolution
(1667-1668) 27
War of the Grand Alliance 21
War of the League of Augsburg 21
War of the Spanish Succession vii, xi, 38, 44, 61, 206
Webb
Major-General 99-100
Welsh
Christopher xi, 24
Welsh
Kit 97
Welsh
Richard vii-viii, x, xii-xiii, 18-20, 22-24, 42, 44, 52, 64-69, 81-82, 84, 86-87, 105-06, 108, 110, 112, 126-27, 142-44, 191
Wenendal 99
West Indies 6, 45, 164
Westminster xiii, 112, 177-78, 186
Westminster Abbey 177
Westminster Ferry 112
William III x, 1, 5, 7, 10-11, 15, 21, 25-26, 29-31, 34, 37, 40-42, 47-48, 120, 168, 171
William IV
(Prince of Orange) x, 7, 143
Williams
Frank 201
Williamstadt 25
Willow Walk 178-79
Wills
General Charles 178
Wilson
Dr J. xiv, 1-3, 16, 20, 35-37, 50, 59-60, 65, 81, 112, 119-20, 142, 160, 167, 169, 175, 180, 182, 189
Windham
Sir William 168
Wirtemberg 30
Withers
General 131
Wood of Lanières 123-25, 129, 131-32, 134-36, 138
Wood of Sars 123
Wood of Taisnieres 123, 125, 141
Wood of Tiry 134
Wylich und Lottum (von Lottum)
Count Carl Philipp 102

Y

Yelabuga 198
Ypres 115-16, 165

Z

Zoutleeuw 30, 79

Other

1st English Foot Guards 57
3rd Carabiniers (the Prince of Wales Dragoon Guards) 38
4th Dragoons 38
4th Earl of Orrery x, 24, 151
5th Royals
(formerly Lord Orrery's Regiment of Foot) x, 151
45th French Regiment 38

About the Author

Tony Matthews is a Welsh/Australian author who has dedicated most of his adult life to writing and researching Australian and world history. He also writes extensively on military and espionage history with a specific emphasis on both world wars. Tony is the author of more than thirty books including several novels. He worked in the television industry for many years, writing, producing and directing, and during that time wrote a number of highly acclaimed historical documentaries which were broadcast on the Seven Network and ABC Television. He has also written and narrated more than five hundred historical programmes for ABC Radio. Tony Matthews' books and articles have been published in Australia, England, the United States and Europe and his television documentaries have been widely distributed to schools, universities, colleges and libraries across Australia.

Please visit the author's website for more details of his published and broadcast works: https://drtonymatthews.weebly.com

OTHER BOOKS

By Tony Matthews

PUBLISHED BY BIG SKY PUBLISHING

Tragedy at Évian

How the World Allowed Hitler to Proceed with the Holocaust

In July 1938 the United States, Great Britain and thirty other countries participated in a vital conference at Évian-les-Bains, France, to discuss the persecution and possible emigration of the European Jews, specifically those caught under the anvil of Nazi atrocities. However, most of those nations rejected the pleas then being made by the Jewish communities, thus condemning them to the Holocaust.

There is no doubt that the Évian conference was a critical turning point in world history. The disastrous outcome of the conference set the stage for the murder of six million people. Today we live in a world defined by turmoil with a disturbing rise of authoritarian governments and ultra right-wing nationalism. Now is the time to reflect on the past to ensure we never again make the same mistakes.

QUIET COURAGE

Forgotten Heroes of World War Two

What could induce a young pilot to walk out onto the wing of his burning aircraft at 13,000 feet?

Why would a plucky young woman descend into the bowels of a sinking ship knowing that she would almost certainly die there?

Why did a family remain on their farm, tending crops while suffering four long years of deadly artillery shelling?

How did a former fishing trawler sink one of Hitler's deadliest U-boats, and who were the two Australian nurses who protected wounded patients with their own bodies while experiencing a savage machine-gun attack?

Why did a young naval apprentice keep rowing when his hands had been so badly burned they were literally glued to his oar? And who were the two selfless 'Dad's Army' soldiers who miraculously saved the lives of hundreds of their comrades even when it meant sacrificing their own?

These and many other fascinating questions are answered in one of the most remarkable books of gallantry, fortitude and self-sacrifice you will ever read. *Quiet Courage — Forgotten Heroes of World War Two* is a book about thoughtful, intelligent actions and above all, an enviable capacity for bravery.

Sea Monsters

Savage Submarine Commanders of World War II

The true story of a deeply murderous intent that lurked menacingly beneath the waves during World War Two.

The torpedoes strike explosively and nine thousand people die — five thousand of them are just defenceless children.

Another ship founders after being attacked by a brutal submarine commander and the ship's crew and passengers are used in a murderous kind of blood-sport.

Merchant seamen are savagely machine-gunned in the water, callously slaughtered with hand-grenades or simply left to the circling sharks.

And hundreds of doctors, nurses, ship's crew, ambulance drivers and hospital orderlies are viciously killed without compassion, despite being protected by the Geneva Convention.

From the heart-rending account of the sinking of the German liner *Wilhelm Gustloff* in 1945 — the worst maritime disaster in world history — through to a variety of other brutal actions carried out by numerous submarine commanders, including the sinking of the hospital ship *Centaur* in 1943, this book comes from the deep shadows of a tragic past. It reveals the terrible truth of a secretive war that was responsible for the deaths of unimaginable numbers of innocent people.

Sea Monsters includes powerful and poignant interviews with survivors — never before published.

INSPIRED BY A TRUE STORY

ENTOMBED

Six Men Buried Alive for Six Years

The year is 1945. Six German soldiers led by Captain Hans von Roth, have been accidentally buried alive deep underground in a military stores bunker at the port of Gydnia, Poland. At first they believe they will be rescued, but as the hours drag into days, months and finally years, it is appallingly clear that the men will almost certainly face a terrifying death in the grim darkness that surrounds them. They struggle to find a way out of their personal hell, but each fierce attempt leads only to failure and despair. Unaware that they will be trapped for six terrible years, the men face debilitating disease, violent death, and even madness as they attempt to understand the horror of what lies ahead.

This is a story of immense struggle against immeasurable odds but it is also a story of great love and anguish — the anguish of Erika von Roth who, unaware that her husband, Hans, is still trapped underground in Poland, and believing him to be dead, is fighting to survive in a brutal post-war Germany. Erika must find her own way through the love she retains for her husband and the growing, unexpected and self-betraying love she is experiencing for a man who was once one of her sworn enemies.

Inspired by actual events, *Entombed* is an agonising struggle for survival and one of the most important untold stories to emerge from the era of the Second World War.

SPIES, SABOTEURS AND SECRET MISSIONS OF WORLD WAR II

What kind of courage does it take for an ordinary married couple to confront the Nazi regime of Hitler's vicious Third Reich?

And why did two men betray their fellow secret agents after landing on American shores with the intention of carrying out sabotage attacks on a massive scale?

Why did the Germans murder more than two hundred and sixty innocent men in retaliation for a botched Resistance attempt to steal a simple truckload of meat?

From technical wizardly that goes disastrously wrong, to underwater warfare with a sting in its tail, this new book by Tony Matthews delves into a wide range of top-secret stories, including black propaganda missions, calamitous Resistance operations and accounts of espionage activities at the very highest level.

Spies, Saboteurs and Secret Missions of World War II is a fascinating insight into some of the most astonishing clandestine activities of the Second World War.

INVISIBLE

The Essential Guide for Aliens Stranded on Earth

Have you ever wondered why you can't wait to get away from the party, go home and put your feet up alone?

As a boy, and right through his entire life, Tony Matthews has craved anonymity and invisibility — a state of being that is not only well beyond the laws of physics as we know them but also one largely at odds with his chosen profession of novelist, historian and poet.

In this brightly humorous autobiographical account of his strange life, Tony Matthews takes us on a mystical journey through the highly unusual world of 'Invisible Man' — living as gently, quietly and unobtrusively as possible in a brash, noisy and sometimes overly disruptive world.

Reflecting his own young confusion, he questions why he appears to be a round doughnut irrevocably stranded in a square biscuit-tin. His quest for understanding takes him on a roller-coaster ride until he realises finally that he is about as comfortable on Earth as a crocodile in a handbag factory.

In this funny and, at times, exquisitely insightful book, Tony Matthews tells us how the world is viewed through the eyes of an intensely introverted and overly self-conscious writer, film-maker, recluse and ethical vegan.

This is a true and extraordinary story that, at times, is emotionally touching and at other times touchingly comic.